# EXTREME WEIGHT LOSS

# Extreme Weight Loss

*Life Before and After Bariatric Surgery*

Sarah Trainer, Alexandra Brewis, and Amber Wutich

NEW YORK UNIVERSITY PRESS

New York

NEW YORK UNIVERSITY PRESS
New York
www.nyupress.org

References to Internet websites (URLs) were accurate at the time of writing. Neither the author nor New York University Press is responsible for URLs that may have expired or changed since the manuscript was prepared.

Library of Congress Cataloging-in-Publication Data
Names: Trainer, Sarah, author. | Brewis, Alexandra, author. | Wutich, Amber, author.
Title: Extreme weight loss : life before and after bariatric surgery / Sarah Trainer, Alexandra Brewis, Amber Wutich.
Description: New York : NYU Press, 2021. | Includes bibliographical references and index.
Identifiers: LCCN 2020028182 (print) | LCCN 2020028183 (ebook) |
ISBN 9781479894970 (cloth) | ISBN 9781479803958 (paperback) |
ISBN 9781479879274 (ebook) | ISBN 9781479857265 (ebook other)
Subjects: LCSH: Obesity—Surgery—Popular works. | Gastric bypass. | Weight loss. |
Obesity. | Obesity—Social aspects. | Ethnology—Methodology.
Classification: LCC RD540 .T73 2021 (print) | LCC RD540 (ebook) | DDC 617.4/3—dc23
LC record available at https://lccn.loc.gov/2020028182
LC ebook record available at https://lccn.loc.gov/2020028183

New York University Press books are printed on acid-free paper, and their binding materials are chosen for strength and durability. We strive to use environmentally responsible suppliers and materials to the greatest extent possible in publishing our books.

Manufactured in the United States of America

10 9 8 7 6 5 4 3 2 1

Also available as an ebook

# CONTENTS

# Introduction

Today, in much of the world, a fat body violates widely held social norms about how people should look. A body with weight deemed excessive by social or medical standards also brings social, economic, political, and emotional consequences, precisely because it does not meet now-dominant norms. Across different cultures and communities, fat individuals are perceived to be lazy and undisciplined. Perhaps the most powerful, overriding meaning currently associated with a fat body, however, is failure. The idea that one fails as a person because of one's weight increasingly dominates in both local and global discussions about health, beauty, and other forms of human capital. This environment, in turn, may feed profound personal self-doubt among those who feel out of sync with body norms because of their weight—and this self-doubt may grow over time into outright emotional misery.[1]

The broader context—a widespread avoidance and despising of weighty, fat bodies—is the starting point for the ethnographic case study we explore in this book. Here, we consider what it means to be fat, obese, and overweight through a detailed analysis of the words of patients undergoing a body modification commonly known as bariatric surgery or weight-loss surgery (WLS) in one large hospital system in the United States. "Why pay attention to bariatric patients?" we are often asked. The reasons are twofold. On the one hand, bariatric patients are uniquely placed as keen participant observers of the social meanings and implications of "being fat," because they come to surgery with long, often fraught histories of having lived with a very large body. On the other hand, the surgery then rapidly transforms their bodies, triggering pronounced weight loss over a very condensed period of time. Postsurgery, it is common to lose half of one's excess body weight within a year. This transformation of the physical, biological body thus provides us with a particularly illuminating lens for examining the role that body weight plays in how Americans in the twenty-first century United

States define themselves and each other, in social, interpersonal, and emotional terms.

Our ethnography traces out the body and identity transformations that people underwent as a result of massive, surgically induced weight loss. It is also an intimate portrait of the "hard work" that people with larger-than-average bodies are willing to do to live up to current societies' stringent norms of thinness. In this book, we share stories of the sacrifices people were willing to make to meet these norms, the triumph that came when they attained them, and the deep sense of disappointment that emerged when they could not. The journey to profound postsurgical weight loss for bariatric patients is a far-reaching and painful one—and not just in physical ways. Many bariatric patients, who undergo surgeries that alter their stomachs and intestines in order to facilitate drastic weight loss, spend years before and after the surgeries struggling with their weight. They do so in part to be healthy but also because of a deep need to find thinner "true selves," ones that align with wider social norms.

The notion that every individual should be struggling to reach and keep a certain weight resonates with an astounding number of people today, whether they identify as thin, fat, or in between. Around the planet, doctors routinely weigh people from birth onward, give advice about how to achieve healthy weights through lifestyle choices, and talk about the pathological consequences that will ensue if a healthy weight or lifestyle is not maintained.[2] People living in a country like the United States are subjected to a constant barrage of advertisements selling the idea that weight loss is easy—with the right product and the correct amount of personal willpower. Images of allegedly successful and desirable thin people are everywhere. People are accordingly enjoined to compare their bodies constantly to those of others, both real and airbrushed, and to constantly worry how well they are doing with personal body-based "improvement" projects.

In this (now widely globalized) paradigm, weight loss is read as a personal success, whereas weight gain is seen as a personal failure. Many people who pick up this book, for example, have probably already worried at least once today about eating the "wrong" food or not putting enough effort into exercising. Many probably start the day with a look at their weight as told to them by a scale and then interpret the results not simply as pounds up or pounds down but as a commentary on individual worth. Up five pounds? That means one has "lost control" or is "not working hard enough." Down five pounds? One must have been "good," and the proof is staring back at them, reflected in the numbers on the scale.

In this context, the emotional and social struggles of people dealing with extreme weight allow us to examine ideas about which bodies belong, which do not, and how that belonging is enforced or not. To have so many millions—actually, now billions—of people working daily to lose or maintain weight, even while the average weights of most populations continue going up,[3] is one of the strangest contradictions of modern human society. It demands investigation. It requires explanation.

This fundamentally complex cultural phenomenon is the departure point for this book. The expectation that people must engage in everyday weight loss is now deeply socially ingrained in countries like the United States. The science of weight loss suggests that the more people try to lose weight through dieting, the more likely they are to gain even more weight in the long term.[4] Thus, weight-loss efforts are only loosely related to actual weight, and they are only loosely related to success at weight loss. Moreover, obesity itself does not always equate with ill health. There are plenty of skinny people with diabetes, high cholesterol, and other physical pathologies that are commonly portrayed as co-occurring with obesity.[5] There are also plenty of people who, if weighed in a doctor's office, would find themselves diagnosed with morbid obesity and quickly thereafter classified as diseased from a medical (and social) standpoint . . . but who would have no other symptoms of disease aside from a higher weight-to-height ratio. In other words, weight deemed excessive is viewed as inherently diseased, whether or not it correlates with lived experiences of illness symptoms and diseases such as diabetes, cardiovascular disease, and the like.[6] In other words, social beliefs about obesity map poorly onto current scientific and medical evidence. Making the situation still more confusing, "fat" and "obese" are slippery words/concepts that are often used interchangeable by many people. What is clear, however, is that it has become a basic social fact in many countries in the world today that fat bodies are unacceptable, are unhealthy, and reflect a lack of personal commitment to other valued traits that include hard work, personal responsibility, and goal-oriented individual success.

In this book, we use detailed ethnographic data collected with bariatric surgery patients in one hospital case study to understand how and why the cultural obsession with weight loss is such a prevailing characteristic of our modern, media-connected societies. We stress that this obsession is at its core a cultural one, although it uses medicalized rhetoric and many of the flows of power and influence happen in and between clinical settings. This book unravels how and why weight and our efforts to escape it have become such a collective and heavy burden, taking up so much of our attention and causing so much daily worry. Our story is about understanding how and why weight norms are core to so many people's basic senses of self. Our case study in based in one city in the United States, but in many ways it is a universal story about life in an increasingly globalized world in the new millennium.

## It's Not Just about Weight—It's about Fitting In

The lifelong struggles with weight and size, as described by the bariatric patients we got to know, are not unique. However, the avenue that they eventually chose to go down to lose weight—that is, opting for bariatric surgery—does make them unusual. The surgery and its consequences also give people who undergo it unusual insights into both weight and weight loss. This is one of the reasons why we chose to focus on bariatric surgery as a rather unique lens for understanding (and, hopefully, disentangling) weight-related experiences. Where else, in the early twenty-first century, might one find a community of people who have—collectively and individually—experienced the social and physical consequences of extremely high weight, followed by the loss of a significant portion of that weight?

Among other things, this expensive surgical intervention facilitates rapid weight loss to an unparalleled degree. Bariatric surgery encompasses a number of different types of surgical interventions on the stomach and intestines, usually through the reduction of stomach capacity and gut length. All trigger weight loss because they profoundly alter how the body takes in, absorbs, and excretes food. Bariatric surgery is also sometimes referred to as metabolic surgery because it manipulates (via surgery) a normal organ system to change an individual's biology to improve their metabolic health. The surgery has a relatively short history, corresponding to the relatively short history of global concern with obesity and metabolic health.

Surgeries to promote weight loss via malabsorption of nutrients and/ or restriction of volume in the stomach and gut began to appear more than sixty years ago but did not become popular until the 1990s, and then primarily in the "advanced economies" of North America, Europe, and Asia.[7] Not coincidentally, the 1990s were also a time when public and medical attention to rising rates of obesity in populations around the world became acute, along with a concordant demand for solutions. A cluster of conditions, including high blood pressure, high blood sugar, excess weight around the waist, and hyperlipidemia, began to pop up routinely in populations—a disease profile commonly known as metabolic syndrome. With the increase in metabolic syndrome, then, we see an increase in metabolic/bariatric surgery.

Bariatric surgery, as other researchers have observed, may not be a perfect solution to promote increased overall health; but it is the most effective weight-loss mechanism currently available, and it is also effective as an intervention for certain diseases. By that, we (and others) mean that the surgery is effective in reducing weight, type 2 diabetes, hyperlipidemia, and joint pain.[8] It also, however, has a host of unpleasant side effects precisely because it causes malabsorption and alters anatomy.

Surgeries categorized as bariatric, weight loss, and/or metabolic come in various forms and via different types of programs. The most commonly used surgeries currently are gastric bypass, sleeve gastrectomy, adjustable gastric band, and biliopancreatic diversion with duodenal switch. Of these, the gastric band is very popular in the United States, despite the fact that it triggers less weight loss than the others and has a less pronounced effect on diseases like type 2 diabetes. It is popular because it is the only one that is potentially reversible: the band can be removed. The most commonly performed bariatric surgery types within the program we studied were laparoscopic vertical sleeve gastrectomy and laparoscopic Roux-en-Y gastric bypass. In a gastrectomy, a bariatric surgeon removes much of the stomach, hugely decreasing the capacity of that organ to take in and process food and forcing everything to go more or less straight into the intestines. One patient described her new stomach as a "small banana" in shape and size. In a bypass, a bariatric surgeon creates a small walnut-sized stomach pouch, seals off the rest of the stomach, and then reattaches the small intestine to that small pouch, "bypassing" much of the stomach and part of the small intestine. Weight loss occurs because the redesigned stomach-intestine combination cannot tolerate food in any quantity or foods high in sugar and fat and because the redesign promotes malabsorption of food. Although the surgeries themselves are typically straightforward, the long-term consequences of the stomach and intestinal rerouting cannot be overstated. They necessitate an entirely different, lifelong approach to one of the most basic of human activities: eating.

The massive weight loss precipitated by bariatric surgery gives people who go through the process special insight and understanding into what it means when bodies do not, then suddenly do, fit in. In other words, in choosing to focus on weight in this research, we are in fact looking at the very human struggle to "be normal," to adhere to the norms accepted by most people. This is the heart of our story. How does a person know whether they fit in or not? Why do people care so much? What happens when an individual is unable to meet basic social norms about how they are meant to look and act?

Although this book is first and foremost an ethnographic account of what it means to undergo extreme weight loss, it is also fundamentally about understanding norms around body, weight, and appearance.[9] Norms are shared but unwritten rules about how humans should act and be. Norms help people understand what is expected and what will be accepted by a wider group. What are the processes by which norms infuse themselves into people's lives? In what ways do these norms form our sense of self and identity, and how do individuals accept and resist them? How do people define success or failure in relation to them? What are the implications when norms change, with regard to the effects on human society and biology?

Our focus in this book is on shared body norms and shared experiences of struggling to meet them. As such, our analysis focuses to a large extent on drawing out core experiences that cut across diverse participants' experiences over time. In doing this, we focus on similar themes that emerged for people, despite the many differences within our sample with regard to each person's weight, dieting history, marital and familial situation, socioeconomic status, age, gender, race, and ethnicity. The literature tells us that all of these factors may impact people's experiences of fat stigma, their sense of self, and their experiences in society. For example, the Centers for Disease Control (CDC) notes that Non-Hispanic Blacks and Hispanics (quoting CDC categories verbatim; we use Black and Latinx in our own descriptions) are at higher risk for obesity and associated chronic diseases than are Non-Hispanic Whites and Non-Hispanic Asians.[10] There also is considerable research examining how obesity in the US correlates with lower socioeconomic status and how this in turn creates greater obesity risk among communities that have experienced systematic and systemic marginalization.[11] Recognizing this, we address in this book how key socioeconomic differences shape people's experiences, at least to the extent that is possible given our sample composition.

This study's sample supports comparisons around gender and, to a much lesser extent, race. The limitations of our race-oriented analysis stem, in large part, from the nature of the clinic itself. It is extremely difficult to gain access for long-term ethnographic studies to clinic settings where patient populations are typically deemed vulnerable. The clinic where we gained permission to do the study was primarily a White space: most providers were White; most patients were White; the bariatric education program was built on medical research reflecting the concerns of mostly White scientists; people in the pictures on the walls of the clinic were mostly White; the anthropologists lurking around the bariatric program were White; and so on. The overall result in this clinic, as in many others, was the production of remarkable cultural uniformity oriented around a (mostly unexplored) set of White norms and interactions.[12] One consequence of this, for our analysis, is that telling detailed stories around the experiences of this study's non-White participants could compromise their confidentiality, making clear to readers who have knowledge of this clinical practice who the specific participants are and what they said. As an experiment to test anonymity and community knowledge, for example, Sarah tried describing one non-White patient to a health-care provider in the clinic, with a few key demographic identifiers—including familial country of origin—changed slightly. The health-care provider immediately identified the patient correctly, thus providing a clear example to us of how insufficient are slight modifications to demographic information for some non-White participants. For us, our ethical obligation to protect participants' identities and right to privacy far outweighs the inducement to produce highly nuanced theory about race and bariatric surgery in this particular instance.

That does not mean we will ignore race in this book, however, or even intersections of race and gender. One important group of participants, Black women, was numerous enough to produce analyzable data that can be effectively anonymized. Our analytic focus on Black women in a bariatric program provides an especially valuable lens because, as the literature indicates, Black women's unique intersectional experiences of racism, misogyny, and fat stigma give them keen insights into dominant body norms in the US and the enormous harm the norms can do.[13]

Socioeconomic status is another important—and often problematic—factor in our analysis. Bariatric surgery itself can be expensive; follow-up surgeries, either for skin removal or to correct a problem, can also be expensive. The Norwegian government offers bariatric surgery to all its citizens whose weight and comorbidities qualify them (a situation that has its own benefits and disadvantages); the United States does not offer the equivalent.[14] In the US, therefore, any person interested in bariatric surgery must first figure out a way to cover the substantial associated costs of the surgery before they can proceed. For some, this means paying out of pocket for an expensive surgery with an accredited provider; others are able to get their health insurance to cover the same types of surgery with an accredited provider. Other lower-cost options, however, include going abroad or electing to use an unaccredited program in the US.[15]

In the accredited program we studied, hospital staff worked hard with all prospective patients to get as much of the surgery covered by health insurance as possible. Over the course of our research, we asked patient-participants how they funded their surgeries and how it related to their economic circumstances. If they did not want to discuss their finances, however, we did not push the point; we were already asking many sensitive questions at a very tumultuous time in people's lives. What we learned from those who did talk about financial matters in some detail was that the patient-participants lived all over the city and surrounding areas, in neighborhoods that ranged from wealthy to lower income, worked a variety of blue- and white-collar jobs, and expressed varying degrees of worry about covering the substantial expenses associated with their bariatric surgery.

While we acknowledge the—often profound—ways in which gender, socioeconomic status, and race shape experiences around weight, as well as the ways in which we live in and through our bodies, it is also important to show how weight can be an unusually powerful "master status" that effectively swamps people's many other social identities and achievements.[16] Transecting race, class, gender, and place, weight has become a new shared cultural preoccupation, an increasingly universal personal concern, the basis for a billion-dollar weight-loss industry, and a phenomenon that seemingly demands immediate government action. Weight is thus also is a perfect lens for exploring how cultural norms are shared by different people, in different communities.

The dark side of failure to meet norms that are so socially important is stigma. Stigma is a concept that social scientists (ourselves included) have been discussing for a long time in the context of other traits, especially stigmatized infectious diseases like HIV/AIDS. What traits become stigmatized in a particular time and place is socioculturally constructed, meaning that it depends on the views and values of each society. Traits judged as socially unacceptable vary widely across cultures and throughout history. Stigma toward people with fat bodies has a relatively brief history. Understanding what it is to live with fat requires us to directly address the processes that push people who fail to meet body norms downward and even out of society.

Stigma, as a judgmental response to nonconformity with social norms, is also understandable as a broader political tool for keeping people in line and penalizing them if they stray.[17] For example, Americans who pride themselves on their tolerance and open-mindedness toward diversity in other aspects will often display high levels of unexamined fat stigma. Fat stigma remains widely acceptable and accepted across many sectors of society; unlike other prejudices that characterize modern American life, it also cuts across social classes, ethnic groups, and geographic areas. We ourselves encounter it on a regular basis within academia, when we describe what we study. "Why would you worry about what a bunch of fat women have to say?" was one such comment from a colleague.

The power that is implicit in such negative judgment about who and what has value also speaks to the power that sociocultural norms possess for shaping both health and the health system. We concentrate in this book on norms around weight, fat, and body, paying particular attention to the ways the acutely aware bariatric participants articulate and react to these norms, both through interviews and more generally during our participant observation in their clinic. We also consider the implications for people's longer-term engagement with weight-related issues once they leave the clinic, because the sociocultural contexts of weight and weight loss matter greatly—and in myriad ways—for both long-term physical and mental health.

## The Path to This Book

We started laying the groundwork for our study on bariatric patients in 2012 and began formal ethnographic research in the clinic in 2014, but we have been engaged in studying weight and weight-loss issues for much longer. In fact, our individual research trajectories are very illustrative of the major shifts that have happened around health, weight, bodies, and nutrition research in our lifetimes alone. Alex began her ethnographic fieldwork in the islands of the central Pacific thirty years ago, when anthropologists were still overwhelmingly engaged with many smaller-scale and subsistence societies that placed a high value on weighty bodies. Alex's long-term research in Samoa, in particular, has tracked shifting preferences and beliefs, showing an accelerating seismic shift from that traditional plump ideal to a vague preference for being thinner (which made an appearance two decades ago) to today's strongly negative ideas about fat. Sarah's research in the United Arab Emirates among female university students in 2009–2011 revealed that young women there expressed considerable worry about weight and invested time and energy in often-draconian efforts at dieting, in stark contrast to the pro-fat attitudes that predominated in their grandparents' youth. Similarly, Amber's decade of work in Paraguay has uncovered profound ambivalence around changing body norms. Many urban Paraguayans reject anti-fat discrimination while also holding harsh anti-fat views, which manifest themselves socially through men's and women's teasing and judgment of bodies identified as fat.

In 2010, we conducted a set of standardized surveys across a range of different low- and middle-income countries in East Africa, the island Pacific, and South America. We found that consistently strong anti-fat sentiments had become normalized across all the cultures we surveyed.[18] This was a shocking finding at the time because many of the cultures we studied were still thought of as fat loving. Yet people consistently identified fat as unhealthy and unwanted and categorized fat individuals as lazy, uneducated, and unmotivated.

Of course, this was not a monolithic attitude; our samples were biased toward urbanites, who were regularly exposed to transnational media messages that equate fatness with badness and public health messages that stress obesity as a risky health condition. Additionally, there were people across all settings who stated that they found large bodies (including their own) not only acceptable but even good. Existing ethnographic research in diverse cultural settings also shows that people may simultaneously hold positive and negative ideas about fatness versus obesity and may focus on the negative frameworks when asked in an official capacity to provide ideas. In other words, long-standing cultural ideas that value larger size still retain power in many settings worldwide.[19]

Nevertheless, those survey results showed that more people overall see fat bodies as unacceptable and bad and will say so. In the survey data, we established that no cultural context we studied—no matter how fat positive it had been historically—was immune to the anti-fat attitudes and rhetoric that gathered momentum throughout the last half of the twentieth century. Moreover, the range of socially acceptable bodies seems to be narrowing in all of these cultures. On the other hand, the strength of expressed anti-fat convictions and the effort, money, and time people are willing to expend to meet new body norms differ from place to place. The US remains one place in the world where the drive to be thin is consistent and internalized and where people with identified fat bodies struggle across many spheres of life, including the workplace, educational settings, and social and familial circles.

Despite several decades of collective work related to weight and body in places as diverse as Paraguay and Bolivia (Amber); Mexico, Samoa, South Korea, Japan, and the US Southeast (Alex); and the United Arab Emirates and the US Southwest (Sarah), we often found ourselves listening to people who did *not* identify as either clinically obese or socially fat. We are certainly not alone in this. In the past few years, a critical corpus of ethnographic work engaging with obesity, fatness, and body issues has developed within anthropology and sociology, exploring the various ways that people engage with globalizing messages that vilify obesity and fat in daily life. With a few exceptions, such work has not explicitly focused on people at the high end of the weight spectrum, those most pathologized by the medical world. Where this work has had such a focus, the research tends to have tiny sample sizes; self-studies ("autoethnographies") are common. This work also tends to be oriented around fat acceptance and/or fat positivity. "Health at Every Size," an agenda that advocates accepting all body sizes as part of a holistic view of health, is also a common framework and point of departure for this research.

Our conclusion is that outside of Fat Studies, anthropologists have not been comprehensively attending to the stories and ideas of those who most struggle to fit dominant body norms because of high body weight, especially in contexts that are highly fat stigmatizing and spurn fat acceptance ideals. For example, the bariatric participants with whom we spoke, who were very large people in a virulently anti-fat setting, were not interested in a revolution that overturns the current stigmatization of fat. Rather, they devoted their emotional efforts, time, and money to changing their physical bodies to better fit current body ideals. Most of the clinic patients we got to know articulated deeply held beliefs that being fat is unacceptable. Even patients who did question anti-fat norms and registered lower levels of fat stigma nonetheless fundamentally believed there was something wrong with their size and therefore with themselves prior to bariatric surgery.

We think another reason that anthropologists have not focused much ethnographic attention on understanding how very large Americans relate to the extreme body norms circulating in the US today is because of the difficulty of the fieldwork. The study of norms, at least as anthropologists approach it, requires that researchers talk to enough people to understand shared concerns and themes. For what we wanted to do, including thematic analysis, one or two cases was insufficient. We needed a robust sample size that was big enough to accommodate loss of participants over time while still meeting the minimum requirements for participant observation and qualitative data analysis.[20] Moreover, recruitment in anthropology in complex urban settings (we based our study in a city in the western US) commonly needs some point of entry. This is even more true when researchers want to study a vulnerable population and are themselves outsiders.

In our case, we could not rely on a politically oriented or community group of "stigma sharers" because the few that do exist are oriented around fat acceptance and "Health at Every Size" goals. We wanted to talk to people who internalized fat stigma and felt it was making their lives miserable, rather than the more studied proponents of the fat acceptance movement. We also wanted to talk to people who knew what it was like to live with fat and live without fat, medically and socially. At a time when medical, public health, and media commentary tends to make it sound like the entire planet is careening toward an "obesity epidemic" (the terminology most often used), studying a group of people who have experienced the reverse trend (extremely fat to not fat) in a fat-stigmatizing context like the US can give us insights into both the experience of unwanted physical weight and its emotional, moral, and social implications.

These considerations meant that the bariatric clinic was an excellent point of entry. However, it took a substantial amount of both administrative approvals and one-on-one relationship building to convince clinicians, who in this case understood the sensitivities and vulnerabilities of their patients, to trust us enough to fully engage in long-term participant observation and patient recruitment within the clinic. Alex spent two years prior to the study launch building trust with hospital administrators. Sarah and Alex talked to most of the bariatric providers and clarified the details of the study before the study began. Sarah provided similar explanations to preoperative and postoperative patients in meetings of the bariatric support group and the behavioral change classes on a routine basis. All three of us went through a variety of quite complex and time-intensive research clearances at the clinic and our own research institution.

One of our goals was to track the patients' changing understandings of their bodies as they lost weight postsurgery. This required a longitudinal (over time) design. The study incorporated repeated interviews of the same set of thirty-five participants, all of whom were at different points in their pre- and postsurgery trajectories. We also conducted two years of clinic-based participant observation in the public spaces of the clinic, focused on interview participants who were patients, patients who did not participate in the interviews, and health-care providers. Lastly, we sent out two waves of surveys (spaced a year apart) to the entire hospital bariatric-patient pool, with a survey sample size of three hundred. Our methodology was thus a technically and practically complex one. The administrative side demanded constant relationship management at high levels. The data collection required highly consistent interviewing styles maintained over time. The analytic methods demanded high levels of technical expertise. It was a large job for the three of us to collect and analyze the array of data with the consistent quality needed, while maintaining the necessary multilevel clinic and participant relationships that allowed the study to continue successfully to its conclusion.

For us, working collaboratively was intellectually and emotionally rewarding, and this helped counter many of the practical and ethical difficulties associated with the project. Now, many years after we first started building our recruitment methodology, we doubt the study could have succeeded if it followed the more traditional approach of a single anthropologist managing all aspects of the study. A team approach made possible the sheer volume of labor involved in managing the complex politics of working in the hospital structure, the fieldwork within the specific clinic with both staff and patients, and the volume and complexity of data our study produced.

It was also helpful that all three of us had our own extensive prior ethnographic experiences, each having conducted long-term field projects in very different places. We had all experienced field research gone wrong, where community relationships were compromised by misunderstandings or miscommunications. We had implemented multiple ethnographic methods many times previously. As a result, we were not learning how to implement various parts of a collaborative, multiyear project on the fly as we rolled the project out. Working in a high-profile, highly regulated clinic means there is not a lot of room for error or do-overs: a serious error and we would have lost access to patients and staff. We have provided details of the methods we deployed in this study in the appendices, for those who are interested in how we went about data collection.

Our particular three-person ethnography in a clinic produced two major interpretive limitations, however. The first has to do with us as individuals. One of the major critiques of social science studies of stigma is that many studies are conducted by people who do not have insider status with the group being studied; in other words, they do not share the vulnerable trait. In this case, none of us have personally experienced extreme obesity or gone through bariatric surgery. Our perspectives are built on multiple years of carefully listening to people who have experienced both of these embodied states, but we have not lived/embodied them ourselves. Sometimes—given rampant fat stigma across many sectors in the United States—this has proven to be an advantage in our work. In certain settings, we are perhaps given more credence than we would be if we were read as fat people (just think of the uphill battle obese physicians face with regard to respect from patients and other providers). At the same time, however, our "outsider status" almost certainly affects what people do and do not feel comfortable sharing with us. Our findings should be tempered with this understanding.

The other interpretative limitation stems from the particular nature of our relationship with the clinic. As was hopefully obvious in our earlier descriptions of our relationship building within the clinic, in order to conduct research within this space, we had to adhere strictly and revert consistently to the authority of clinic rules and norms. There was little space for negotiation over the form of the social science research in which we were involved, compared to what we have previously experienced working within nonclinical settings. Our human-subjects research application (which any US-based researcher who wants to conduct research on humans must submit in order to be in compliance with current international ethical standards) went through the clinic's review process first, before our own institution would even review it. This oversight was ethically and pragmatically necessary, but it did impose certain restrictions on the degree to which we could ask critical questions within clinical spaces. For example, once question sets for interviews were approved administratively, we could not then follow emergent ideas in new directions to the extent we are able to do on other ethnographic projects. Similarly, basing ourselves in a clinic meant that some of the boundaries of the clinic-patient relationship also applied to us. If a patient dropped out of the clinical program, for example, we tended to lose sight of them as well. This was particularly frustrating in some cases but does help to explain why data on the postoperative lives and health of bariatric patients in the long term, more than five years after surgery, is lacking more generally (although there are exceptions).[21]

Finally, we feel it is important to note that as ethnographers, our overriding ethical commitment in any project we undertake, whether individually or as a team, is to depict the cultural worlds of our participants in a way that does them no harm. Because they were bariatric patients, most of our participants had suffered a great deal of stigma and social devaluation, and we therefore felt this duty especially strongly on this project. Although we are well aware that other theoretical lenses, including a critical lens, could be applied to our research, we have opted not to do so ourselves. Instead, we provide enough ethnographic depth and rich description to support alternative readings and leave such analyses in the hands of the reader.

## Organization of the Book

The anthropological ethnographic tradition once idealized the notion of a single researcher heroically collecting data (often while awkwardly appropriating "native" dress), analyzing it, and then going home to write it up in his study (and yes, it was usually "his"). The reality is that this research approach could never handle all the complex realities posed by on-the-ground, in-depth research. The ideal still retains great power, but we have found working as a collaborative unit on this project allowed us to comprehensively approach many methodological, theoretical, and practical challenges. Writing about our research as a collaborative unit has been more difficult. For one thing, first-person narration dominates much of the current compelling ethnographic writing. Most of the ethnographies written recently, for example, are framed firmly in the first person with careful attention to what the writer did, said, and saw—and how their own experienced self influenced what they did, said, and saw. This avoids the problematic third-person omnipotent narrator perspective, but it puts multiple authors, who necessarily were in different places at different times performing different tasks, in a bit of a bind.

After a great deal of internal debate and some external consultation, we decided to rely mostly on the use of "we" and "our" in the introduction and conclusion, which give more of an overview and a theoretical framing for the chapters that form the rest of the book. When necessary, we refer to ourselves in the third person by name. In the remaining chapters, the content- and participant-driven chapters that give primacy of place to participant-patient narratives and experiences, we again write mostly from a "we" perspective, but we more frequently refer to ourselves in the third person (again by name) because there are more instances within the fieldwork in which only one or two of us were present at any given time. Sarah, for example, conducted the interviews that form the core of the ethnographic research described in these chapters. Alex shouldered the task of managing the potentially fragile relations with hospital administrators. Amber devoted substantial time and effort to working out the methodological ramifications of different aspects of what was an extremely complex ethnographic project in an ethically sensitive context. We thus attempt to capture all of these individual experiences within our three-person team via a thoughtful, patchwork use of first-person-plural and third-person-plural perspective. In this book, no one wrote sections for which they themselves were not present. The shifting voice, however, hopefully highlights the fact that our points of view are just that. We do not and cannot know all that occurred in any given situation.

In *Steering the Craft: A 21st-Century Guide to Sailing the Sea of Story*, Ursula K. Le Guin writes about first-person narration, saying, "In nonfiction narrative of any kind . . . the *I* . . . is the author. In these forms, we normally expect the author/narrator to be reliable: to try honestly to tell us what they think happened. . . . The memoirists and nonfiction writers I respect are fully aware of the impossibility of being perfectly factual."[22] We strive to be reliable, even as we wrestle with our limitations, and to give due respect and attention to those ideas and experiences that our participants most wanted communicated to a broader audience.

In our writing, we also decided to organize the book around four key themes that emerged over and over again in our analyses: (1) weight as pathology, (2) weight as judgment, (3) weight loss as success, and (4) weight, worry, and perpetual surveillance. These themes are discussed in a semilinear fashion that roughly tracks the before, during, and after phases of the patients' surgical journeys. Each chapter explores a different way in which the "burden" of weight is experienced in individual lives, acting as a prism for broader social processes. These are themes we see as important not just for anthropological discussions but also for clinicians and the general public.

In chapter 1, "Weight as Pathology," we focus on the ways in which weight becomes a problem for people because it is framed as a medical issue. By this, we mean that obesity in medical terms is considered a disease and public health concern. In chapter 2, "Weight as Judgment," we discuss how and why weight is a problem based on the fact that it has become a signpost and signal of a lack of individual moral worth and social standing. In contrast, in chapter 3, "Weight Loss as Success," we show how lack of weight and/or weight loss signals worth and greater social integration. Finally, in chapter 4, "Weight, Worry, and Surveillance," we focus on the ways in which weight maintenance, "healthy lifestyles," and constant monitoring of eating and exercise are commonly perceived as signs of a strong personal work ethic, good moral fiber, and dedicated willpower. We also show how the high levels of worry and stress associated with constant tracking and monitoring are normalized or ignored.

## A Word about Language

Throughout the introduction, we have used a variety of words to describe bodies. These may have included "fat/fatness," "obese/obesity," "extreme weight," "weight," "morbid obesity," "higher weight-to-height ratio," "high body weight," "very large people," and (less often, given our focus) "skinny." At first glance, our usage probably appears casual and haphazard; in fact, it is purposeful and reflects quite a lot of thought.

Common working definitions of all of these terms tend to draw dichotomies between them. For example, "fat" is often treated as a slippery social descriptor, used casually in conversations to self-describe or to describe someone else but without basis in objective physical measures. In other words, someone may be "fat" in certain settings but not in others and to certain audiences but not to others. Moreover, in some settings, using "fat" is derogatory and stigmatizing: "She's fat and ugly!" would be an all-too-common example of this type of usage (and yes, it is more likely to be "she"). On the other hand, there has been considerable recent pushback in Western settings like the US to this type of deployment, and many activists and adherents of feminist-influenced body-positivity movements now insist that "fat" be used in a positive, empowering sense.

Some researchers focus on "obesity" as a medical term, defined by weight deemed "excessive" after height and weight measures have been obtained from an individual and used to calculate that person's BMI, or Body Mass Index. "Normal weight" only applies to people whose BMI (based on those height-to-weight ratios) is between 18 and 24.9. "Overweight" applies to individuals with BMIs 25 to 29.9, and "obese" applies to individuals with BMIs of 30 or above. "Obese" is then further subdivided into different categories: Class 1, with BMIs 30 to 34.9; Class 2, with BMIs 35 to 39.9; and Class 3, with BMIs 40 and above.[23] People whose weight pushes them into that last category, Class 3 Obesity, are also categorized as "morbidly obese" and, less often, as "extremely obese."

Does this sound scientific and neatly delineated? In fact, use of "obesity" is almost as messy as use of "fat" as a descriptor. Two major problems emerge upon closer examination. One is that BMI categories are woefully inaccurate and do not take into account muscle mass at an individual level, population-level differences, and gendered differences in weight distribution, to name just a few well-known problems.[24] The second is that in everyday practice, Americans often use "obesity" somewhat interchangeably with "fat," even though the connotations of that usage remain slightly different.[25]

What does all of this messiness mean for the way we use descriptors here in this book? After some reflection, we decided to deploy all possible descriptors both that we hear used in everyday language in the United States today and that surfaced as influential and common words / embodied states for patients in the bariatric practice where we were engaged. In relating our research findings, we also decided to use these terms in the ways that are faithful to what we observed—that various terms are used interchangeably, fluidly, and very problematically. In the introduction and conclusion, we engage with the literatures that analyze and critique these terms and how they are used to (dis)establish social norms. We hope our approach will help readers become aware of these same terms, and their power to set and challenge norms, in their own lives.

It is nonetheless important to note that the clinic definitely did not share our approach to language and categories. Several health-care providers within the clinic could and did talk very knowledgably with bariatric patients about fat stigma when that arose. In general, however, the clinic relied on traditional BMI-based obesity categories. Indeed, in order to qualify for the surgery, would-be bariatric candidates typically needed to present with a BMI of 40 or above, indicating "morbid obesity." In this, the clinic reflects common medical and public health practice in the twenty-first century, which overwhelmingly (1) acknowledges that BMIs are conceptually and practically problematic and (2) continues to use them for lack of a clear-cut alternative.

## Questions to Frame Subsequent Reading

If, as we argue, fear of fat is a globalizing phenomenon, the United States has been ground zero for the contradictory, swirling waves of the "obesity epidemic," the massive transnational diet industry, thin-promoting and body-acceptance movements in social and traditional media, and bariatric surgery. We hope our work with bariatric patients will bring attention to some very challenging questions about what bodies mean in our society and what this signals about being "normal." We ask, Why do we struggle so hard to be "normal," when our ideas about normal are so far from the statistical average? What are the repercussions of these struggles? Why does fat stigma remain so entrenched, and why are body norms so very powerful and resistant to change? We will revisit these questions in the conclusion and discuss the implications of our work for broader social issues and concerns. In the meantime, we will use the following four chapters to delve into the experiences of the bariatric patients, as articulated to us across the years of our study.

1

# Weight as Pathology

Toward the end of our years collecting data in the bariatric surgery clinic, Sarah and Alex traveled to Canada to attend "Obesity Week," a large professional conference focused on "fixing" obesity. After we had spent years thinking deeply about the pernicious effects of fat stigma, as well as the complex dynamics between medicalized perspectives on obesity and social perceptions of fat, the conference was a cultural shock. People, all thin and mostly in suits, wandered the brightly lit halls of the conference center, passing between presentations on sedentarism and weight circumference, brain chemistry, new weight-loss technologies, and epidemiological increases in weight across a plethora of different countries and regions.

Ducking into one lecture, Sarah watched a presenter talk about the importance of physical activity in metabolic flexibility, with a slide comparing a cartoon figure of an enormously fat man with a slim, young woman. Entering the vast exhibition hall, she was confronted by booths selling a variety of products, all aimed at helping to monitor or disguise or lose weight. Pictures of obese bellies and rippled, cellulite-plagued thighs were prominent everywhere; actual breathing, talking fat people were entirely absent.

This conference typifies an approach to large bodies that has come to dominate medicine and public health—and, indeed, science more generally—in recent decades. It is, in many respects, a simple and straightforward approach: obesity is a pathological disorder that overwhelms the epidemiological profiles of many societies worldwide, a result of increased sedentary living, consumption of calories, and consumption of high-fat and high-sugar foods.[1] This approach assumes that both policy and individual practice must change to bring bodies back into a "desired" range. To do this, proponents have continued to amass data presenting obesity and overweight as profoundly negative medical conditions, as well as an economic and social burden. Images of fat bodies (especially bodies with BMI ≥ 40, categorized as "morbidly obese"),[2] were everywhere at the conference we attended, but only as pathological sites that required intervention.

Part of the cultural shock we experienced at the conference stemmed from the blatant and pervasive stigma of large bodies, the persistent messages focused on lifestyle change as an antidote to obesity, and the casual assumptions that large bodies are inherently pathological. Of course, these are not at all unusual attitudes. In 2013, for example, coincidentally just a few months before we officially embarked on our ethnographic project focused on bariatric patients, the American Medical Association ruled that obesity should be classified as a disease.[3] This landmark ruling solidified the prevailing view within medicine and science that obesity not only increases the risk for "comorbidities" but also is a morbidity itself. Fat activists and scholars (among others) have fiercely criticized the conflation of obesity with pathology, but it nonetheless informs medical practice, scientific practice, and public opinion throughout the US and, increasingly, worldwide.[4]

Much has been written in the social sciences about processes and techniques of medicalization and pathologization in modern society, whereby certain traits and conditions are reframed as diseased states and inherently "risky."[5] During the past half century, we have seen a profound shift toward treating fat/obese bodies as diseased. Being fat/obese in a country like the US is seen not only to be undesired on aesthetic grounds but also to be unhealthy and out of control.[6]

From this perspective, these out-of-control bodies that pose a risk to others require medical intervention, particularly because of the presumed expense they will impose on society through their alleged lack of work productivity and higher health-care needs. Bariatric surgery is one such intervention aimed at (re)exerting control and (re)establishing a healthy state and "normal" weight. Bariatric surgery also draws our attention to the intertwined relationship between clinic and society. What exactly constitutes a normal body in a sociocultural context where medicalized ideas about health and thinness influence public discussion, morph during these same discussions,[7] and then leak back into the clinic, informing views there?

The ways in which medical professionals use the hierarchically structured space of the clinic (where the MD is the ultimate authority) not only to advise on health but also to express dominant social norms, ideologies, and forms of control is a well-established field of analysis. Likewise, social scientists have focused on the processes by which patients resist medical decrees, construct counternarratives, and modify health-care consumption through doctor shopping, selective adherence to recommendations, and outright avoidance of the clinical space.[8] The clinical encounter in the twenty-first-century United States is reported to be particularly contentious for obese patients.[9] However, while social science critiques have focused on medicalization and the ways in which the clinical space reinforces broader social norms such as anti-fat attitudes, the medical, public health, and nutrition fields continue to medicalize, pathologize, and rely on hierarchically structured clinical visits.

What is perhaps more interesting in this context is that "our" clinical spaces—the hospital and clinic facilities within which we observed and interacted with bariatric patients and providers—were far less overtly stigmatizing of obesity. Indeed, part of Sarah and Alex's cultural shock at the conference stemmed from the fact that we had become accustomed to a more person-based and sympathetic approach to obesity and fatness in the bariatric program within which we were embedded. Listening to conference presenters, Sarah—who did the interviews with bariatric patients—kept thinking, "*My* bariatric clinicians would never say that!" However, while this might be true, the bariatric program we observed, as well as the patients and providers housed within it, still espoused the same underlying perspective that obesity is a pathology and therefore needs to be "fixed." After all, bariatric surgery as a technological intervention would not exist without that assumption.

As we mentioned in our introduction, bariatric surgery as a medical "fix" for obesity has only been offered in the relatively short span of time that obesity has come to be viewed as a global problem: roughly speaking, since the middle of the last century. With the increase in the surgery's popularity has come a proliferation of programs offering it: just Google "bariatric surgery near me" on your computer and look at the results. What may not be immediately apparent from a Google search is the variation in the programs that offer these surgeries. Arguably the most significant difference has to do with whether a program and facilities have been accredited or not. The accreditation process (the Metabolic and Bariatric Surgery Accreditation and Quality Improvement Program, or MBSAQIP) was developed by the American College of Surgeons and the American Society for Metabolic and Bariatric Surgery as a way to standardize training, safety, surgical practices, and patient follow-up practices.[10] According to the American Society for Metabolic and Bariatric Surgery, accredited programs show lower rates of mortality and have more consistently enforced high-quality care.[11] All programs nevertheless face challenges. Long-term follow-up with (and data collection on) patients remains difficult, affecting what we know about bariatric patients' experiences after the first decade.[12] The surgeries, as we remarked earlier, are effective at triggering weight loss but do have their own health consequences precisely because they change fundamental anatomy and biological processes. Moreover, despite well-documented concerns with the accuracy of the standardized BMI categories,[13] even some accredited bariatric programs will perform a gastric bypass or sleeve gastrectomy on individuals who exhibit no comorbidities if they have a BMI of 40 or higher.

One common and reasonable critique that arises in the social science work of clinics has to do with the medicalization of healing. This perspective illustrates that the biomedical worldview of treating diseases rather than people can be experienced as profoundly dehumanizing by patients. Clinicians, as the people with the most authority and power within such settings, are sometimes cast as the "villain" in these narratives, the ones who make patients feel harmed while they seek healing. In recent ethnographic work documenting clinical spaces, some social scientists have engaged more comprehensively with hospital staff and administrators to bridge misunderstandings between academic and applied perspectives on how patients should be viewed and hence treated.[14] When it comes to obesity, however, medical guidelines and practices do not tend to reflect social science work on stigma and lived experiences around fatness. Instead, practitioners in Western biomedical health care overwhelmingly weigh patients, note weight gain, and lecture patients who are subsequently identified as "overweight" or "obese" about weight loss and healthy living.[15] Insurance and medical-practice guidelines ensure that even health-care practitioners who do not particularly want to follow this pattern must. For our part, most social scientists have not seriously attempted to bridge the gap between medical practice and the social critique of medical practice around obesity/fat.

In the hospital where we did our ethnography, however, concern for patients' well-being and the maintenance of a high quality of personalized care were repeatedly stated to be core values within the system. We observed multiple interactions between patients and caregivers in which these values were clearly and immediately obvious as a set of well-rehearsed practices, thus showing that routinized observed practice did, in fact, underscore articulated values. In fact, Amber and Alex have for some years been patients themselves in the same hospital system (though admittedly not in its bariatric program), getting treatment for their own complex illnesses, and have similarly observed, from a patient perspective, the consistently patient-centered ethos at work.

Stigma around weight was likewise not directly evident in the way medical experts in this system interacted with patients (and we were looking closely for it). The patient-participants, too, almost universally articulated that they believed the staff and practitioners were working to help them and that they generally felt respected as people. This made bridging the gap between the medical establishment and the academics conducting research much easier. Nevertheless, we were working within the creative tension produced by recognizing the insights generated by social critiques of the pathologization of obesity on the one hand, and the data supporting a view that sees obesity as a medical condition impacting health, on the other.

Bariatric patients with whom we interacted also saw the surgical procedures they were going through as a necessary medical fix for a medical problem. This explanatory framework rests on the understanding that obesity is a disease and bariatric surgery is a medical technique that, at minimum, alleviates some disease symptoms. We should note that such a framework is at odds with widespread US social norms that see bariatric surgery as a freakish medical intervention for exceptionally fat, "lazy" people.

Such a perspective is also at odds with the views of some scholars who are more sympathetic with respect to fatness itself but not necessarily to the surgery. Fat Studies scholarship, for example, has provided an important stream of critique of the "medicalization of obesity" and fat stigma in recent years but tends to see bariatric surgery in a very negative light. One Fat Studies scholar with whom we spoke while researching and writing this book, for example, said that bariatric surgery can be understood as a body mutilation and that the medical emphasis on the surgery obscures the problem posed by fat stigma and discrimination. Other discussions within Fat Studies have developed layered perspectives, noting "soft opposition"[16] to the surgery among fat activists but also support among most for an individual's right to decide what to do with their body.[17]

The aim in this chapter is to explain why people decide to undergo bariatric surgery, particularly by teasing apart people's reported suffering prior to arrival at the clinic. We focus on both experienced bodily illnesses and the ways patients and providers construct obesity-as-illness in conversation. In doing this, we can explore how weight and disease / ill health are connected and constructed and how people define "too much" weight in both medical and personal terms. We outline some of the current social science critiques of the conflation between weight and poor health status, while also presenting arguments from biomedicine that show compelling links between morbid obesity status and certain disease states.

## Life before Surgery: The Physical Suffering of Morbid Obesity

When Sarah began interviewing patients within the bariatric program, she started by observing the weekly behavioral change classes that presurgical patients were required to attend, to meet patients and also to better understand how groups of prospective patients interacted and interfaced with the program. As an anthropologist with a background of in-depth conversations with women about their experiences with fatness and body ideals, her perspective at the onset of fieldwork was a tendency (mirrored in much of the existing anthropological, sociological, and Fat Studies research) to approach obesity as highly socially constructed. In this view, suffering relating to obesity is predominantly the result of stigma. She discovered almost immediately, however, that prospective bariatric patients had a very different perspective.

In the first presurgery "Change" class series Sarah observed, obvious pain and mobility issues affected many of the attendees. Martha was one such case. In her midsixties, Martha had enrolled in the program a second time after an unfinished attempt several years prior. Her health conditions had become so acute and her size so burdensome that her life was becoming severely circumscribed. The first time Sarah and Martha met, Martha asked Sarah, "What on earth are *you* doing in this class, skinny?" (Sarah had never been called "skinny" so much in her life as she was during the years doing participant observation in the bariatric program.) Chatting about weight, food, and children, Martha did not look well. She moved slowly, dragging a leg, and her face was an odd gray color. By the end of class, she had a sheen of sweat on her face, and her hair was damp. Her husband arrived to help her to the car right outside the clinic entrance, but she still had to stop and rest several times along the way.

Over the next few months, Martha's appearance deteriorated still further, enough so that Sarah became worried and inquired about her health. Martha told Sarah she had debilitating high blood pressure and arthritis, both a result of her weight, she felt. When Martha's surgery was slightly delayed because of insurance complications, we began to fear that Martha would not live to have surgery—or would not live *through* surgery. Thankfully she did both.

As this vignette illustrates, physical weight can be uncomfortable in and of itself. Charles, whom Sarah encountered in a support group meeting eighteen days after his gastric bypass, described it the following way:

> I was tired of being 450 pounds. It's a lot of weight to carry around. People who aren't heavy don't know the amount of work that's involved in actually being heavy. They think you're fat and lazy. Well, you're maybe lazy, . . . but it's a lot of work to carry around that much weight. It's that our daily lives are a lot of work. People take for granted just bounding up the stairs. When you're 450 pounds, you just don't go bound up the stairs, you know?

Charles did not have the serious comorbidities that other bariatric candidates had, nor did he register that the weight had impeded him socially or professionally; but he was tired of carrying 450 pounds on his five-foot-ten-inch frame.

In his narrative, Charles clearly felt that his weight impeded his mobility, that it affected his energy levels, and that it was exacting avoidable wear and tear on his body, a toll that was becoming more apparent now that he was in his midfifties. His own experience was that being "heavy" and "fat" involved a huge amount of daily effort and labor just to get around, and this was exhausting in its own right and also discouraged him from a variety of different activities. This, in turn, was read as laziness and sloth by others he encountered (a point we will return to in chapter 2).

A survey of the larger patient pool at the program reinforces these ethnographic observations. As a supplement to the ethnographic research, our team also sent out a two-wave survey to all individuals who had undergone bariatric surgery within the previous ten years (see appendix B for survey details). Of the 296 responses, 91 percent said that health concerns were "very important" factors in their decision to have the surgery, and 56 percent said that mobility issues were "very important" factors. Over 60 percent of the survey respondents reported suffering from hypertension, high cholesterol, and sleep apnea before surgery, and roughly 40 percent reported suffering from type 2 diabetes before surgery.

We are not arguing that larger body size necessarily equates with a diseased state, and indeed, we will critique this core component of the medicalization of obesity later. Similarly, we are very cognizant—as chapter 2 will show—that a great deal of the suffering inflicted on obese bodies today stems from stress and discrimination. The category "obesity" is highly problematic, relying on inconsistent and arbitrary BMI designations based on weight and height. Similarly, the science linking "obesity" to ill health is murky, especially given how difficult it is to parse out the effects of fat on the body from the effects of chronic psychosocial stress (triggered by experiences of fat stigma).

That said, our data shows that many of our participants were close to being immobilized by their weight and that some of them were also in horrific pain. The participants in this study tended to be both very large and very ill as a result of physical conditions that could be traced to their size—and they were all exceptionally clear and articulate about these connections. This acted as a powerful motivating factor in pushing people to at least consider bariatric surgery. Brad, a man in his sixties whom Sarah met through the support group two years after his gastric bypass, put it bluntly: "I feel now that I was just kind of sitting around, waiting to die. I didn't do anything. I had pain trying to do things. Whenever I got up out of a chair, it was difficult just to get up, and I had to wait. Because my knees would hurt so bad, I had to wait a minute to make sure I had my balance and stuff before I walked, things like that."

## Enrolling in the Program: "You Have to Buy In"

People came to the bariatric program we studied as a result of physician referrals, word of mouth, or their own research. Once there, the first step toward enrollment in the required presurgery program was an all-day intake. It was a grueling but efficient way of comprehensively assessing a new patient. An "exciting ordeal" was how one woman, named Tiffany (more from her later), described the intake. The day included completing the necessary medical and insurance paperwork with bariatric administrators, as well as an assessment by a variety of providers—including but not limited to a bariatric surgeon, the program's psychologist, an endocrinologist, the program's nurse practitioner, and a psychiatrist. It also included a meeting with a scheduler to plan the presurgery clinic visits and classes, as well as the actual surgery date.

The intake had a certain flavor that reminded Sarah of a college freshmen orientation, albeit minus the sweet treats and excited teenagers. That same atmosphere of nervousness, intensity, and excitement, as people attempted to cram as much information about the program as possible into a condensed parcel of time, was much like watching freshmen move into their new university dorms during orientation week.

After the intake day, the arc of presurgery preparation was extensive and included participation in behavioral change classes, food diary recording, and more individual visits with a nurse practitioner, dieticians, a psychologist, an endocrinologist, and a surgeon. Throughout all of these, the content of the visits mattered: it was not simply an issue of showing up and getting cleared for surgery. Patients had to demonstrate some degree of weight loss presurgery coupled with weight-management techniques, reflected in regular weigh-ins during the behavioral change classes and individual clinic visits, as well as in the food diaries. Ideally, patients also demonstrated that they were working on their emotional states to the satisfaction of the team psychologist, namely, through willingness to verbally engage on a variety of personal topics. They were also asked to self-reflect both to the psychologist and in their food diaries, which patients used to track meals, calories, portion sizes, and emotional states at each meal or snack.

Sarah spent a lot of time in the behavioral change classes, especially during the first year of fieldwork. Each patient attended an eight-week cycle of "Change" classes that met once per week. Patients could choose among three specific time slots for each class every week. In the first year, Sarah tried to attend all three sessions of each weekly class, thereby observing three groups of different patients in each week's sessions.

Dieticians taught three of the classes, two of them early in the cycle. These sessions focused on general nutrition-related topics such as guidelines on reading food labels and shopping at grocery stores and the need to achieve a correct balance of protein, fiber, carbohydrate, and fat for general health. Many patients, especially women, had a working knowledge of the general nutrition reviewed by the dieticians in the two early classes, particularly as it pertained to dieting and food restriction. As one woman commented, "We are all expert dieters by now. I bet this class has collectively lost thousands of pounds over the years."

People interfaced with the classes, as well as with concurrent visits to the psychologist, in different ways. The bariatric program's nurses taught the other five classes in the series, covering a wide range of different topics, such as social experiences of weight-related and surgery-related stigma and the emotional components of what it means to binge eat. Not everyone wanted to talk about their feelings, let alone their feelings while eating. As one man commented in frustration during class, "I just keep writing, 'I feel hungry' or 'I feel fine,' in those sections [of the food diaries that asked for his emotional state] because that's all I feel!"

Although patients' refusal to examine their own emotions worried some of the providers, it did not seriously impede patients from getting cleared for surgery, as long as they could prove they were "buying into the program." This meant losing weight, following dietary and exercise guidelines, and demonstrating an understanding of the medical directives and physical limitations associated with their bariatric surgery. On the other hand, some individuals did not lose weight before surgery but did consciously engage in a great deal of self-reflection and emotional work—in class, in the food diaries, and with the psychologist. These patients, too, were usually cleared for surgery. In other words, the program offered some flexibility with regard to the way "buying into the program" was defined for different prospective patients.

The last "Change" class that the dieticians taught occurred in the seventh week of the eight-week class cycle and focused on the dietary needs and specific limitations imposed by a Roux-en-Y gastric bypass or a vertical sleeve gastrectomy, stressing the importance of eating enough protein (sixty grams a day) and staying hydrated (sixty-four ounces of water a day). This class also went over dietary progression after surgery. The first week after surgery, patients were supposed to drink Gatorade only. By the second week, they could progress to pureed food in medicine-cup-sized portions, avoiding sugars and fats so as not to trigger nausea or dumping (dumping occurs when undigested food is "dumped" from the stomach into the small intestine, triggering a range of acutely unpleasant symptoms felt by the person attached to that stomach). From pureed food, they progressed to "mechanical soft," still in small portions. A year after surgery, people could eat most foods, just in smaller amounts.

The dieticians recommended avoiding alcohol, slider foods such as peanut butter (which, in the immortal words of one health-care provider, "go down easy but slide right through your tubes," promoting weight regain), high-fat and high-sugar foods in general, and carbonated drinks for the rest of people's postoperative lives. The goal, each of the dieticians would tell people in the class, was to gradually ramp up to about twelve hundred calories daily and then to maintain that energy consumption. The seventh class often daunted people because of the permanency of the surgery and its lifelong restrictions.

The eighth class, again taught by one of the bariatric program's nurses, intimidated them even more. Part of this final lecture was entitled "Lifetime Commitment." It reiterated that the keys to long-term change after surgery were being aware of eating patterns and amounts, recognizing eating triggers, tracking the difference between hunger and cravings, and changing behaviors. In the lecture, the nurse would emphasize the life-altering nature of the surgeries. One nurse would repeatedly tell would-be patients, "These [sleeve gastrectomies and gastric bypasses] are really not reversible surgeries to all practical intents and purposes."

These tactics were highly intentional, as the presurgery preparation was designed to leave patients scared but prepared, with realistic expectations of what would happen postsurgery. Patients and providers often drew contrasts between the preparation for patients in their own program versus most other programs in the country, which cannot or are not willing to invest in the same degree of preoperative preparation. Even after the "Change" classes finished, prospective patients still needed to attend nutrition follow-ups with dieticians, counseling sessions, and at least one support group meeting. They typically had a clinic visit right before surgery to review health history and lab work and to get a chest x-ray and an EKG. They also needed to complete their insurance requirements and, if applicable, apply to their workplace for permission to take time away.

Thus, by the time patients in this program arrived at the hospital for their surgery, they had already been under intense medical scrutiny, accompanied by medicalizing discourses and technologies. The surgery itself was, in a sense, the proverbial icing on the cake.

## The Effects of Gender, Race, and Age on Program Enrollment and Experiences

As we just mentioned, the required, presurgery classes covered a range of different topics, and people responded to the topics in various ways, depending on their own personal histories and experiences. We also noted that many patients, especially women, had prior knowledge of the general nutrition reviewed by the dieticians in the classes. In fact, some of the women we met were told during their individual visits with the dieticians that they needed to eat more calories or to stop avoiding carbohydrates or other food groups. In other words, they were restricting themselves too much, with unfortunate metabolic consequences. Similarly, women and younger people generally were more apt to self-classify as emotional binge eaters. They were also more prone to feel that their physical bodies were not just medically obese but also socially "too fat" (more on these points in chapter 2). They therefore came into the program with more fraught histories of dieting and more self-identified emotional issues.

In contrast, a small portion of the male patients and, in particular, men who were in their fifties or older, came to the classes with little knowledge of nutrition, no history of dieting, and no past engagement with food beyond an attitude of eating as much as possible. These were the patients who, if they listened to the dieticians' lectures and "bought into the program" (in the words of one participant), tended to lose a lot of weight even before the surgery because they were managing their nutrition and diet for the first time in their lives. This subgroup of men had not previously identified their eating habits as pathological or abnormal, although they had identified their bodies as medically obese. This latter realization, after all, is usually what propelled them into the program in the first place. They had not, however, made in-depth connections between their everyday eating habits and their weights.

Many of these men commented that their workdays had never left them time to manage their eating or to think about their diets, beyond a fuel-in, fuel-out mentality, and that typical workdays were grueling and intensive enough to discourage planning around diet. This is certainly true—the observation that the average American workplace is not conducive to health has been made by many obesity researchers and industry consultants.[18] We would, however, like to draw attention to the fact that most women, no matter how grueling their workdays, did find time to worry about diet and nutrition. Thus, gender profoundly influenced people's experiences with dieting and food before they set foot in the program. This is not surprising; other research clearly indicates that women have faced substantially more pressure to conform to thin ideals, and substantially more fat stigma if they violate those ideals, than have men.[19] There is also evidence that certain types of eating, and particularly restrictive types of eating and dieting, are characterized in the US as traditionally feminine.[20]

Gendered stereotypes themselves have shifted dramatically in recent years in the US, as have feminine and masculine body ideals, which may account for the fact that it was the older men in the bariatric program who seemed the most likely to enter with a less intimate knowledge of nutrition and food restriction. Major changes in American society have increasingly emphasized the male body as a toned, muscular object to be worked on and seen as such. As a result, we have begun to see dissatisfaction levels expressed by men about their bodies rise, although women still surpass man with regard to pressure and dissatisfaction vis-à-vis body ideals.[21]

Gender and age also impacted the ways people interpreted other components of the classes, as well as concurrent visits to the psychologist. The bariatric program's nurses taught the other five classes in the series, covering a wide range of different topics, such as social experiences of weight-related and surgery-related stigma and the emotional components of what it means to binge eat. Many of the older men resisted both the idea that they could be impacted by social stigma and that their eating had any emotional component. In the preceding section, we quoted the man who said, "I just keep writing, 'I feel hungry' or 'I feel fine,' in those sections because that's all I feel!" One of the medical providers often presented a case study for prospective patients that indirectly attempted to prompt people to think about gendered stereotypes around emotional eating. In the case study, the provider contrasted movie portrayals of the grim, stoic male hero drinking his sorrows away at a bar with movie portrayals of the sad, weeping heroine sitting at home on her couch eating a tub of ice cream. In this way, the program itself tried to tackle pervasive social stereotypes about how gendered emotional eating affects people in everyday life.

Another man said, in reference to a class discussion about negative outside reactions to the surgery, "The way I look at it, this is all about me. . . . If other people don't understand, then screw 'em. . . . End of story." Many patients struggled with setting boundaries with others, but gender also influenced the forms this took. Women, for example, often reported trying to carve out time and attention for themselves, but they definitely did not frame this as "screw 'em" if others were not understanding of these attempts. American ideas about nurturing women and independent men made the social repercussions for women who were overtly attempting to tend to themselves rather than others more severe.

Race also influenced an individual's interfacing with the clinic, but as we mentioned in the introduction, there are a variety of reasons why we have a much more difficult time drawing out common themes and threads around race. These reasons include the fact that there were vastly more White people in the classes and in the program more generally, and this both shaped the tone of the conversations and also brought up issues around confidentiality.

A short story here is illustrative. Sarah met an individual over the course of the classes whose gender, race, and age combined to make that person quite unique within this particular program. The individual was a lovely person to chat with and contributed extensively in the classes. One day, Sarah and this individual were standing by the front door of the clinic, casually talking after a class ended. The person finally looked at Sarah and said, "You know I wish you well with this study, . . . but I will never agree to be in it." Sarah, who had not actively recruited the person precisely because she did not think the person wanted to be recruited, was mildly startled by this sally. After a moment, she asked whether the person's reasons were due to time constraints or other concerns. In response, the individual said that no one from their life knew they were considering surgery, it was not considered acceptable in their social circles, and they did not believe there was any productive way to talk about their experiences to a researcher without getting into identifiable background information. Although Sarah did not completely agree with this last statement, as social scientists have increasingly developed ways to talk about important thematic findings without using identifying information about participants, she did not think it worth stressing the person with a debate about advances in anthropological methodologies right before a life-altering surgery. One motivation for this study, after all, is to shed light on the unintended and often overlooked suffering before and after bariatric surgery, not to cause more stress and suffering among would-be patients. Sarah and the person parted amicably and never discussed the issue again.

Most of the people quoted and described in this chapter are White. One or two just did not want to discuss race, and so we do not, at least in the context of their particular experiences. We do recognize that there are problems in this approach, but the themes discussed in this chapter did dominate patient narratives across our general participant observation and in our interviews, regardless of race and ethnicity. In other words, experiences of weight-related illness and medicalized frameworks for both obesity and bariatric surgery cut across racial groups in this sample.

We do know, from the existing literature, that race impacts enrollment in bariatric surgery programs in the United States more generally, as well as experiences thereafter. Most of the research that has explored race and bariatric surgery within the American context has focused on Black and Latinx populations and has not been ethnographic. Summarized, this literature says something to the effect that people who are Black and Latinx do not opt for bariatric surgery at the same rates as do White people; if they do undergo surgery, then their outcomes postsurgery are worse; socioeconomic factors impact their access to surgery; they tend to be more "obesity positive"; and their behavioral patterns pre- and postsurgery are different.[22] Although data supports these assertions, each does need to be teased apart and further examined. Why? For one, if you look at the comments sections below some of the publicly accessible news bulletins reporting on this type of research, online commentators have immediately used the data to argue that the observed disparities in access and outcomes between Black people and White people is due to higher rates of "reckless behavior" on the part of Black people.[23] This is not how the data should be interpreted—decades of research by medical anthropologists and sociologists, among others, tell us otherwise. It is certainly not relevant to an analysis of our own sample of bariatric patients, which did include people who identified as Black and Latinx.

In chapter 2, we delve into the history, usefulness, and often-problematic use of "fat positive" frameworks by researchers to explain higher rates of obesity among Black women. We also will look at the effects of fat stigma and stress on the emotional and physical health of people identified as fat, while considering the potentially amplifying effects of experiences of racism and stress for fat people of color, inside and outside clinical spaces. In the introduction, we already discussed the ways in which US-based research on obesity portrays Black and Latinx people as more at risk for obesity, relative to White people, as well as the ways in which socioeconomic factors that impact weight trajectories currently do disproportionately affect certain communities of color within the United States. Some of these same factors are certainly at play when it comes to bariatric surgery.

For now, two additional observations about race, obesity, and bariatric surgery need to be made. The first is that Asian Americans have, until very recently, been invisible in US-based research on obesity, and they remain largely invisible in the research on bariatric surgery.[24] This invisibility seems to stem from the fact that Asian Americans register lower rates of overweight and obesity across all of the fifty states, relative to White, Black, Latinx, and Native American people.[25] In other words, Asian Americans were, until very recently, perceived to be more "successful" at weight management and, therefore, not in need of attention. Recent research has rendered this assumption more complex, showing significant rates of fat-stigma experiences among Asian Americans, on the one hand, and greater tendency toward abdominal fat and elevated risk for metabolic and cardiovascular disease at lower BMIs, on the other.[26] There was a small but steady presence of Asian Americans in the clinic program we studied, and they also numbered among our participants.

The second observation is that indigenous communities in the United States have been hypervisible in US-based research on obesity, but there are nonetheless persistent gaps in the current research on bariatric surgery experiences among indigenous people. Indigenous communities in the US have had a particularly fraught experience when it comes to obesity/fat and diseases like type 2 diabetes. For those of us who remember obesity and chronic disease research in the 1980s and 1990s in the mainland United States, reservations were ground zero for much of the early work, theories about supposed "thrifty genotypes" among southwestern tribes like the Akimel O'odham (Pima) proliferated, and billions of dollars were spent trying to isolate the genetic factors that allegedly made Native Americans more at risk for weight gain and metabolic disease.[27] We ourselves had no participants who identified themselves to us as tribal members, and thus we cannot comment on indigenous experiences around bariatric surgery. It is certainly an area, however, that needs more social science work informed by critical race theory to be done, and it needs this urgently. Bariatric surgeries are increasingly being recommended to specific tribes as an "obesity fix," at a time when the political economics, histories of oppression, and structural inequities that have contributed to sky-high obesity and diabetes rates on reservations are also receiving attention.[28]

## Framing Bariatric Surgery as Medically Necessary

In the clinic we studied, medical providers very intentionally framed bariatric surgery as a medical necessity, often a dire one. For example, periodically, extremely ill individuals would enroll in the program but would not attend the required classes and clinician visits. From a provider perspective, it was intensely frustrating to engage with people every day who were dying from heart disease, diabetes, and organ failure and to be unable to concretely help those individuals.

The attitudes of bariatric program providers (which we learned about via our extensive participant observation in the clinic) were based on the bedrock assumption that morbid obesity—at least in the patients in the program—represented a diseased state and that bariatric surgery could alleviate this condition. Beyond this core belief, attitudes differed markedly, but this did not diminish cooperation among the bariatric providers at this clinic, because its mandate for patient-centered care provided a uniting framework. As a result, members of the bariatric medical team consistently framed bariatric surgery as medically necessary, focusing on the ways in which gastric bypass or (less often) sleeve gastrectomy resolved life-threatening illnesses. This approach dominated the preoperative "Change" classes and clinician visits as prospective patients cycled through the requirements presurgery, as well as the first-year postsurgery.

One provider explained early in fieldwork that such verbal framings were for her a very intentional effort to combat negative stereotypes of bariatric surgery. She pointed out that many prospective patients come to the program after years of failure at weight loss. They have been told repeatedly that such failures are their own fault and then must face additional judgments that they are now "cheating" at weight loss by opting for surgery rather than "losing weight on their own" (both common phrases bandied about by patients' family, friends, and colleagues). The provider argued that learning not to self-blame or allow others to attach blame to weight were pivotal components of long-term success in the program.

This provider drew a powerful comparison between her previous work with cancer patients and her current work, saying that she used to wheel lung-cancer patients out of the hospital for smoke breaks between treatments and yet they still did not receive the same level of casual but toxic blame and shame from others that her morbidly obese patients do. Research on obesity stigma and the stigma around smoking and other behaviors that are seen to elevate one's "risk" of disease indicates very interesting parallel trends in blame and stigma between smokers and people labeled obese/fat. However, smoking has additional connotations of addiction and nefarious activities by "Big Tobacco" that remove some of the blame from individuals.[29] Food, by contrast, is not usually classed as an addictive substance.

One of the nurses, echoing the techniques examined in sociologist Natalie Boero's work,[30] actively combated rhetorics of blame, shame, and personal responsibility by medicalizing morbid obesity and bariatric surgery. In the very first presurgery class of each cycle, for instance, she reviewed an impressive list of the health conditions that drive individuals into the bariatric program. These included extreme weight, fatty liver disease, sleep apnea, joint pain, heart disease, type 2 diabetes, abnormal blood fats (hyperlipidemia), and high blood pressure (hypertension). Most of the people in the class could identify with more than one of these pathologies, because they have become much more common in the US in recent years and they are all (albeit problematically) associated with higher weights. Nonalcoholic fatty liver disease is a bit of a kitchen-sink category for a range of liver conditions, all characterized by too much fat getting stored in the liver, which leads over time to chronic liver inflammation and eventually a damaged liver.[31] Sleep apnea is a condition that sounds comical to many outsiders because the most obvious and frequent symptom is loud snoring and gasping during sleep, but it is potentially very serious because a person who has sleep apnea actually stops breathing repeatedly during the night while they are ostensibly asleep.[32]

"Heart disease" is another term that actually refers to a range of different conditions, this time all affecting the heart. Coronary artery disease, caused by plaque buildup in the walls of the arteries that supply blood to the heart and the rest of the body, is the most common type of heart disease in the United States today. That plaque buildup obstructing vital blood flow throughout the body is caused by cholesterol deposits, and over time, the obstructions weaken the heart muscle and increase an individual's risk of a heart attack.[33] Type 2 diabetes is loosely defined as a chronic condition that occurs when the body stops properly using insulin—a hormone produced by the pancreas that helps the body take circulating glucose from the bloodstream into the cells, where it is used for energy—resulting in elevated blood-sugar levels.[34] Hyperlipidemia refers to elevated levels of fats in the blood, mainly two types of fats: cholesterol and triglycerides. Both are essential to normal cellular functioning (in other words, it would be a bad idea to try to eliminate fat from one's diet entirely), but higher levels become unhealthy. In particular, chronically increased levels of cholesterol are associated with plaque buildup on the walls of the arteries, as we just mentioned in our description of heart disease.[35] Hypertension, or high blood pressure, is alarmingly termed the "silent killer" because it often has no symptoms from the perspective of the hypertensive individual. The term refers to increased pressure in the blood vessels, as the blood pushes with more force against the walls of the arteries. If pressure stays elevated over a prolonged period of time, this can increase a person's risk of having a stroke or a heart attack.[36]

One of the major risk factors for developing many of these diseases is simply age, but obesity—as we have mentioned—is typically associated with all of them as well. Although the science behind these associations is sometimes less clear than Americans, for one, tend to think (because of the complicating health effects of fat stigma, which we will discuss in more detail later, as well as complex nutritional, epigenetic, and genetic factors), it is certainly true that, at the population level, (1) obesity rates have soared in the US population; (2) rates of fatty liver disease, sleep apnea, joint pain, heart disease, type 2 diabetes, hyperlipidemia, and hypertension have likewise soared; and (3) obesity and the associated diseases are co-occurring in increasingly younger age cohorts.[37] In other words, having more Americans in their sixties, seventies, and above explains some of the increases in heart disease and the like, but it does not explain why more Americans in their forties and below are suffering from them.

Also significant is the fact that all of the diseases just mentioned can be managed through medication, but the first recommendation for long-term management—whether one goes to the doctor, reads a self-help book, or looks at the CDC website—is typically lifestyle change, that is, get regular exercise and "eat healthy." Here, eating healthily most often means avoiding heavily processed foods and foods high in sugar, salt, and saturated fat. Fat activists have correctly pointed out that people with higher weights who follow this exercise and dietary regime but do not lose weight may, in fact, be healthy. However, given the fact that most Americans, regardless of weight, are essentially sedentary creatures at this point in the twenty-first century (meaning, on average, we use our legs to walk around our houses and offices and out to the car) and given the fact we primarily eat premade, prepackaged foods that are high in sugar, salt, and saturated fat, implementing exercise and dietary changes does cause weight loss in most people. The trick is that neither the changes nor the weight loss typically last all that long for any given person, because most of the environmental cues in the US are obesogenic. In other words, work days and child care make it more difficult to exercise than not to exercise; most urban built environments now encourage driving rather than walking or taking public transport; gyms cost money; preparing healthy food takes time and/or money; and so on.

In this context, bariatric surgery is particularly interesting because it leads to pronounced reductions in the "bad numbers" and symptoms associated with type 2 diabetes and hypertension and the like, both through weight loss and (this is the interesting part) independently of weight loss. Moreover, the effects are more likely to last. As a result, bariatric surgery is increasingly viewed within medical programs nationwide as one of the few medical fixes in existence for obesity and diseases traditionally associated with obesity.

After describing all of the diseases that bring people to the clinic, the nurse in the "Change" class asked her audience to list the potential effects of type 2 diabetes. That is, she asked them to describe the negative consequences of having uncontrolled, elevated blood sugar over a sustained period of time. Patients mentioned neuropathy, blindness, fatigue, and amputation. The nurse used this discussion to emphasize that type 2 diabetes needs to be tightly controlled because of the devastating long-term effects and that gastric bypass is the best resolution for diabetes in the morbidly obese. She also discussed how both the sleeve and the bypass are effective interventions for heart disease, joint pain, sleep apnea, hypertension, and more. The nurse never used the word "cure" when describing bariatric surgery and in fact explicitly stated that this term should not be used since the mechanisms by which many of the pathologies improve are not yet well understood. The patients, however, did routinely use that word.

Other provider tactics also contributed to the framing of morbid obesity as pathological and bariatric surgery as medically necessary. These included frequent references to serious comorbidities and the preprogram screening that emphasized serious illness and/or extreme obesity as a prerequisite for surgery. Other ways of reinforcing this framing involved discussions of how to navigate insurance coverage and the presence of many patients who were referred by outside physicians in primary care, orthopedics, organ transplant, and endocrinology.

Finally, there was the powerful influence of the space itself. All of the activities we have just described took place in medical settings: "Change" classes were run at both the out-patient clinic and the in-patient hospital, as were individual visits between providers and patients and the support group meetings. Simply being situated in the clinic and hospital highlighted the medically supported nature of the surgery and its program.

## Teaching Participants the Biomedical Framework

People came into this bariatric program primed to think about morbid obesity as a pathological state simply because such attitudes are so pervasive in American society today. As a host of other social scientists have documented, the dominant biomedical frameworks for a range of conditions including obesity have expanded out of the clinic and now increasingly shape popular and public health understandings.[38] This has profound repercussions for how people categorize normal versus diseased states and healthy versus risky lifestyles.

Within such frameworks, large bodies have specifically been portrayed as embodying a particular type of out-of-control riskiness. Although scholars and activists have extensively challenged such assumptions, casual conflations of obesity/fat with pathology still dominate most people's thinking.[39] The bariatric patients were no exception.

Patients also learned through the presurgery preparation a specific, partially exculpating language to frame their diseased state and the resolution of it through bariatric surgery. The fact that illnesses often improved dramatically in a matter of weeks to months after the operation meant that patients could track their own lived experience of feeling "cured" within a condensed period of time. This was certainly true for Martha, Charles, Brad, and other people we encountered in the support group meetings, as well as most of the survey respondents.

Both in interviews and in discussions in the presurgery classes and postsurgery bariatric support group meetings, the patients' narratives showed a distinct pattern, focusing on the medical necessities underlying their decisions to undergo bariatric surgery. Stories from four very different patients provide personalized examples of these patterns.

## Anita

Sarah met Anita, like many of our research participants, in the presurgery behavioral change classes. She was part of a chatty, small, all-female, racially diverse class. Friendly and talkative, with coiffed red hair and freckles, Anita asked many questions about bariatric surgery and its aftermath. She also volunteered details about her own health, as well as about her job as an administrator at a large, local institution. It was not until the first formal interview, however, that we learned personal details, such as the fact that Anita had divorced five years previously and had two adult sons. She was only in her early fifties but had been diagnosed with type 2 diabetes some years previously. Anita reported that she began gaining weight in her thirties and said, "Once I hit 200 [pounds], there was no going back." She reached her highest weight of 340 pounds during her divorce because, she said, of the associated stress.

When asked during a presurgery interview what made her consider having bariatric surgery, Anita settled more firmly into her seat, looked at Sarah, and responded frankly:

> My diabetes. And they've pretty much put me through or put me on a lot
> of the diabetic medicines. And it's not controlling my blood sugars the

way they want it to control them. And the next step would be insulin, like a slow-release insulin, and I really don't want to go there because insulin usually makes you gain weight. And being heavy as a diabetic isn't a good idea to begin with. So for health reasons, for my diabetes . . . Last year, I changed lots of habits. I went on Weight Watchers, and I walked. I slowly increased my walking. I walked two to three miles during the week. And then on the weekends, I walked five to eight miles on the weekends. . . . So I made all these changes, and my A1C [a blood test that measures average blood-sugar levels over a multimonth period] was still at like 7.6, 7.8. And that wasn't good enough, so in January of this year, they switched my medicine. And the medicine made me hungry 24/7, and it also made me gain weight. I gained like close to thirty pounds in a month. . . . And I had lost about forty pounds the previous year. So bam, I'm done. One month, I'm back to square one. And so, it was frustrating. . . . And the doctor had been asking me if I would consider [bariatric surgery] for like a year and a half already, but I was like, "No, I can do this myself." . . . And then in March, I was talking to my sister about the surgery because the doctor recommended it. And she started reminding me of all the problems that family members have had with diabetes. My mom went blind in one eye. My grandma actually died in a diabetic coma. And so it's like, all right, I guess I should go through the process.

In her narrative, Anita highlighted that she was stuck in a frustrating loop, where her weight gain (in conjunction with a family predisposition) triggered diabetes, but then diabetes and diabetes medications prevented her from losing weight and reducing her dangerous blood-sugar levels "on her own."

Anita mentioned elsewhere in the interview that she was already experiencing neuropathy in her feet and that her insurance would cover a gastric bypass procedure because it was the only intervention that would effectively break her downward medical spiral. Later in this same interview and again in her final postsurgery interview, Anita noted that "evidence indicates" that people who have bariatric surgery for health reasons are "more successful than those who just do it to lose weight." In this way, Anita expressed her complete adoption of an explanatory framework based in a biomedical understanding of her presurgery condition and body. Anita repeated a version of this narrative (minus some of the personal details) in the classes, in a support group meeting she attended, and in subsequent interviews postsurgery. She had established a clear origin story to explain her reasons for bariatric surgery and did not deviate from it substantially.

Medicalizing tactics were also deployed by patients who suffered from less obvious comorbidities, in this case highlighting the inherently "risky" nature of morbid obesity. Extended excerpts from two interviews with Tiffany—one presurgery and one postsurgery—illustrate how this played out in one such patient.

## Tiffany

Sarah met Tiffany in the behavioral change classes many months before her Roux-en-Y gastric bypass surgery. After a great deal of informal chatting before and after the classes, they eventually sat down for a formal interview. Tiffany, both because of her background as a nurse and because of her size, had been considering bariatric surgery for years and was very open with her professional and social circles about that process. In a presurgery interview, she said,

> I've been morbidly obese for most of my adult life, since like puberty set in. . . . And I think I always thought about it [surgery] because when I first heard about it, I was like, "Oh, that sounds really neat. It's a solution." You know, at first this is what I thought. And I did research. I did do my research on the different types. And I was at first gung ho about the lap band. And then working in the medical field, I saw patients that had had it and would hear, "Oh, I have a graduation to go to" or "I have a party to go to, and I can loosen the band so I can enjoy it." That doesn't work for me. Every day would be that for me if I was put in that scenario. So lap band was out. Then I looked at things like the sleeve, and I did all my research on bariatric surgeries. And I think it was just something that was in the back of my head, like, you know, "It's a solution. It's going to help me. And, yeah, someday I'll do it." And then a friend of my mom's about ten years ago had it done, and that really pushed me because I saw the weight on her come off, like melting off of her. And I'm an active soul in a large body, and it doesn't work, you know? I want to go hike. . . . I want to go to the Caribbean and snorkel and scuba dive.

I'm going to get emotional. But I want to do those things, and I can't. I can't, physically I can't.

In this narrative, Tiffany's weight itself was the problem. Tiffany primarily focused on the frustration she felt as "an active soul in a large body."

Tiffany's reason for getting gastric bypass surgery specifically was not because it was associated with better resolution of comorbidities (the reason that many medical providers said they preferred bypass). Instead, she thought the weight-loss results would be better than they would be with a procedure such as gastric band or even a sleeve gastrectomy, in part because she physically could not "cheat." The surgery was a "solution" to her near-lifelong morbid obesity.

Tiffany's narrative shifted in significant ways in the second interview, conducted several months after the first and also after her gastric bypass. Sarah had run into her by chance a couple of weeks before this second interview, so she already knew that Tiffany was thrilled with the way things were unfolding for her postsurgery. However, when they sat down for the formal interview, Tiffany had a few lingering complaints:

I feel—I will be—on the twenty-sixth, I will be forty-four years old, and I feel like I'm twenty-two again. My energy level has plummeted [gone up] through the roof. . . . Just crazy. I have a little bit of a setback going on right now with my left knee. . . . Well, for many years I've had, you know, degenerative arthritis and stuff, obviously weight issues causing that. And right after my surgery, it was great. I mean, nothing. But since going to the gym, I did my first 5k [and she tweaked her knee and is having to rest it, to allow it to recuperate]. . . . [On the other hand,] I know my lab numbers are completely changed, and I've done a complete 180. Even my cholesterol levels have—I'm off cholesterol meds.

By this time, Tiffany had lost 102 pounds. She talked at length about her excitement over losing the weight, but in this interview, she also focused on medical issues stemming from her obesity that were resolving themselves. A few, like the knee, had gotten worse in the short term, but Tiffany said that her doctor was confident that the surgery and weight loss would be pivotal in her recovery.

In the first interview, Tiffany had reported that she was basically healthy, but in the second interview, she mentioned that in fact, her lab results had improved since surgery and weight loss. Her comments imply that she knew her numbers were less healthy before and immediately after surgery and that they improved exponentially afterward. Thus, there is a medicalizing shift in her narrative, in which she focused more on the pathology of weight after she began to lose weight.

Other study participants drew even clearer linkages between high body weight and disease, even when they themselves were healthy in all other respects.

### Charles

As mentioned earlier, Charles was less than a month postsurgery when Sarah first met him at a support group meeting. He was one of the most even-keeled patients that she met; very little rattled him, and he had experienced little social stigma during his lifetime. Partly this stemmed from his supportive family structure, especially from his wife, who managed a rare and exceedingly difficult balance of being supportive (she changed her own diet to accommodate his needs) without policing his food intake or being critical of his weight. Externally imposed weight-related stigma therefore did not encourage Charles to choose surgery. Neither did existing disease. Instead, it was his interpretation of what his future would be like if he did not lose weight that motivated him. In his first formal interview with Sarah, conducted postsurgery, Charles said,

> I am fifty-four. . . . Okay, I am relatively very healthy. Now I was a big man. Okay, I was 450 pounds, . . . [and] I guess I'm five foot ten. And so my weight was not healthy, but physically I was pretty healthy. I didn't really have high blood pressure. I used to take high blood pressure pills, but then I came off them because my blood pressure was fine. So I didn't really have a high blood pressure. I didn't have diabetes. I didn't have any of that stuff, okay? So I told my wife, I said, "I need to do this now because it's not that I'm not going to have that stuff. I just don't have it now." So I needed to lose the weight because I needed to remain healthy. I'd like to live a nice, long life. So I went ahead and

decided that the surgery would be appropriate for myself for what I want with my life.

Charles had no comorbidities at the time of his gastric bypass, so in the absence of current illness, his emphasis shifted to potential future risks. He felt his morbid obesity was eventually going to cause illness and even early death. Thus, he decided to undergo surgery for health reasons, but to prevent future illnesses rather than to alleviate existing ones. By losing a lot of weight through surgery, Charles hoped to live a "nice, long life."

Charles, Anita, and Tiffany all had their gastric bypass surgeries covered by insurance because their BMIs were high, despite the relative absence of serious comorbidities. Lisa Campo-Engelstein points out that people make strong linkages between a "real" disease and the necessity and legitimacy of insurance coverage.[40] Insurance is thus another key component in the medicalization of obesity, and insurance providers are fundamental in shaping both health-care-seeking behaviors and attitudes toward bariatric surgery. According to the National Institute of Diabetes and Digestive and Kidney Diseases, bariatric procedures in the United States typically cost $15,000–$25,000 at the time of this study, which was similar to the cost of surgery in our study's clinic at the time.[41] The clinic we studied accepted patients covered by Medicare or Medicaid, as well as those without insurance who were able to pay privately. Sometimes, the program was also able to provide surgeries and accompanying care gratis, which made providers and patients alike happy.

As we have pointed out elsewhere, however, despite the fact that the surgery was frequently covered by insurance at the clinic we studied, bariatric procedures are generally considered "elective" rather than essential and life-saving.[42] This has all sorts of ramifications, with regard to both how people perceive the surgery and who is able to access it. For example, at the time of this writing (the first half of 2020; after the research described here was completed), most novel bariatric procedures have been put on hold worldwide as a result of the COVID-19 pandemic.[43]

*Fred*

While drafting an early version of this book, Sarah attended a support group meeting. After two years, most attendees knew her well, regardless of whether they were actively participating in the research interviews. The few exceptions tended to be sporadic in their attendance. One of these, an older gentleman named Fred, cornered Sarah after the meeting to quiz her about our project.

Listening to Sarah's explanation of the research, Fred said that he was very much driven by numbers and "big data" but that before his own surgery, he did not know what any of his own numbers (e.g., A1C, vitamin D, blood pressure) were or what they meant. Now, several years after his gastric bypass, he was proud to say that he did. He announced that the numbers were what had power for him. He insisted on returning to the clinic multiple times a year for a checkup. He said that he wanted to see the numbers and to track the way some were going up and some were going down.

Fred even created his own spreadsheets and graphs using his health records. For twenty years prior to his surgery, he said all of the "bad" numbers had steadily increased while the "good" numbers were too low, and now both those trends had reversed. He felt better physically, and this feeling was amplified (or arguably cocreated) by the positive feedback that his normal A1C levels, blood pressure, and other numbers gave him.

Fred's example illustrates the overall theme of this chapter: that ideas about weight can be both scientifically based and also deeply culturally constructed. Both strands are unavoidably embedded in most of the discourse around obesity, especially morbid obesity, and the cultural framework of medicalization has created an especially strong pathologization of obesity. This pathologization, along with the movement toward medicalization within our society more generally, interweaves personal experiences of suffering (in which disease and stigma-induced distress become entangled) with cultural beliefs about the importance of medical "facts." Such facts include clinical interpretations of diagnostic disease categories that establish high body weight as a problem and an array of tests that show that comorbidities and obesity are interrelated.

Fred also made a series of comments that are significant in the context of chapter 2, where we will explore weight-related stigma. When

Sarah told Fred that we were interested in how people register weight-related stigma, Fred said that when he compared the current obesity rates in the US with forty years ago, he felt "embarrassed" that nothing had changed in private-sector activities, federal policies, and individual behavior with respect to the "national disgrace" of our collective weight gain. Fred thus expressed strongly stigmatizing views about being a part of a fat and lazy country. Fred is certainly not alone in his judgments about weight, and this is the topic we turn to in chapter 2.

2

# Weight as Judgment

As medical anthropologists, we were interested in how respondents—in their roles as patients and in their lives outside the clinic—talked about stigma. We particularly focused on weight-related stigma, or being judged by others as a failure because of one's body size. Feeling stigmatized can be a heavy emotional burden. Patients tended to react to stigma in two very different ways. They would recount personal stories of the hurt of experiencing teasing, snide comments, or other forms of weight-related stigma, or they would, like Fred in chapter 1, completely dismiss weight-related stigma as a relevant issue. This dismissal did not mean Fred was inattentive to fat stigma; rather, he was expressing that the pathological weight itself was the problem, and he believed fat people (his past self included) deserved to be judged. Some people even exhibited both tendencies: they noticed when they were judged harshly by others but identified themselves as to some extent deserving the blame.

Individuals who entered the bariatric program at this clinic by definition had a clinical designation of morbid obesity; they would not otherwise have qualified for the surgery. Regardless of whether they perceived large size and heavy weight to be pathological and deserving of condemnation, most of them would (when asked) detail many indignities that they had encountered while being identified as fat in contemporary American society. These issues ranged from self-condemnation for not achieving normative American body ideals of thinness to experiencing acute episodes of stigma inflicted by another person(s) to the daily misery of attempting to squeeze into chairs that did not quite fit their frames.

In all of these cases, an individual's weight became a measure—or sometimes a proxy—for sweeping judgments and assumptions about personal worth. Most of the men and women with whom we spoke also internalized that stigma to some degree. Indeed, given the depth and power of the societal blame-shame framework in which all of our lives are currently embedded, it would be difficult not to internalize it.

This chapter explores what we call "fat stigma" and others refer to as weight-related or obesity stigma. We use the word "fat" here again because we pay particular attention to both its ubiquity and its power. Bias against fat people is virulent and widespread across all sectors of American society, and it is also normalized. In other words, it is tolerated by many people, including those who would not tolerate other types of prejudice, and—despite a slew of recent challenges—it is still mostly legal in forty-eight states at the time we write this.[1]

Activists inside and outside the social sciences have critiqued recent cultural ideas that idealize thinness as well as related notions of risk, morality, responsibility, and control.[2] A recent surge in social media activities around body positivity (think of @TessHolliday and her @EffYourBeautyStandards, as well as all of the hashtags like #IWokeUpLikeThis) has had some impact, too, at least on young people. These insights do not appear to be making much of a dent in widely held societal attitudes about weight and size, however. Several factors—including the uneven inclusion of people of different races, genders, and body sizes in these movements;[3] the continued popularity of moral-thinness-as-personal-project; and the rewriting of the movements by some obesity researchers as "increasing risk"[4]—leave us pessimistic that the US is going to experience a sustained reduction in fat stigma in coming years.

A personal experience with the popular media reminded us recently just how deeply seated our cultural notions about weight and size are and added yet another layer to the perspectives and experiences emerging from the participant data. We wrote a public opinion piece intended for the general news media, in which we discussed the ways in which antiobesity campaigns increase stigma and are ineffective because they overfocus on individual behavioral change—a point that is supported by robust scientific evidence. The editor responded to this by saying, "At the end of the day, it is all about the individual, so I don't understand your point." Clearly, it is incredibly difficult to unseat deeply held cultural beliefs that have been rewritten as universal human truths.

A good deal of scholarly literature indicates that not everyone in the US holds to and is judged by the same body norms. This research— some of it excellent and some of it very poor indeed—has attempted to demonstrate cultural differences in the ways in which different communities view fatness, the ways in which these line up with mainstream

American racial categories, and how this produces differences in attitudes and behaviors around body image, diet, nutrition, exercise, and so
on that show demographic patterns. The experiences of Black women in
the bariatric program we studied, fleshed out with writing from Black
women scholars, provides us with a valuable insight into these literatures. Black women's experiences with body norms have been widely
discussed and debated across many sectors of American society, and
they are often depicted as a more "fat positive" cohort in the United
States today.[5] Mimi Nichter's work, now two decades old, talked about
the power of this positivity to resist stereotyping "Barbie doll" ideals and
to have a healthier self-image.[6] Recent work on this topic, often written
by Black women scholars, makes clear that Black women experience racialized fat stigma in profoundly harmful ways and that pressure to lose
weight and attain unrealistic body shapes and weights is increasingly
prevalent.[7]

Our participant data are rife with various people's experiences of
different types of burdens stemming from ill treatment related to their
obese/fat status presurgery. We organize this chapter to walk the reader
through these burdens. Judgments, for example, were levied by close
family members and random strangers, and they were also produced
internally as people blamed and shamed themselves for their undesired
weight status. Structural stigma further increased the emotional and
physical burden on people, as they attempted to negotiate airplane seats,
chairs, clothing, and store aisles into which they did not fit. All of this
added up to make many patients feel they could not experience normal
lives until they lost significant weight.

## Burden #1: Fat Bodies Are Consistently Devalued

The physical body has long been a visual marker of identity and social
connectedness (or lack thereof), both cross-culturally and throughout
history. However, the way bodies are "read" (in other words, perceived
and interpreted) has varied significantly.[8] In many cultural contexts, fat
bodies have been read as signals of abundance and meaningful social
connections and have therefore been considered desirable. Such models
still hold power among many populations globally, but increasingly, we
see a worldwide shift toward valuing and even idealizing thinness.[9]

As thinness is increasingly valued, the fat body becomes not just patho-
logically obese but also socially disgusting, unaesthetic, and displeasing.
Such attitudes are extremely pronounced in the United States, where the
"cult of thinness" has penetrated people's thinking about bodies across gendered, racial, socioeconomic, and age divisions.[10] To date, however, women
have borne the brunt of the idealized thin body norm, and although men
also appear to be experiencing increasing pressure to adhere to a toned
body ideal, the onus is still primarily on women.[11] This was certainly true
in our participant sample, in which women were far more likely to cite
aesthetics and external and internal rejections of their fat bodies as motivations for undergoing bariatric surgery. Research also indicates that
men and women—at least in a Western context—respond to fat stigma in
gendered ways, with social cues prompting men to think about weight in
the context of "normal" body function (like mobility) and women to think
about weight in the context of "normal" body aesthetics (like beauty).[12]

## Clara

Clara, who was in her early thirties at the time of the interviews, had
been coping with a serious health issue since her early teens. The condition made it difficult for her to lose weight and keep that weight off,
which was intensely frustrating for her. She had gone through prolonged
periods in which she had shrunk her frame down to 180 and even 150
pounds through intense exercise and liquid diets, but she had never
been able to sustain either the draconian lifestyle or the lower weight.
Clara arrived at her first meeting with Sarah in immaculate makeup and
upscale yoga pants. Initially quiet and reserved, she quickly became talkative and sociable. Clara said,

> I hate it [being "fat"]. Like I don't ever want to go out. I don't even want to
> see my friends, family. I hope to God no one dies so I don't have to go to
> funerals. . . . Okay, here's a perfect example. I have a friend in town who
> used to live here. And I hadn't seen her in a few years. And she's been
> blowing up my phone: "Let's get together. I want to see you, da da da."
> And I'd love to see her, but I don't want her seeing me. That's sad. Stuff like
> that. Like my close friends that know I'm fat, and it is what it is, yeah, I'll
> go out to a certain degree, but not like I would have.

One of the striking things about this conversation was how much disgust Clara expressed toward her own body. Clara absolutely hated the weight she carried.

Presurgery, Clara received little overtly negative feedback about her weight and size, but she herself felt disgusting and out of sync with her surroundings. Self-directed shame and dislike of her own appearance kept her from seeing family and friends. Also, because Clara had lost significant amounts of weight at certain points in the past, she tended to compare the absence of positive feedback from others when she was heavy with the compliments she had received when thinner. This made her aware that an absence of verbalized negative reactions to her higher weight(s) did not necessarily mean that people viewed her positively at those weights.

*Shannon*

Shannon commented that she had spent roughly thirty years of her life—since she was a small child—dieting, and she was tired of and frustrated by the endless cycles of weight loss and inevitable weight regain. In her first, presurgery interview, Shannon said,

> Well, actually I've thought about it [bariatric surgery] on and off for probably ten years or more. . . . When I was seven years old, . . . my parents started me dieting then, so I've been dieting on and off . . . since I was seven. . . . My dad used to always tell me, "You're too fat. You're too ugly. You'll never find a man." All when I was growing up, that's what I heard. . . . Yeah, junior high and high school were really hard. I heard it a lot. College at least is better as far as that goes, but it's hard not to notice sometimes when people turn and give you a second look as you walk by because of your size.

In contrast to Clara, Shannon raised many specific instances when she was subjected to weight-related teasing, negative comments, and shaming attempts by family and outsiders alike. By the time she sat down with Sarah for that first interview, she had internalized much of this stigma and was reflecting it back; she felt that she was ugly and unattractive because of her weight. At the same time, she registered how unfair this was, as were all of the stigmatizing comments about her appearance that she received from others. She felt intensely frustrated trying to reconcile all of these opposing and stressful threads. Unlike Clara, however, Shannon had been called fat since her childhood, so she had no other experience with which she could compare her current body.

The survey, which we sent to all patients within the wider hospital system who had undergone bariatric surgery in the previous ten years, also revealed the extent of patients' distaste for their own weight. Out of the three hundred survey respondents (see appendix B for details), the majority reported that their own negative feelings about their weight were "very important" factors in their decision to have surgery. They also reported, however, that they experienced a high prevalence of weight-related stigma presurgery, especially in the workplace and in public places and also from family members, friends, and medical professionals.

When asked for more specific examples of weight-related stigma, patients described a wide array of interactions. Most of the person-to-person stigma reported was not perhaps blatantly cruel. Instead, it was mostly framed as trying to be helpful to the person identified as having problematic weight: "You just need to lose weight to be pretty," "You just need to exercise a little more willpower," or "That dress is not an appropriate thing to be wearing at your size." Good intentions notwithstanding, the effect as felt by the people receiving the comments was anything but helpful and was, in fact, experienced as cruel. Shannon's parents, for example, explained all of their many comments and everyday interventions around her weight, exercise, and diet as helping her to be happy, popular, and successful. Yet Shannon remembered that these constant efforts were easily the biggest contributing factor to her deep unhappiness as a child and teenager.

Large bodies in the US today indisputably generate a great deal of hate across many different social, political, and media outlets.[13] Large bodies do still signal positive social worth in certain contexts, even within the US, but the key point here is that "large" cannot be too large. Where more full-bodied ideals retain power, "full-bodied" is a relative term, especially for women.[14] Indeed, much of the more size-inclusive language that seemingly rejects the feminine waif look simply replaces it with an hourglass body-shape ideal. This ideal still suggests that bodies (and particularly female bodies) should be thin at least in certain areas (such as the waist) and toned. Belly aprons and rolls are verboten.[15] With this in mind, let us return to a point we made earlier: current American body ideals are increasingly misaligned with most bodies now found in this country.[16] The disjunction results in a lot of suffering for both men and women, although the suffering appears to fall more heavily on women; and there are racialized implications as well.

Our data, for example, illustrate some of the complex dynamics Black women must navigate around weight and racialized body norms. We remarked at the outset of this chapter that Black women are often characterized as "fat positive" but that this does not fully capture the experiences and attitudes our participants discussed. These would be more aptly described as holding curvier (but still thin) body ideals than mainstream White culture, while striving to embrace self-love at any size. This is not the same as being fat loving. Beyond this, Black women in our research stressed that struggling with misogynoir was at the heart of their lifelong experiences with fat. Participants did not use the term "misogynoir," but the concept, used in other writing and activism, does reflect many of their personal experiences. Misogynoir refers to the unique combination of anti-Black racism and misogyny, especially as it is propagated through popular media (including medical media), that Black women must contend with in their daily lives.[17] The two study participants whose reflections on stigma we focus on here strongly ground their perspectives in their experiences as Black women. That these experiences were common enough in the bariatric program that these women are not identifiable tells us something significant about the ways in which race, gender, and fat are currently operating in the United States.

## Joyce

We first met Joyce in the morning "Change" classes that she attended for the required eight weeks before her Roux-en-Y gastric bypass. Although reserved in the group settings, Joyce was very forthcoming during interviews. Joyce's comments in the classes, which focused on her concerns with her ability to cook for family gatherings after surgery, had highlighted her role as the nurturing family matriarch. In interviews, however, Joyce talked more about how much she disliked her weight gain over the previous twenty years and how this weight interfered with her love of shopping and fashion. She said she was finding it difficult to date, although she was interested in doing so. Finally, she pointed out that as a heavy (one), middle-aged (two), Black (three) woman (four), she felt she had four strikes against her whenever she went up for a promotion at work.

Joyce was very up-front that she opted for surgery "purely" because she wanted to lose the weight. She had a number of friends her own age and younger (mostly through her volunteer work) who had undergone bariatric surgery, lost weight, and now looked the way she wanted to. This was a big motivating factor for her. At the same time, Joyce was clear that she did not want to be thin per se, especially at her current age. She simply wanted to get back to the shape that she possessed until her forties and not to be typecast in the role of "everyone's mama" (quoting her). In her first interview before surgery, Joyce explained,

> So, I do think that we should be a healthy weight, but I don't necessarily believe in what the doctors—in their scale. In fact, I remember going to a doctor, and he wanted me to get under weight, and I told him, I said, "That's a white girl's." And I told him just that. And he laughed about it. . . . And he was saying, "You know, you can get down." I looked at him, "Are you kidding me?" . . . I think a lot of people, women, see us—because a lot of us are getting heavier, and it's accepted because we're a certain age, and it's expected. "Well, you're not twenty-five anymore. Oh, you're not thirty-five." . . . Men, of course, I think they always want to see prettier and slimmer, and they want all those things. . . . At church, they call me "mama." I hate that. And they "ma'am" me a lot. "Yes, ma'am."

Although Joyce does not explicitly cite anything but her own experience, her reflection echoes major themes in the writing drawn from Black women scholars: my beauty standard does not need to be White, and I do not want only to be everyone's mama figure.[18]

In the third interview, conducted many months after her surgery and after Joyce had lost a lot of weight, she spoke more broadly about the many ways that Black women's bodies are judged negatively by comparing them against White US body norms. She said,

> It's not that it's acceptable if you're African American and you're overweight, but we've been beat down so much about so many things: you're not pretty enough, your hair is not long enough, your lips aren't thin enough, your nose is too big, your butt's too big—which now big butts are

in style, and we all talk about that. All of a sudden—our big butts used to be—we were criticized for it. And now everybody wants to have one. . . . But I think what it is, it's not that you are—it's okay to be big, but it's always such a hard battle. And it's big people in every culture. But don't beat yourself up anymore. . . . Because you've been beat up enough about other things. So it's like, come on, learn to love yourself. And so, if I'm big and busty and have a big butt and my hair is short and nappy and my skin is dark and my nose is big, love yourself. Because if you don't love yourself, nobody else will. And I think that's what we teach our children. . . . I think being fat is not acceptable. Like I said, it's just that if I'm fat, I just got to love myself until I can do something better.

Joyce expressed some important points in her narrative, ones that circulate widely in popular and scholarly discussions occurring across the US. Namely, she said that being fat is not acceptable, but it is also important to acknowledge that White beauty standards (including body norms) have been deployed against Black women in a host of harmful ways.[19] Given this onslaught, she said, a woman's most powerful defense is to love herself.

Joyce's thinking echoes widely shared views among Black women scholars and activists about the essential nature of self-love,[20] self-preservation,[21] and self-care[22] in the face of misogynoir. As others before us have often observed, this response to the systematic marginalization of Black women is often misconstrued in the public health literature on obesity as a problem in need of intervention.[23] It is an exasperating but illustrative point, because it so clearly shows the intractable problem at the heart of intervention-based approaches to obesity. As many commentators we cite here have said—and as Joyce herself said—not caring and lack of awareness are not the issue. Moreover, embracing self-love in the face of hate is a radical act of health affirmation, not a rejection of it.

*Ava*

Ava was in her forties when she had her Roux-en-Y gastric bypass. By Sarah's second interview with her, shortly after surgery, Ava had not yet lost significant weight and was still ruminating on the changes she was about to experience as a result of her weight loss. By the third interview,

however, eight months later and seventy pounds lighter, she was beginning to wrap her head around many of these changes. In this third
interview, Ava talked about her own experiences of how race and gender
intersected with worry and stress over weight:

> To be obese in the Black [community] . . . Women do it [lose weight] to
> get men, or to change their lifestyle or circumstance. Because I mean,
> you see news and videos, and all you see is people popping booties and
> all that kind of stuff, so they think that's what they have to gravitate to.
> Men say, "I'm a man." They have the machismo. . . . "I got the machismo.
> I got it, whatever. I can just talk, suave, get through this." And it does. I
> mean, how many times have you seen larger men with very petite, small
> women? You see it all the time. It's just different needs. . . . And different
> expectations. Men are more critical of how women look than women are
> of their men. They look for two different things. And that's just how it is.

In Ava's opinion, there are clearly fat-stigmatizing body norms circulating in the Black community. While these norms may tolerate some
body fat, they are still restrictive and limiting in that only certain body
shapes and sizes are celebrated. Further, Ava explains, Black women
have to conform to far more rigid body and beauty standards than do
Black men. Like Joyce, Ava clearly believed the social pressures were
profoundly unfair, and she was by no means attempting to whittle her
body down to some sort of social ideal. Nonetheless, Ava did want to be
not fat, and she wanted it badly.

Ava's story shows how having a body that is physically displeasing—by
one's own and/or others' standards—is not only inherently upsetting on a
daily basis but also results in blocked social and economic opportunities.
There is much evidence that discrimination at school, in the workplace, inside social circles, within health care, and in other settings is severe for people labeled obese/fat.[24] Approached from a different angle, other scholars
have written about the ways bodies accumulate differing amounts of "capital," depending on how well they meet prevailing current beauty, aesthetic,
and sexual preferences.[25] Although there are many differences across various social and cultural cohorts in the US when it comes to the perceived
attractiveness of certain distributions of fat, people with morbidly obese
bodies in the contemporary US have very little body capital anywhere.[26]

Burden #2: Excess Weight Is Immoral

A participant described the following interaction with an ex-husband:

> Yeah, I had a very terrible marriage. It was really bad. We're civil now. . . .
> And so we went to a family birthday. . . . When we were eating, when we
> sat down to eat, the next day the kids said, "Dad, the food was so good at
> the birthday. . . ." And everybody was talking about how good it was. And
> they said, "Did you eat?" He said, "I got some cheese and crackers, but I
> was okay. I looked at your mom eating and I got full."

Comments of this kind were not unusual experiences for many of the
people enrolled in the bariatric program, even if the circumstances in
this instance were particularly fraught.

Commentaries aimed to shame and blame larger bodies, often using
humor, are in fact very common in the US.[27] Such commentaries typically focus on how the targeted individual is behaving in a way perceived to contribute to her "out-of-control" fatness. If the target reacts
to the stigmatizing humor, then she "can't take a joke," so she is judged
humorless as well as fat. Comments like these underlined for us our
outsider status when it comes to being in the world as a fat person.
Sarah, for example, gets comments all the time on her eating. A friend
recently watched her finish a meal and remarked that Sarah has "the
eating habits of a teenage boy." The reason that these comments are
even marginally funny (assuming you find them so) is because Sarah
is not fat. They are not without some moral overtones (i.e., Sarah is
judged to be something of a pig), but they do not sit alongside judgments of Sarah's weight. Thus, the teasing does not have the nasty hook
of shame-blame attached to it.

One reason that a thin body ideal has such power in the US is that
it is widely seen as a state that is achieved through hard work, self-
surveillance, and self-denial. These hard-work and self-control tropes
have far deeper roots in Western culture than the thin body ideal.[28]
Americans place great value on individual hard work, where the work
is seen as important in and of itself. Self-improvement projects are likewise valued, including work on the physical body, via dieting and exercise, to make it conform with current body ideals.[29] As a result, fat

bodies are seen not just as unaesthetic but also as physical manifestations or embodiments of individual laziness and disorder.[30]

In other words, a fat body is seen (at least on a day-to-day basis) neither as a signal of happy abundance nor as symptomatic of the larger changes in American foodscapes but rather as an individual failure to work hard and meet social expectations. Thus, weight becomes equated with immorality, and it is this conflation that truly produces stigma.[31] In other words, fat bodies are judged not just as aesthetically displeasing but also as signals of an individual's flawed and tainted character. In the bariatric survey, for example, many respondents said that others made assumptions that they commonly struggled with binge eating, an overall lack of control of their lives, and underlying emotional pathologies. Such assumptions are currently common. The "I looked at your mom eating, and I got full" comment slyly judged not only the woman's eating at that one event but also all of her presumed "excessive" eating up to that day.

Scholarship on stigma that traces its thinking back to the sociologist Erving Goffman has explored a range of stigmatized health conditions, from HIV/AIDS to schizophrenia, as well as stigmatized traits such as race, disability status, and more.[32] Judgments—that a character trait is inherently linked with an arbitrary condition or physical trait—are fundamental in shaping such stigmas. Judgments are not just leveled against a stigma bearer by an outsider. They are also frequently internalized to a significant degree, so that stigma bearers believe the social messaging with which they are being inundated. This not only amplifies the misery that the stigma bearer feels but also makes stigma highly resistant to intervention and alleviation.[33] This is certainly true in people's descriptions of living with obesity/fatness.

Ava's second interview illustrated how stigma creates incessant moral judgments about fat, as well as the ways in which different types of stigma intersect. She clearly depicted the judgments that she routinely faced, which formed part of her motivation to undergo surgery. Moreover, these were not unique occurrences or isolated phenomena; they affected her every single day. In the interview, she said,

> The day I walked into that place again, I was a big Black woman. Well, they weren't even really sure I was Black. I was just a big woman coming in because that's the adjective used to describe. I don't want that adjective. . . .

You do not want to be known as that. You want to be known for the words that come out of your mouth and the ideas that come out of your head. You don't want to be known, you don't want people to refer to you as that because you're more than that. . . . You have to be strong. You have to be self-confident, and you have to know that that's not you. But in a way, you have to know that that's how other people see you. So your self-perception has to overcome the public perception. People don't necessarily know the struggle or can appreciate the struggle, just like people can't appreciate different struggles people do every day for different things.

Ava pointed out that she faced potential judgment every time she walked into a new workplace, volunteer site, or social situation: "just a big woman," as she said. She also pointed out that she was judged for her race and gender, but she did not want to change those. When she said, "You do not want to be known as that. You want to be known for the words that come out of your mouth and the ideas that come out of your head," she meant that a person should not be judged for their large size but for their intellect and contributions—but she also said elsewhere that the weight-related judgments fall more heavily on Black people who are heavier and that this held true across all sorts of settings, especially employment and educational ones. Be confident, know thyself, Ava said—but lose the weight in order to access better opportunities.

From the first day Sarah met her, Ava presented herself as a confident—even fearless—person, and she was tolerant and accepting of difference, including body types. She nevertheless struggled with her own body size and associated dissatisfaction with the way she looked. Some of that dissatisfaction resulted from the constant barrage of assumptions and stereotypes she faced as a "big woman." In the preceding interview excerpt, she clearly pointed out that the linkages people made between her observed size and her inferred intelligence and emotional capacity tended to be negative, assumptions that she had to "struggle" with and "overcome." In other words, Ava felt socially tainted by her size.

Ava was an unusually self-reflective individual, even in a clinical context that encouraged self-reflection. Peter expressed similar sentiments, however, in his first interview before surgery, showing that men also experience stigma across different sectors of their lives. Peter, a highly successful consultant in his fifties, was grappling with many of the same questions and existential dilemmas that other preoperative patients dealt with as they made their way through the presurgical requirements. Here is an excerpt from Peter's first interview:

SARAH: Do you ever notice weight playing a part in the way people treat you?

PETER: Oh yeah.

SARAH: Work, acquaintances, random strangers?

PETER: Everybody.

SARAH: Everybody? Literally everybody?

PETER: Virtually everybody.

SARAH: So what's the treatment?

PETER: Kind of like, stay away.

SARAH: Even close friends?

PETER: Not so much, but—yeah, not so much, but maybe a little.

SARAH: Do you ever get outright comments, or it's more a pull back?

PETER: Just a pull back. . . . And then the other thing that I definitely notice is—this is one of the things I'm kind of interested in seeing is, as far as work goes, I know I'm being held back.

SARAH: You are?

PETER: I know I am, yes. And I talked to some other people I work with who are in similar situations, and we all know we're getting held back. And it's like, "Okay, so if I do lose all this weight and all of a sudden things open up, I'm going to be really pissed off." Because it just has nothing to do with my ability, zero.

SARAH: So who's making that judgment?

PETER: My bosses.

SARAH: Company-wide?

PETER: Yeah.

SARAH: In terms of you're big, ergo you're lazy?

PETER: Right. Or stupid. Or can't control myself, so how could I possibly control multimillion-dollar projects, things like that. Although I've successfully done all of that.

SARAH: Has that happened your whole life?

PETER: Feels like it, yeah.

In this interview, Peter relayed stories of being stigmatized both socially and at work. He described the physical space people—even friends—maintained between themselves and him and also how associations of laziness, stupidity, and being out of control with larger body size had systematically held him back in his career. He also pointed out that this happened to other people he knew at work, which indicated a wider pattern of size-based discrimination.

Despite all of these experiences, Peter went on to say that workplace discrimination was even worse for the larger-bodied women he knew. Men do face negative social and clinical consequences as a result of being labeled "morbidly obese," but research indicates that it is still worse for women, who are held to far more rigid body norms and eating habits.[34] Most of our interviewees, both men and women, mentioned this disparity.

The dramatic increase in morbid obesity in the US in recent decades appears to have amplified, rather than alleviated, weight-related stigma. The scope of fat stigma in the United States is now so vast and so seldom problematized that it is difficult to parse out the effects.[35] We do know that people labeled "morbidly obese" experience blocked opportunities at all levels of life, not just because their bodies do not fit cultural expectations of thinness, curviness, and/or muscled fitness but also because of assumptions made about their work ethic and moral fiber. A fat person is demonstrably less likely to get a callback for a job interview or a promotion at work not only because of their physical appearance but also because they are presumed to be less likely to have the requisite knowledge and expertise, as well as the willingness and ability to work hard.[36]

Many people who identify as fat internalize these negative stereotypes, and this only adds to their suffering. For example, Clara, whose earlier quote described her own hatred of her body, also drew a number of unflattering connections between her fat body and her fat persona. Clara's self-identification as a fat person frustrated her. She stalked into a behavioral change class one day, clearly exasperated, and told Sarah that she had just had an unsatisfactory meeting with a dietician, who "just does not understand how fat people think!" She made comments in that vein often, explaining many of her behaviors and thoughts as part of her "fat" mentality. This mentality was also why she felt she needed a surgical intervention, since she could not seem to bring herself under control and into dietary compliance otherwise.

Weight-related stress and stigma are so pernicious that, at this point, they probably account for a great deal of the ill health currently attributed to the physical state of being obese.[37] To give some idea of the depth of weight-related stigma, consider that people who have lost weight and are now viewed as "normal weight" are still stigmatized if they reveal that they used to be fat.[38] Put another way, the moral taint of obesity is so great that it persists even when the physical body no longer reflects that state.

This last fact seems particularly ironic, given the constant social messaging about weight loss to which Americans—and especially overweight Americans—are subjected. The social stream of prompts to work hard and make lifestyle modifications to achieve a "good" body, or at the very least a "normal" one, are everywhere.[39] Traditional diet and exercise tactics remain the primary focus of weight-loss endeavors in the US,[40] despite the fact that they have been comprehensive failures at the population level. This failure is not due to a collective lack of moral fiber and willpower; Americans have not suddenly become lazier since World War II, popular perception notwithstanding. Instead, the increase in average body size is the result of macro-level obesogenic policies. Yet these tactics remain popular because they appeal to the same core cultural values that link thin bodies with hard work, morality, health, and willpower.[41]

Within this somewhat overwhelming cultural context, we routinely saw participants express these same themes of work, morality, willpower, and self-control. In fact, to combat stigmatizing stereotypes linked to both their fatness and to their decision to have bariatric surgery (commonly perceived as a low-effort form of cheating at weight loss), patients in the program repeatedly "performed" productivity and self-identified hard work.[42] This is not an isolated phenomenon, and other research on bariatric populations has uncovered similar themes.[43] This is not to say that the bariatric patients in this study accepted the societal views that bariatric patients and fat people are inherently lazy and lack willpower. Indeed, patients routinely reframed the surgery to combat this judgment. Nonetheless, their counterarguments were based on the same framework of productivity and hard work.[44]

Because bariatric patients focused on their own work before and after the surgery and on the value of the surgery itself, some of them did also sometimes disparage other bariatric programs and other patients using the same stigmatizing language of laziness. As one participant, Louis, said about bariatric surgery recipients he had seen on a TV program, "They were eating a gallon of ice cream and doing foolish things that you shouldn't be doing. If you don't buy into the program or buy into wanting to make a lifestyle change yourself, you're not going to do it no matter how good the surgeon is or whatever."

Such counterframing strategies rely on the same tropes of moral work, individual responsibility, and behavioral change that were used against the program participants themselves. Few patients with whom we spoke actively challenged this moral framework that, at its core, is based on stigmatizing fat bodies and the (presumably) fat characters associated with them.

## Burden #3: Judgment in Clothes and Spaces

Media coverage over the past couple of years has highlighted the recent increase and diversification of attractive plus-size clothing lines. Comedians-actresses Melissa McCarthy and Rebel Wilson, singer Beth Ditto, and model Ashley Graham all started their own plus-size clothing lines. Target has increased the size range of its swimwear. Plus-size fashion bloggers like GabiFresh, The Curvy Fashionista, and Nicolette Mason have attracted international attention and loyal followings.

Spend time reading, watching, and listening to these women (and yes, it is mostly women), and you will get a generally positive view of current trends in beauty, body, and fashion. The emphasis is on plus-size women breaking traditional rules by loving and showing off their bodies at a time when there are more clothing lines available for them. However, this was not the reality for the male and female bariatric patients we spoke with, who repeatedly expressed frustration and difficulty in finding clothing, prior to their surgeries, that fit, was flattering or looked professional, and was not terribly expensive. As one participant, named Robert, explained in his first interview, "I want to be able to walk into any store and say, 'Give me that one right there,' and my size is there. And it isn't a 'Well, let's see if we have it,' or the jacket's too long."

Many women, both during the presurgery classes and in presurgery interviews, complained about the "huge grandmotherly" underwear and the unflattering dress styles ("think muumuus," said one woman), which were often all they could find. Many people in the classes, the support group meetings, the interviews, and the survey complained about the lack of options for larger sizes, as well as the tendency for larger sizes of clothing to be shoved into the basements and backs of stores. The abundance of data around this theme suggests that an inability to find appropriate clothing was a major issue that plagued most people before bariatric surgery.

Self-presentation is a core component of many people's identity, and dress plays a central role in presentations of self.[45] Being unable to fit into an off-the-rack but nice suit for a job interview or having to wear lingerie that reminds one of one's grandmother on a date is confidence shaking. An inability to control one's own presentation profoundly impacts an individual's sense of "fitting" into the surrounding environment, and research has shown that too-small clothing worsens people's anxiety, dissatisfaction, and sense of not belonging.[46] Moreover, this sense of a "misfit" extends well beyond clothing. For example, the same research showed that too-tight seating had a similar effect on people's sense of not belonging.

Disability studies research on "disabling environments" similarly describes the ways in which places are designed and built for particular bodies, marginalizing all other bodies in the process.[47] An ethnographic study based in New York City translated such disability-based research into the context of fat bodies specifically, exploring the ways in which larger bodies failed to physically fit within public spaces such as seats in public transportation.[48] This lack of fit affected individuals' ability to freely move about their chosen urban spaces, as well as their sense of belonging in these spaces. As other research has indicated, people navigating through space that feels too small for them often register the daily indignities of these structural forms of stigma as especially demoralizing.[49] The stream of negative feedback is constant, and the feedback seems unbiased because it is not interpersonal in origin—instead, it is built into the very structure that surrounds us.

The combination of not fitting in a seat or space while in front of an unsympathetic audience of outsiders is often especially distressing for people. In this way, a layer of interpersonal stigma is added to the environmentally produced "misfit." This was certainly true for many of the bariatric patients with whom Sarah spoke. One woman, named Olivia, for example, said, "When I was large, there was a lot more—people would give you more room. . . . I never thought people kept me at arm's length, but I did notice that moving around or moving around in small spaces, it was—they stepped back."

Airplane seats are another space that makes people with larger bodies feel like they do not fit while being judged by others for that failure. Airplane seating has attracted a great deal of media commentary in recent years. The width of the average economy class seat has markedly decreased over the past two decades, and at the time of this writing, policies allow airlines to force people above a certain size to purchase two seats and to prevent them from flying if they do not. Participants told Sarah that flying was incredibly uncomfortable and emotionally stressful.

All of the participants who flew (there were some who avoided it) spoke about the stress of getting on a plane while trying to calculate whether they would fit into the seat assigned to them. There was the worry over whether their seat was a middle versus an aisle (allowing more spillover) and anxiety around what kinds of bodies and personalities would be sitting next to them. Would they also be big? Would they be understanding, or would they be judgmental and angry?

Seatbelt extenders also loomed large in these conversations. People reported holding their breath and just praying that the regular seatbelt would snap closed around their middle. Many said that even if the seatbelt closed with difficulty and/or pinched them terribly, that was preferable to the humiliation of getting up and finding an attendant to ask for an extender. One woman asked plaintively, "And why are they always bright colors like neon orange?" pointing out that she did not want to advertise that she needed an extender, but she had little choice in the matter, given that the extender color palette seemed aimed to draw attention. Ava reported that if the regular belt did not close, she just put a blanket over her lap and hoped the attendants would not notice the gap.

## Burden #4: Weight Is Seen as Risky and Burdensome

In the introduction and chapter 1, we talked about how weight has been pathologized in scientific and medical thinking and about the processes of medicalization that occur within clinical spaces. Weight, however, is also routinely pathologized by the general American public, by people who hold no degrees in fields remotely connected to biomedicine. Ideas about sickness, disease, deviance, and risk have leaked from clinical spaces and public health programs into society at large—and then been reinterpreted, often with substantial input from the commercial diet industry and the media. The "fact" that fatness and/or obesity represents elevated risk and sickness is typically accepted by most Americans, including by many of our participants.[50]

Many people believe that to be fat is to increase your own personal risk for ill health and to place a burden on all those around you, to be a bad member of your community and even a poor citizen.[51] Debates currently rage over whether fat people are responsible for global climate change, the breakdown of many national health-care systems, lack of productivity in the workplace, and even the degradation of some urban systems. From this perspective, bariatric surgery represents the intervention of outside clinical forces on the deviant, erring body to reduce risk, not only to the body itself but to everyone around that body. Such fat-as-burden-on-others judgments were prevalent in conversations with patients such as Sofia.

## Sofia

Sofia caught Sarah's attention in a presurgery class early on when she remarked that she wished each patient had to meet more often with the psychologist. The vast majority of the pre-bariatric-surgery patients complained mightily about having to meet with the psychologist at all, so her attitude stood out. Sofia was a thorough woman, who liked analyzing a situation from every side before proceeding. She noted in the first interview, "I'm in my head a lot, and I like to think through all of the plans of the eventualities."

In her late forties at the time of our interviews, Sofia had gone through cyclical patterns of weight loss (through rigid dieting and hours of exercise every day) and weight regain since childhood. In her first interview, Sofia talked a great deal about the responsibilities she had juggled over the years, from helping her immigrant Latinx parents at an early age to caring for three very ill close family members more recently. She explained,

> Like last year, especially with everything we had and everyone knowing the stressors on me as a caregiver and all of that, everyone was super

concerned about my health. And I kept saying, "I'm healthy. Leave me alone. I'm healthy." And they really weren't believing that I'm healthy . . . [because of] my weight. . . . "You can't be healthy and overweight." I don't have high blood pressure. I don't take any medications. . . . Like I've never been someone that needed anything. Pretty healthy, strong. But they were convinced I'm not healthy.

Sofia did not actually believe the views stated here but was reporting the prevailing attitudes she encountered.

Sofia opted for gastric bypass surgery because she was tired of her weight, tired of her inability to lose that weight, and tired of thinking about food all of the time. She very clearly articulated these motivations, as well as the fact that medically, she was perfectly healthy. As she told us, she looked up her chart after a clinic visit one day and saw a doctor's comment calling her a "formidable, obese woman" who was "otherwise" healthy. As a working mother who also took on caregiving for family members, Sofia said she had to stay strong and energetic in order to fulfill her many familial and social roles. At the same time, because of her weight, many of her friends and family—the "everyone" she referred to in her narrative—tended to view Sofia as inherently unhealthy and at risk of illness. Among other things, she was tired of that dual burden of staying strong while being perceived as "at risk."

Social science research tells us that to be at risk is popularly conceived as being "out of control," with regard not only to habits but also to the way these habits have become physically embodied in particular ways. Modern societies and governing systems, as well as public health systems more specifically, are founded in part on notions of individualized risk. This refers to an underlying belief that people should restrict certain behaviors in order to reduce the perceived "risk" of an undesired future condition such as illness or even fatness in the absence of illness.[52] This belief certainly underpins some of the anti-fat discourse in the US today.

The bariatric patients with whom we interacted tended to focus less on a macro rhetoric of blame and more on the very specific ways in which they saw themselves as burdening their loved ones. In other words, they were not worried about being a burden on society generally but instead about imposing on their nearest and dearest. Discussions with two very different women show how these feelings may play out in diverse circumstances.

## Emily

Emily easily qualified for the Roux-en-Y gastric bypass when she entered the program. Only in her midforties, Emily was motivated to undergo surgery because of her knee problems, but she also detested her size, saying she had been "fat" since she was nine. Moreover, she saw her size as an increasingly difficult problem for her daughter. In her first interview presurgery, she said,

> You know, she's [Emily's daughter] one of the reasons. . . . I want to see her get married, grandkids. . . . And you know, she says, "Mama, I want you to play on the floor with me," and I can't. And that's a bitter pill to swallow. So when we were in class and they said children with one obese parent are 50 percent more likely to become obese, children with two obese parents are 75 percent more likely to become obese, that about brought me down because what I went through as a child being overweight, I don't want her to ever experience any of that. You know, kids are cruel, period. They can be. But when they can look at you and say, "Haha, you're fat" . . . In [the neighborhood], it seems like there are a lot of fit people. And when we go to school, when I drop her off at school, you know, I am incredibly self-conscious at that point because there are very few women who are overweight. Same thing with the fathers. And someone has said something. One of her schoolmates has said something to her about me. And you know, and she was like, "But you're beautiful." She's the sweetest child in the world. But I think that she now sees us in a different light. And you know, she'll come over and she'll grab your belly and shake it and laugh. And you know, and she will, "You've got a fat belly. Why is your belly so fat?"

One of Emily's main expressed reasons for getting a gastric bypass was to lose weight in order to be more mobile and present for her daughter, who was still only in elementary school. Emily had severe knee problems before the bypass, which the weight was exacerbating, but her health was not otherwise poor. Nonetheless, in her narrative, she mentioned a possible early death if she did not lose weight, and she focused on how this would lead to a loss of valuable time with her daughter.

Emily's narrative also contained a series of imagined medical and social impacts down the road. For example, she cited a statistic that her own obesity was more likely to make her daughter obese and then reflected on the social impact this might have on her daughter through teasing, bullying, and interpersonal stigma. Emily also mentioned that children at her daughter's school were beginning to make fun of her daughter for having a fat mother. Emily therefore saw her own weight as affecting her child in a myriad of different negative ways. By getting a gastric bypass and losing weight, Emily hoped to remove her daughter's present and future burden.

## Martha

Martha, who was introduced in chapter 1, entered the bariatric program with a very high Body Mass Index and a range of serious health issues. Her health issues loomed large during the presurgery classes and in the first interview before her gastric bypass. Martha seemed confident and matter-of-fact about her own size during these first encounters, in part because she had a strong social network and an extremely close-knit family. Sarah was therefore slightly taken aback when Martha indicated during the second interview, a few months after her surgery, that she felt her size was a burden on her marriage.

Martha, who typically took a humorous and motherly approach in conversations, became uncharacteristically emotional as she described the tipping point when she decided to get bariatric surgery. It began with a picture at a party, the first picture of herself that Martha had really looked closely at for years. She said,

> I was crying in the car on the way home. And he [her husband] said, "What's the matter?" And I said, "This," and I showed him the picture, and he said goes, "What?" And I said, "I'm so big." And he looked at me, and he goes, "Yeah." I said, "John, I had no idea I looked like this." And he goes, "Well, hon, you are a big woman." I just cried. . . . I could tell . . . it must've been quite a weight on him [how big she was]. I've never really approached it and probably won't until maybe further on down the line [after losing

more weight] because he might not be willing to open up. . . . So I'll have to wait until I've lost [weight] and shown more of a success with it, and then I'm going to ask him. And that makes me feel horrible that I could have lessened the quality of his life [by being so big], but the only thing I can do is improve it now. I can't go back. I mean, I could live a long time on regret.

Martha very bluntly said that she felt her size and limited mobility had prevented her from being the equal partner to her husband that she had promised to be. They had not traveled as much or socialized as much as they would have liked because of her size and limited mobility. Her husband was still as thin as when they first married, whereas she had begun (she said) as "a hottie" and now was simply "a huge woman."

Martha also articulated in both an interview and in a support group discussion that she worried about being a burden on her husband and children as she aged. Specifically, she worried that she had a degenerative condition that would worsen over the years. Already, she could not drive, and she foresaw a time when she would be even more dependent on her family. Under such circumstances, she felt strongly that she had to reduce her weight to at least mitigate "the burden" she would impose on her family, so that it would be easier to help her in and out of vehicles, chairs, toilets, and beds. She did not tell her family that she opted for surgery to make life easier for them; she simply analyzed the situation, drew her own conclusions, and then moved quietly ahead with her weight-loss plan.

## Moving from Shame to Success

This chapter has explored the fact that although most of the bariatric program's focus is on the medical factors necessitating bariatric surgery, many individuals are motivated to undergo surgery because of their past experiences of weight-related stigma. Also involved is their internalization of the idea that fat equates with diseased, bad, and burdensome. In other words, the trade-offs between the physical limitations imposed by surgery and those inflicted by weight felt worth it to many people.

In chapter 3, we move on to the next stage in the bariatric patient's journey: the aftermath of surgery. It is generally a much more positive period for patients but not straightforwardly so, as we will explain.

# 3

## Weight Loss as Success

Tiffany stuck her head in the door and gestured frantically at me, so I went out to see her. I hadn't seen her since the day after her surgery, although we had exchanged texts, and she looked really good. I didn't tell her, but I didn't notice a drastic difference in her size. . . . The main difference I noticed was that she was beaming, and energetic, and generally thrilled with herself—so proud of herself for doing so well and so excited about the weight loss. She told me that her weight is just sucking off her legs, but that she's also lost her "fat pack" around her neck that was making her hunch over and she "only has one chin now!" She hasn't really gotten new clothes yet, but one of the nurses apparently told her she needs to do it ASAP and she is also going to go in and get a haircut soon, since she wants to try to revamp her "very thin" hair. . . . After the class, Tiffany really came into her own [and started talking about her experience with all of the preoperative people attending]. I think she just wanted a chance to share with people. So she talked about her experience with Tessa [another study participant] and L and the woman in maroon. . . . Mostly, Tiffany just talked about all of the things that have been getting better: her medical history is looking better, she's lost a lot of weight, she feels great. She feels successful. She said she feels so much more confident now and wishes she had done the surgery years ago. She said to me, "What are you going to do when I'm smaller than you, eh?" mostly playfully but not entirely.
—Sarah's field notes, fall 2014

Tiffany appeared to be a very extroverted, talkative, and kind person from the first time Sarah met her, months before her surgery. The most striking thing about this chance meeting described above, however, was that she positively radiated pride and happiness, well beyond anything seen in her previously. She was so excited about her weight melting off and her increased energy that she was virtually bubbling over with the felt success of it all. As the end passage of the field notes suggest, she was also beginning to feel out her position vis-à-vis others, attempting to gauge where her increasingly "normal" body would place her socially. Like everyone else who had attended the "Change" classes, she had been well prepared for the fact that people would treat her differently when she began to lose weight.

Both patients and providers referred to the year after bariatric surgery as the "honeymoon period." It is the time when the weight peels off most easily, the sensation of hunger is almost entirely absent, blood-sugar levels and other numbers improve markedly, and positive affirmation from others is at its greatest. Some negative feedback occasionally also characterizes this period, including accusations of "cheating" at weight loss, jealousy from others, and relationship destabilization. Patients may also internally question their decision to undergo surgery if symptoms such as dumping, fatigue, and nausea are persistent. Nonetheless, during the honeymoon period, the weight loss almost always outweighs (pun intended) everything else. As a result, hope and self-confidence are high.

The clinic patients' views, as heard and observed across the years of this study, were idiosyncratic and individualized (of course), but all of them saw weight loss as a marker of success. Other numbers were felt to be important as well, especially diabetic- and blood-pressure-related biomarker indicators such as A1C tests (which measures average blood-sugar levels over the previous two to three months) and blood-pressure readings (which measure systolic blood pressure over diastolic blood pressure). Weight, however, is visible to everyone and requires no needles, no testing, and no complex interpretation. Even if an individual did not attend follow-up visits, was medically "noncompliant" in many respects, and had no further testing (which sometimes happened), they could track their weight themselves. And for the most part, their weight trended very reassuringly downward.

In this chapter, we explore perspectives from both survey and interview data to describe people's own interpretations of what they felt was "successful" weight loss, as well as what it felt like to be "not fat." These stories are set against a background of medical data that document the expected, standardized weight-loss trajectories after bariatric surgery. More broadly, we also consider why losing physical weight is such a powerful and important marker of overall "success" in the US today.

## Weight Loss, "Controlled" Eating, and Compliance

In the first six to twelve months after bariatric surgery, weight loss is rapid and massive. No other technique currently available can achieve equivalent weight loss. The medical literature shows that people typically lose about half of their excess weight after bariatric surgery, where "excess weight" is calculated as the weight that puts someone in a BMI category above the "normal weight" cut-off. Most of this loss happens in the first year.[1] Among the patients we interviewed for this study, weight loss during the first year was a minimum of 50 pounds. Some patients lost a staggering 150 pounds. Importantly, the people we knew lost fairly similar percentages of excess weight in the first year after surgery. Most of the individuals who lost closer to the 50-pound minimum, for example, were those who were not quite as heavy when they had surgery and/or their weights were still trending downward at our last meeting. As Charles remarked, "I mean, you're going to lose weight if you have the surgery. You can't help but lose some weight."

Similarly, of those 195 survey respondents from the hospital system's bariatric programs who provided information on their weight, all reported losing substantial amounts. Their mean weight at the time of bariatric surgery was 280.4 pounds, dropping to 207.6 pounds by six months postsurgery, 189.2 pounds by twelve months postsurgery, and 186.4 pounds by eighteen months postsurgery. Furthermore, because we sent out two waves of the same survey to the same respondents, we were able to examine potential weight change over time in this survey population. The average weight of respondents was 185.4 pounds at the time of the first survey and 187.6 pounds by the second survey, sent out a year after the first.

These numbers illustrate several central points about this particular hospital's patient population, at least among those willing to send surveys back to us. First, major weight loss occurred in the six months immediately postsurgery. Second, weight loss was still substantial six to twelve months postsurgery. Third, weight loss was negligible by the second year, but neither was there a large weight rebound in the years immediately after surgery. We saw a similar pattern among those whom we interviewed.

Weight loss was not new to most of the patients. Most reported that they had experienced some weight loss at previous times in their lives before opting to undergo bariatric surgery. However, the rapid disappearance of a significant portion of their bodies in such a concentrated period of time was a completely new experience. One mother with a child in elementary school commented that she had lost the equivalent of her child's weight—"an entire little person!" as she put it.

Many patients said they found the rapid, pronounced weight loss confusing but exciting. Narratives around the dramatic initial post-surgical loss of weight over and over reflected a mixture of euphoria over successful, sustained, visible weight loss and confusion around the momentous physical changes. For example, Luke said in his first interview postsurgery, "And now I look in the mirror, I don't recognize myself. . . . Every Monday I weigh myself, and then every Wednesday, which is today actually, I have to have my wife kind of take a front and side picture so I can mentally keep myself focused on my changes. . . . I literally shrank." Several other participants also carefully documented their shrinking bodies, not just by watching the numbers on the scale tick steadily downward but via other means like taking weekly photographs. The photo documentation, for example, both reaffirmed people's excitement over their visible progress at losing weight and also provided something of an anchor, an external, seemingly neutral chain of evidence to which they could turn in the midst of all of the confusing weight, health, behavioral, and interpersonal changes.

At the same time that patients were making adjustments for their new (albeit still changing) size, they were also negotiating the new limitations that surgery imposed on their eating patterns. Eating for humans has never simply been about nutrition in, nutrition out; it is one of the most fundamental social activities in which we engage. It is a basic way of establishing connections, and it is a powerful identity marker.[2] The changes in eating induced by bariatric surgery necessarily alter the roles that eating plays in people's lives.

Holly, for example, said, "Last year [the first year after her bypass], I did no baking whatsoever. I didn't trust myself. And this year, I'm trying it, and I give it away, but it's one of those things that I'm known for. In fact, my oldest son said when I die, they're not going to have a wake. We're going to have a bake sale." Other women and men—but, in particular, women who, like Holly, were mothers or grandmothers in an extended family network—also resumed baking and cooking for their families at some point postsurgery. They did so even if they were unable to eat the products or even taste test during the process, because their roles as bakers, cooks, and providers were so central to their children's perceptions of them. The six to twelve months immediately after surgery, when many of these women were consciously abstaining from active participation in food preparation and consumption, was a correspondingly difficult period for some of the families.

On the other hand, many of the changes in people's relationships with food were positive. This is perhaps not surprising given how many men and women in the program had felt "out of control" and unhealthy with respect to their own eating behaviors presurgery and felt deeply judged by outsiders over their eating habits. Other bariatric research has highlighted the emphasis that patients place on feeling more in control and self-monitoring effectively in the wake of surgery,[3] and that was certainly true among these participants as well.

Many participants said that they enjoyed feeling more in control of their eating habits through self-monitoring and portion control, compared to those around them currently, as well as to their past selves. As Luke put it,

> Yeah, we eat together [all the coworkers] at lunch. And so I eat very, very slow now, and I eat very, very little. . . . And they're watching what I eat. And I'm watching what they eat too, and it amazes me sometimes how much they eat when I know that I ate that much before. But now I can't even possibly think about eating that much because I would be so sick if I ate that much, you know?

Luke raised many interesting themes in his narrative, including eating surveillance, both self-directed and coming from others.

Surveillance of eating was a theme that resonated deeply across most participant experiences and is something we will delve into in detail in chapter 4. Here, we want to draw attention to Luke's description of his eating before versus after bariatric surgery. He said that it "amazes" him how much people (his prior self included) who have not undergone bariatric surgery put away at mealtimes and contrasted that with how slowly he now has to eat and how little he can pack into his resized stomach. What is particularly significant in this narrative is that in Luke's description of mealtimes, the new normal was his postsurgical manner of eating—not the way his coworkers eat or his prior self ate. Luke went on later to remark that what did continue to feel abnormal to him was that he did not eat rice postsurgery, which he said felt profoundly out of sync with his culture. Luke is Asian American, and he stated that daily rice consumption was one of the ways in which his family expressed that identity but was also something that he started conscientiously avoiding after surgery.

In Luke's reframing of eating norms and standards, he was certainly not alone. Indeed, such reframing was common among the patients postsurgery. Charles, for instance, expressed similar sentiments. He remarked,

> Prior to the surgery, I probably would have told you I didn't eat that much. I ate, don't get me wrong, but I didn't eat six plates of food, which is what people would think, right, when you're 450 pounds. . . . But now postsurgery, seeing what I eat, realizing how much I used to eat, I still did overeat [before surgery] even though I didn't feel like I overate. Because I think of the amount of food I eat today, and I'm sustaining myself and my lifestyle just fine life-wise, energy-wise.

In his narrative, Charles pointed out that prior to surgery, he would have told you he did not eat that much. The subtext here is that he did not eat that differently from most of the other Americans around him and so felt that his eating habits were normal. Postsurgery, however, he eats drastically less and yet manages to "sustain" himself "just fine life-wise," and this new perspective has made him realize, he said, that he was in fact eating too much before. Common attitudes in the US toward bariatric surgery often paint the surgery as skewing daily eating habits, but here Charles is registering a very different perspective: his frame of reference for what was appropriate consumption was skewed before surgery, and the surgery has reset this in a healthier direction.

In chapter 2, we discussed how cultural mores place a great deal of importance on virtuous self-control, restraint, and discipline with regard to one's body. We also showed that participants in this study had suffered greatly from social judgments that they must be lazy, greedy, and out of control because of their fatness (note Charles's preceding comment about six plates of food). In other words, their size supposedly signaled their lack of moral fiber, and because many participants accepted this external moral framework, many also suffered from self-directed judgments. As a result, being able to show moral self-control through a thinning body, as Luke and Charles discussed, was a huge relief for many patients, even though restrictions imposed by the surgery certainly facilitated this restraint.

Unless there are complicating factors (such as a hernia repair performed simultaneously), the surgery itself only takes about an hour (most surgeries are laproscopic), and recovery is typically swift. It is certainly not an out-patient procedure when done at an accredited program, but patients are expected to get up and begin walking the hospital corridors the day after surgery. This trajectory held true for most of our participants as well, although a few did experience complications that prolonged their stay in the hospital. Eventually, however, everyone ended up at home and then spent the subsequent week unenthusiastically following the medical directive to drink lots of Gatorade (the last time their medical advisers would suggest consuming sugar-sweetened beverages) and trying to increase their activity levels. By the second week (sometimes sooner, if an individual really developed an antipathy to Gatorade), people transitioned to eating tiny portions of pureed food and were supposed to follow directives to begin gentle exercise. This period went on for a while for some of the men and women, as they got used to their lack of appetite and more limited digestive processes, whereas others transitioned more rapidly into eating soft foods and moderate exercise. The soft-food period was not a whole lot more inspiring than the pureed-food period (chicken pounded, pulled apart, and cooked into submission was common), but most people we spoke with did not mind, since they were not particularly interested in food— and were excited that they were not hungry.

Three to six months post-op, most people are expected to be exercising regularly and eating an approximation of "normal" foods, but in far smaller and extremely well-chewed portions. They also typically must avoid fats, sugars, salts, and spices. People approached this period in a variety of ways, depending on their family habits, whether they were back at work or not, preexisting food preferences, and the often-idiosyncratic food preferences, intolerances, and limitations that emerged postsurgery. Pressure cookers were popular with some people, both because they could be used to break down foods and also because quantities of food tailored to an individual could be made ahead of time and stored. One woman kept string cheese in her purse at all times, while another kept packets of protein powder to add to her coffee in place of sugar and milk; yet another had little Tupperware containers with low-fat snacks in the glove compartment of her car.

Post-op patients are expected to follow an approximation of this regime for the rest of their lives, although the physical restrictions imposed by the surgery usually ease after the first year. The emphasis throughout this process is to prioritize (low-fat) protein and water intake above all else, since these are essential to basic cellular functioning. People are told frequently to ingest at least sixty grams of protein and sixty-four ounces of water per day. Supplements are also prescribed for life, including a daily chewable multivitamin, an iron supplement, and monthly B12 shots (or sublingual B12 supplements). The latter is absolutely essential because B12 from food cannot be absorbed in a bypassed gut or by a reduced stomach pouch.

Failure to follow dietary guidelines during the first twelve months led to a range of uncomfortable symptoms for patients, including nausea, dizziness, diarrhea, sweats, and the dreaded "dumping," where undigested portions of a meal are "dumped" directly from the stomach pouch into the intestine, resulting in extreme discomfort. Tiffany provided a graphic description of dumping in her second interview, four months after her gastric bypass:

> I have a friend. . . . She's into baking the cookies and the candies and stuff. She was making sugar cookies a couple nights ago. I'm like, "I just want to taste the batter. I just want a little." And I literally put a dab on my finger just to taste it. I got sick. . . . I got sick to the point where I could've dumped, but I didn't. I just kind of went and laid down, and I'm like, "Okay, yeah, you can't do this." But I did have a dumping spell with sweet and sour chicken. I tried one piece of that, and I had my head in the toilet for forty-five minutes. It had to have been the sugar, yeah. But I was

thinking—and this was a couple months ago, so hello, two months after surgery? Not a good thing to do. Not a good thing, period. But it had to be the sugar because that's—when I dumped, I could taste sauce. I mean, the dumping is not a pleasant thing. It's a pretty nasty thing. It's not like a normal vomiting session. . . . It's almost like slime. Yeah, it's the most unpleasant thing. So when you dump or vomit, it comes out. I explain it like it's the Nickelodeon green slime. Yeah, it's bad. I know I'm getting graphic and being gross, but you feel that in your mouth. And it is so not nice. . . . Yeah, it's not pleasant to feel that way. And then I had a couple of bouts with some diarrhea where I think I drank something too soon after I ate, and it just kind of went through me.

In her narrative, Tiffany semiapologized for "getting graphic and being gross," but in fact, participants' willingness to get into the physical bodily details around digestion, dumping, and diarrhea that make most Americans delicately squeamish was extremely helpful. We remarked at the outset of this book that we ourselves have not undergone bariatric surgery and so we cannot understand at the embodied level of personal experience—but the same will be true for many readers as well. In this context, Tiffany's willingness to wade into the messy details around sweet and sour chicken coming up as green slime is invaluable to those of us sitting outside the experience.

Some other ethnographic research has detailed the unpleasant symptoms that may follow bariatric surgery, showing how these symptoms negatively impact quality of life and people's sense of well-being and normality postsurgery.[4] The individuals in this study reported relatively few unpleasant episodes of nausea and dumping, but many encountered it at least once postsurgery; 60 percent of survey respondents, for example, reported episodes of nausea or dumping in the months following surgery, but only a few reported experiencing these reactions repeatedly, over the longer term.

Moreover, many of those who did have intense episodes framed them as a result of eating inappropriately with regard to quantity, content, or speed and explained that the immediate physical response helped them "retrain" their food cravings and desires. Clara, for example, described her only experience with dumping in vivid detail:

It's only happened to me once. For whatever reason, I was craving ice cream like, "I need ice cream." And that is so weird because I didn't ever really have ice cream before. But for whatever reason, I was like, "I got to have some ice cream." So I went to the store and got—it was the Dreyer's half—I don't know, half whatever it is. And I think it's like nine grams of sugar in a fourth of a cup. Not terrible. Not great, it's ice cream. But for it being that, yeah. So I measure out my fourth of a cup, and I had that, and it was so good, and everything was fine. So the next day, I wake up, it's a Saturday, weekend, nothing going on. "Ooh, I still got a bunch of ice cream in the refrigerator. I'm going to go for it." . . . So I'm like, "Well, I'm just going to see how this works." You know, just to kind of see. I almost did it as an experiment, honestly. . . . Yeah, so I didn't measure anything. I was eating it out of the container. And I was like, "Oh, I should stop. I've had a lot." I'm like, "I feel fine." And I was even texting people like, "I feel fine. I can't believe I'm feeling fine. Did they even do anything in there?" And oh, just waited a little bit longer, and then I thought death was coming out of my ass. Like, literally it's the weirdest feeling. It's almost like you can almost feel that insulin go through your body, it's the craziest thing. And you just feel—it's so weird. I can't even explain it to you. And then just you think your guts are going to fall out of your bottom. . . . It was bad. I'm like, "I will never . . ." And I haven't had ice cream since. I know it's delicious, but I'm like, "I never want to feel that way again."

Clara's narrative can be read as a classic morality tale, in which she was disobedient and noncompliant, suffered and was punished, and so grew as a person. Again, we see a horrible bodily experience portrayed as a positive retraining to think about food and eating in a different way and to develop new habits and food associations. These stories were not framed by the people telling them to solicit pity and sympathy for what people could *not* eat anymore. They were rather framed as valuable self-teaching moments.

Throughout the cycle of preoperative clinic classes, and especially in the final class before surgery, the nurses stressed that there is substantial and immediate negative physical feedback after bariatric surgery when someone tries to "cheat" on the recommended postsurgical diet. Clinic staff also constantly reinforced the dietary guidelines as an integral and core part of what makes the surgery an effective weight-loss method.

The patients in this study all received the same detailed instructions (modified according to age and specific disabilities), went through the same presurgery program, and had either bypass or gastrectomy surgery performed by one of two bariatric surgeons. In other words, their preparation and surgical experiences were overtly very similar.

Nevertheless, patients had idiosyncratic and individualized interpretations of their postoperative experiences and guidelines. For example, each person we followed created their own, slightly different, diet and exercise regime. Importantly, none of the patients proved fully compliant with the guidelines from a standardized, medical perspective, even if many followed them very closely. This finding—that people get standardized medical advice but then go through a separate process of deciding what to do with it—is to be expected. In medical terms, this is often referred to as "noncompliance," but to anthropologists, the way medical advice is understood and acted on also reflects the other constraints and concerns (medical, cultural, economic, familial, etc.) that people balance and that inevitably shape their decisions and behaviors.[5]

Patients who worked outside the home full-time, for instance, often described how they struggled to balance the demands of the workplace with the stringent new dietary prescriptions. Most people who worked outside the home did take time off in the weeks right after surgery (filing for paid time off) but typically ended up back at work well before they had adapted to their new restrictions. Take the case of those who worked in sterile medical environments; they could not bring their own drinking water to work. This meant they had to rely on drinking fountains scattered throughout their work building. It is very difficult to achieve a water intake of sixty-four ounces per day through a drinking fountain (just try it). Moreover, after bariatric surgery, food and water need to be consumed at staggered intervals, which means that assuming someone newly back at work after bariatric surgery is even given a lunch break (and workplaces increasingly exert subtle pressure on employees to eat quickly while continuing to work), ideally, they should not drink liquid at the same time they are eating solids. Alternatively, consider the challenges associated with trying to take care of oneself and one's postsurgical needs as a stay-at-home mother with children, who have a variety of conflicting needs themselves. Underconsumption of the daily recommended calories due to meal skipping was also very common, especially at lunchtime. People complained consistently about this both in interviews and in the support group meetings. They would literally forget to eat because their hunger cues no longer functioned as they had before.

Also difficult was the fact that family, work, and friend circles continued on with their own established behavioral patterns, and as we described in chapters 1 and 2, patterns among most Americans today tend to involve lots of consumption and very little activity. One woman reported that she started smoking in order to have something to do with her hands and mouth when her coworkers were snacking. About half of the participants exercised daily, as directed. Others did not and explained their lack of exercise as due to persistent fatigue, days that were completely packed with family and work-related tasks, and low motivation.

The survey data also showed dramatic postsurgical differences in reported physical activity. Some people reported virtually no physical activity in a given week, and others reported several hours of activity on multiple days of the week; but the vast majority did not meet the exercise requirements expressly stipulated by the bariatric program (at least forty-five minutes of exercise or walking five to seven days per week). Moreover, many survey respondents said they did not follow the dietary recommendations with regard to quality, instead focusing on control of quantity. For example, some said they drank sweetened drinks and alcohol, which dieticians advised patients to avoid entirely, although most respondents said they did not drink it often (e.g., a few times a month or in social situations). Survey respondents also provided details about their diets over the course of an average week, and analysis of many of the responses shows widespread avoidance of both refined and whole grains, even though the clinic clearly recommends consuming whole grains (while avoiding refined grains). Respondents also apparently prioritized the consumption of animal protein sources over plant protein, even though that was not necessarily a program recommendation. This suggested to us that patients were influenced by highly prevalent and pervasive current American cultural norms that value animal proteins and deem carbohydrates fattening.

All of these examples show that bariatric patients—like patients everywhere—rarely complied completely with medical guidelines, because in real (i.e., nonclinical) life, people were constantly balancing individual needs, social and work pressures, and personal interpretations of the recommendations with their medical patient role. Moreover, people often believed they were being compliant as long as they followed some portion of the guidelines (especially the parts that related to caloric and portion control) and continued to lose weight. In other words, the weight loss—the physical "evidence" provided by the shrinking body—was proof of compliance with diet and exercise regimes regardless of what patients actually did outside the clinic. Most people came out the other end of the first year missing a substantial portion of their presurgery body as a result of the biological and physical limitations on food intake imposed by the surgery.

## Chronicity, Cures, and Not Being a Burden

The category of "bariatric surgery" encompasses a number of different types of surgery, ranging from a gastric band (a reversible surgery that is minimally invasive but not as effective as other types) to a biliopancreatic diversion with duodenal switch (an extremely invasive and rarely performed procedure, at least in our experience). All the patients in our ethnographic study had either the Roux-en-Y gastric bypass or vertical sleeve gastrectomy. Of these two options, the gastric bypass was strongly favored—only two of our ethnographic patients opted for a sleeve. This pattern was mirrored in the survey responses.

In a sleeve gastrectomy, a portion of the stomach is actually removed, whereas in a gastric bypass, a small portion of the stomach is made into a pouch and then attached to the lower segment of the intestine, thus "bypassing" not only the majority of the stomach pouch but also part of the upper intestine (technically, the duodenum and the jejunum). Weight loss from the sleeve therefore relies on the greatly reduced size of the stomach pouch, which cannot accommodate large portions of food, as well as the greater speed with which food, again quoting a program dietician, "goes through your tubes." Weight loss from the bypass surgery relies on both a reduced stomach pouch and malabsorption of nutrients in the smaller stomach and the shorter intestines.

Within the bariatric program, post-op recovery directives and dietary and exercise guidelines were not substantially different for bypass versus sleeve patients. Patients generally did not report substantial differences in how they felt in the weeks immediately after surgery, as long as they did not experience any complications. Weight loss in sleeve patients was slightly less dramatic than in bypass patients, but all patients regardless of surgery type experienced significant, prolonged weight loss.

Most individuals in this program opted for bypass surgery over the sleeve because of the associated expected health benefits. Both procedures are associated with substantial improvements in a range of pathologies, including sleep apnea, acid reflux, type 2 diabetes, hypertension, arthritis, degenerative joint issues, and cardiovascular disease; however, the improvements are more consistent with bypass.[6] Many of these health improvements are a result of the weight loss induced by the surgery, but many of them are not—especially in gastric bypass surgeries. Although the mechanisms behind these health improvements are still not completely understood (both by experts in the field and, to a far greater degree, by the three of us), research indicates that gastric bypass has a profound effect on diseases like type 2 diabetes independently of weight loss, via its effects on tissue-specific insulin sensitivity, intestinal metabolism of glucose, gut microbiota, and other processes.[7]

Before surgery, participants received detailed medical evidence conveyed by the bariatric surgeons and the nurses and used this information to decide which type of bariatric surgery to choose. After surgery, however, their own experience of being "cured" of medical conditions completely overrode any debate within the scientific and medical communities about the use of the word "cure."[8] As Brad said,

> I don't know how to explain it. I'm not an expert, but it [the surgery] saved my life. . . . I'm not very religious, but I feel as though God has given me a second chance and I would be an idiot if I blew it. . . . That's why I have to not regain [weight]. . . . Dr. M. performed the miracle [of the surgery], and now it's up to me. . . . I would like to become an evangelist and open a church proclaiming the news that there *is* a cure for diabetes . . . because I *am* cured.

In this narrative, Brad sounded like he felt passionately, even zealously missionary about the procedure and its effects. Interestingly, however, it seemed that he was very circumspect with his friends and family in day-to-day life.

One of Brad's friends, for example, told Sarah that Brad never really went into detail about his surgery, weight, or eating requirements. Instead, Brad would just "quietly eat his little rabbit-food snacks from his little Ziploc baggies," while the rest of his close friends ate and drank voraciously. Despite the teasing tone of the "rabbit food . . . in baggies" comment, Brad's friend actually expressed a great deal of admiration for Brad's quiet displays of control and adherence to his health regime. This interplay is particularly interesting in light of other research that has specifically focused on the experiences of men who have undergone bariatric surgery.[9] Men appear to face particularly entrenched sociocultural ideas about the importance of being "in control" and of demonstrating responsibility and agency while their everyday lives and relationships are upended by the surgery.

Profound change nonetheless affected everyone, women and men alike, who underwent bariatric surgery with whom we spoke. Among the many changes that affected people in the first year after surgery, the physical experience of watching many medical symptoms wane was pivotal. Most survey respondents who reported suffering from hypertension, high cholesterol, sleep apnea, and type 2 diabetes before surgery said that their disease symptoms largely resolved after surgery. The nature of the survey itself made it difficult for respondents to wax philosophical about "cures"; but symptom resolution feels a lot like a cure in everyday, embodied experience, and the participants in the ethnographic research certainly conveyed that.

Emily talked in her third interview about general improvements in her health during the eleven months since surgery, directly related to her loss of over ninety-five pounds. Sitting outside on a hazy, hot day at a Starbucks in a mountain suburb above our city, she said,

> So the first time I had knee surgery was in 2004, I think. I had one knee surgery, and then . . . in 2008, I had double knee surgery. . . . The doctor told me, "Emily, the only thing that's going to help you is if you lose weight." And I'm like, "I know, but hello. You know, help me lose weight." And you know, there was never any help. It was like, "You just got to do that." . . . Yes, just do it. . . . So I had that surgery. And I always thought—

even going into this and even during it, there was never an expectation that I would walk away from this pain free. . . . [But now] I don't have pain. . . . Probably right before Christmas was when I really started to notice it. [*She went with her family on a vacation into the mountains that involved a hike.*] . . . So it's got that turny road and everything, and there's stairs in between all the roads because that's how steep it is. Well, we went up there, and I didn't realize that that was the way it was, you know? I knew that it was hilly, but I didn't know the extent of it. Well, we walked up our first flight of stairs, and I was just amazed because no pain, I wasn't out of breath, I didn't have to stop—you know, all of those things—and was happy to continue on. . . . That was one of those expectations that I wouldn't even have thought of. . . . And that's amazing. . . . And I mean, it just makes everything . . . Well, we have two dogs, big dogs, and I buy them fifty-pound bags of dog food. . . . I pick up that bag, and I actually feel the weight of it, you know? Before I was just picking up a bag. Now I'm picking that up, and I'm going, "Oh my God, I've lost this twice." And I cannot believe how much I weighed. I just cannot. I cannot believe it.

Emily became emotional at several points during this exchange, talking about the shift in her daily lived experience, from being in pain and limited to pain-free and active. Overall, though, she seemed happy and energized and seemed to glow visibly throughout the meeting.

To try to understand just how earth-shattering such changes in experiences of illness (and, from a biomedical perspective, "disease profiles)" can be, we turned to the anthropological literature on "chronicity." This focuses attention on the other trajectory: the lived experience of chronic disease. Scholars have written about the shift in medical and social understandings of chronic-acute dichotomies, especially as diseases increasingly come to be understood as lifelong, managed conditions. In this view, everyday experience is characterized by constant medical intervention and self-surveillance as well as by coping patterns, diverse interpretations of illness, and attempts to articulate a synthesized notion of self.[10]

The term "chronicity" attempts to describe the ways in which a person's identity and social roles shift in the face of long-term illness or disability, contextualized within a broader political economic framework.[11] Diabetes has received particular attention in this regard, because the technological advances that made insulin (and later drugs) widely available rapidly transformed the condition into a chronic (rather than an immediately fatal) one at roughly the same time that rates of type 2 diabetes exponentially increased worldwide.[12] Acute episodes of felt illness combine to create a chronically diseased identity, but because blood-sugar levels fluctuate, so do illness identities—especially for people in the early stages of diabetes. Sociocultural and political economic contexts also profoundly shape this identity work and the available resources for treatment.[13] Importantly in the context of our discussion here, research overwhelmingly indicates that those who suffer from diabetes are expected to manage (although they cannot cure) their disease through medication and behavioral modification, "working" to gain control of their diabetes so as not to risk being labeled out of control.[14]

Imagine, then, the repercussions on an individual's sense of self and on their roles in their family and community when suddenly they feel "cured" of their diabetes. After years, sometimes decades, spent acclimatizing to an illness identity, everything—blood-sugar levels, A1C counts, experienced illness episodes, energy levels, and so on—reverses, often in a matter of weeks. How exciting, even thrilling for that person—but also profoundly disruptive, because identity and sociality must correspondingly shift. Lenore Manderson and Narelle Warren described these complex dynamics as a "recursive cascade."[15] In such transitions, social context, economic resources, chronic conditions, vulnerabilities and affective conditions, social support, and many other factors all shape particular "social and bodily impairments" in dynamic and constantly shifting ways that loop back on one another. Gastric bypass, and its effects on pathologies such as diabetes, throws these cascades into further disorder.

Even participants who did not experience a miraculous turnaround in every aspect of their health still showed marked improvements. Martha, in her third interview ten months after her bypass, had perhaps the fewest health complaints resolved at that point of any participant we spoke with, but she remained philosophical. In response to being asked whether one of her chronic conditions was improving, Martha said,

No, it won't. . . . And I've lost a lot more [function]. . . . And it's just with the recognition that that's what my life is going to be. I mean, there's nothing to be done. . . . But it's gradual enough that I don't even realize it until I try to do something with someone else, and I realize what I'm incapable of doing. But it's not something that I feel depressed about, and I can't really explain. It's just where I'm at.

Martha was watching one of her core functions slowly leave her and was trying to come to terms with that loss. It perhaps helped that her particular disability was not one that bariatric surgery reliability resolves, the program had been clear with her on that point, and her expectations had been low in this area.

Martha had, however, hoped for significant improvement in her joint pain after surgery. When asked how she felt postsurgery, Martha said, "Great!" But when specifically asked how her knees were doing, she told Sarah,

> Not great. I exercise in the pool, and I come out hobbling. If I don't treat it right, if I try to be too energetic with it, like I go out and I jog in the pool, I can hardly drag myself out. It used to be that way because of the weight. Now my knees are the total problem. And so even walking, I have the driveway to walk up, and then I go up to the mailbox. I've tried walking a little bit further, but when I have, it's made it harder to get back down the drive. . . . But I'm not really in any frame of mind to have knee replacement right now. I've had too many friends and my mom show me what limitations it gives them, even though they do end up pain-free. I'm pain-free. If I can have a moderate amount of exercise in my life, even if it's just walking a little bit in the morning, walking a little bit in the afternoon, and still can keep myself active, that's what I'm going to have to do.

Martha is an example of someone who did not experience the miraculous cure that Brad, Emily, and others did, and yet she still saw herself and her trajectory as a success.

Martha commented that many physical problems had indeed gotten better with surgery and weight loss. She was very proud of reducing her weight from 345 pounds to 254.7, and she went through all of the fitness apps she was using to chart her weight loss. It was also significant to Martha that her weight loss and relative improvement in health would make her less of a burden for her family as her other condition worsened. She raised her concern with age and infirmity repeatedly throughout the interviews, even though, in the final interview when Sarah asked her for a reminder of how old she was, Martha responded, "Only sixty-six!" Sarah told Martha that she was the same age as her own mother, and Martha said, "You could have been my baby girl." Martha had tremendous grace in how she met the world, and this included her approach to her surgery.

As discussed in chapter 2, fatness and "excess" weight were often cast as burdensome on everyone in a participant's intimate circles. This feeling of being a burden was one motivation for undergoing bariatric surgery. Martha was not the only participant who expressed satisfaction that her surgery and weight loss had successfully reduced the burden she felt she placed on the people around her. In fact, this was a common theme among bariatric patients whom we encountered during fieldwork.

## Fitting

One of the biggest social changes participants experienced when they lost so much weight during the first year after surgery was a reversal in some of the major types of stigma they had to bear, both interpersonal and structural. Patients' physical bodies still may not have fit the American ideal of a taut, toned, slim body, but the moral overtones of laziness associated with fatness, as well as feelings of "misfitting," were alleviated by the drastic weight loss experienced. Survey respondents, for example, who reported relatively high rates of weight-related stigma before surgery from coworkers, spouses/partners, friends, family members, supervisors, teachers, doctors, nurses, neighbors, sales clerks, restaurant servers, strangers, and others subsequently reported a dramatic decrease in weight-related stigma after surgery.

In chapter 2, Olivia and Robert talked about their experiences navigating space and clothing with large bodies. After surgery and significant weight loss (Olivia weighed 120 pounds at seventeen months postsurgery, and Robert had gone from 330 at the time of his surgery down to 250 at seven months postsurgery), both reported drastic changes in these experiences. Olivia (who was not a person who typically gushed) did in fact gush about how easy it was to move through the institutional spaces of her workplace after her weight loss, running up and down stairs and weaving around desks and other bodies that now had to make less of a detour around her. She explained,

> You know, it's strange, I keep coming back to the fact that the reason why I went through this whole transformation was I wanted to be healthy and alive for my grandson. . . . And then, you know, everything else has been a bonus. The shopping, the clothes, the hair, you know. It's funny because I never felt this good about myself when I was a teenager. And I am probably about the same size as I was when I was in high school—a little smaller: I wore a size nine in high school, I'm wearing size eights now. . . . And you know, my husband was just saying yesterday, "Oh, you look wonderful."

In her narrative, Olivia registered how weight loss, combined with a more mature perspective and more attention to hair, makeup, and clothes, made her feel that she looked better than ever before. She also noted that her husband reinforced her feelings with compliments about her appearance.

When Robert was asked in his final interview about his favorite aspect of losing weight, his wife—who had wandered in during the interview—started laughing. Robert looked sheepish and said,

> My wardrobe. It sounds shallow, . . . but it really makes a difference. When we went looking—I had to get a jacket on short notice because I had to do the interview [for a new position at work]. And before, it would have been, "Well, I have to shell out so much money because it's the size that I have, and it's only certain places I can go." To be able to get stuff off the rack, and it just fits—okay, it's in the budget, let's do it.

Robert definitely was not alone in feeling this way. Another male interviewee mentioned that it was a huge milestone when his neck shrunk to the point that he could wear ties to work. Several women talked about the thrill of easily obtaining new clothes from department stores, without having to scour the back racks of dresses for plus sizes.

Chapter 2 also discussed the particularly traumatic experience of airline seats for large-bodied people. Not surprisingly, many participants mentioned that fitting into airline seats postsurgery was a particular source of pride and personal satisfaction—a clear marker of the success of their surgery. Ava's comments were characteristic, as she talked about her first experience flying after she lost eighty pounds:

> Usually what I did when I was bigger, I would click the seatbelt behind and sit on it, then put something over me so the stewardess would never know I didn't have my seatbelt on because I didn't want to ask for the extender. So out of habit, I did it again when I was sitting next to these guys [that she had just struck up a conversation with]. And I got busted. And so the stewardess was like, "You got to put your seatbelt on, blah blah blah." And I was just like, "Oh, right." I'm embarrassed. And if this doesn't go right, I'm going to be really embarrassed. So I'm like, "Okay," and Louis was like, "Oh, here's your thing." Cha-chunk. I'm like, "Yes!" You know, it was a great feeling. It's a great accomplishment.

Ava booked a number of flights around the country in celebration of her new sense of fitting. She even shared pictures of herself in the airplane seats. A number of other participants also showed selfies of themselves in plane seats. The experience of being indistinguishable from other passengers registered as a really important milestone and a sign of fitting and being "normal" for many.

Sofia mentioned similar feelings but added an important layer to the discussion by referencing other bodies as well. Nine months after her surgery, Sofia had only lost fifty pounds by her third interview. Fifty pounds was at the low end of the weight loss experienced by our participants, but Sofia felt at peace and happy with her weight loss and her new relationship with food. She also noticed substantial differences in how she fit into the spaces around her:

> This past probably six to eight weeks have been hellaciously busy for me. And I've traveled a bunch, but I probably am able to get through it easier. I don't even mind a couple of things, like, you know, frequent travel, when you're on these five-hour hikes. Because when I go, sometimes I have to go all the way to Florida. . . . It took me a day to get there and a day to get back and a two-hour meeting. It was a long way. And so you don't get the best seat selections sometimes, depending on all that. But before, the thought of being stuck in the middle seat for five hours was enough to

send me—like, I'll sit by the bathroom, I'll sit anywhere. Do not make me sit in the middle seat. And now I've gotten middle seats, and I'm completely fine sitting in it. . . . The assignment of the seat and where it is, I don't have to be so strategic about it. I can just be in the seat. . . . And you're not really sure what size the [other] person's going to be. Odds are you're not going to be the only overweight one in the row these days. So, you know, even if I've got someone a bit bigger sitting next to me, it's not like we're so waffled, because I take up less room there now, just my hip span has changed, and I can feel that. And I can tighten the—I never needed an extender, but just knowing that, "Oh, it moves all the way over to here now instead of here." Yeah, that feels good.

Sofia also felt satisfied that she could fit into smaller clothes, although she did point out that since she was in her fifties, she was trying not to shop too much. She wanted, she said, to dress appropriately for her age, not like her teenagers.

Joyce likewise reported experiencing huge satisfaction from her new ability to wear nice clothes, after feeling trapped for years in unflattering garments she felt were designed for elderly people trying to hide all parts of their bodies between their necks and their ankles. However, her comments about clothes were closely intertwined with other people's reactions to her. Like Ava and Sofia, Joyce experienced better fitting at the same time that she experienced more compliments about her appearance and weight loss. In her final interview, for example, Joyce said,

There's only about four or five single men in my age group at the church [but] . . . I did have some of the younger men—they're married. And their wives are so funny. At the banquet, a lady was telling me—she's younger. . . . And she was saying, "You look so nice, I didn't believe it." And she said [to her husband], "Look, Joseph." And he was like, "*Uh-huh.*" And you know, he's my son's age. And I thought that was so funny, so cute. That was nice, that was nice.

During our years of fieldwork, virtually all of the female participants we observed—as well as most of the women who attended the support group meetings postsurgery—started wearing more makeup, painting their nails, and changing their hairstyles after a few months of weight loss. Although these practices of self-care, self-adornment, and self-work could have been performed at any weight, there was definitely a marked increase in beautification and grooming after surgery.

Previous research on bariatric patients has documented how much easier patients find it to practice what is defined as "good hygiene" after weight loss.[16] We did not observe this as a powerful change for the participants in this study. Indeed, the majority reported careful and detailed habits to maintain good hygiene and cleanliness prior to surgery, and some said that they viewed such self-care habits as pivotal to combating societal stereotypes of being sloppy, lazy, or dirty. Nevertheless, extra grooming effort with respect to appearance (i.e., striving to look good as well as clean) was an additional layer that many women and some men specifically added to their routines once they began receiving positive feedback about weight loss. It seemed to us that the confidence induced by the positive feedback was a key factor in their doing so.

## Compliments and Accusations

Study participants reported drastic reductions in structural stigma, such as being able to "fit" better in the material world,[17] but the quality of their experiences around interpersonal stigma (i.e., comments and reactions from others) proved slightly more complicated. Compliments about weight loss came from people whom patients knew prior to their bariatric surgery. These compliments were occasionally mixed with vague or direct suggestions that getting surgery was cheating at weight loss or with some form of negative reaction to their thinning bodies. Other participants commented that they just grew tired of the constant social focus on their bodies and their weight.

Joyce's musings on this subject are characteristic of the mixed feelings people expressed. As noted previously, she clearly stated that she enjoyed the compliments she received after weight loss and liked creating a completely new look for herself. In the third and final interview nine months after Joyce's bypass surgery, she weighed only 174 pounds. She had new clothes and a new hairstyle and a new job. Like others, Joyce was extremely happy overall with the changes in her life. Nevertheless, the compliments on her dramatic weight loss sometimes irked her, as did her own internal reflection on the way people treated her before versus after weight loss. She said,

> I just notice that people speak to you more: "Hi, how you doing?" I walked into the bank, and the guy spoke to me twice. I'm like, "You just spoke to me. I just went to my car and came right back." I know they have to greet you when you come in the building. I know that's the customer service now. You can't walk in Wal-Mart or Walgreens . . . But I just noticed that they are a little friendlier. And I'm almost insulted. This is from people that I don't know, but I think about how society treats people who they think are not pretty enough, not shapely enough, you know?

As this excerpt shows, Joyce had mixed feelings about the sea change she was experiencing when she interacted with other people. On the one hand, she liked the more positive feedback she herself now enjoyed. On the other hand, she recognized that all kinds of bodies that did not meet social norms were being judged, and she found this distressing and deeply insulting.

In the presurgery classes, the nurses talked to every cohort of patients about the possible ways others might burden them with negative or stress-inducing reactions to their weight loss. The nurses routinely mentioned, for example, that a lot of spouses and family members expressed fear when someone had surgery. They also commented that friends sometimes accused surgery patients of cheating by getting surgery. The nurses had specific lecture points that they always raised with preoperative patients concerning the ways in which other social interactions would evolve after surgery and weight loss. One popular topic of discussion in presurgery classes, for example, was the fact that lots of people had learned to compensate socially for stigmatizing assumptions associated with excess weight by never saying no and always helping everyone else, often at their own expense. "You can no longer be the garbage dump for every unwanted task in your family and work," the nurses would tell the class. The implication was that patients needed to be prepared for occasional negative feedback, including accusations of selfishness.

The nurses' preparation seemed highly effective in giving people a framework for understanding the many reactions that their social and work circles might have. We heard many stories of upended social relationships and less-than-positive interactions, but participants invariably referenced the same key points that the nurses discussed in classes and that came up in the support group meetings. A number of parents remarked that their children complained about their new emotional outlook on life, which the children (ranging from elementary-school-aged to nominal adults) interpreted as "more selfish." Several women in their fifties and sixties shared stories about how their husbands felt intimidated by their thinner bodies and threatened when they got body compliments from others. Having an explanation and a justification ready in such situations made a huge difference for many people, whether the negative reaction was a snide comment about becoming less nice and more uppity after weight loss, an accusation that the surgery was cheating, or simply an overabundance of weight-loss compliments.

Few survey respondents reported that they were told they were not as nice after surgery and weight loss. Roughly a quarter, however, said that they had been told by someone in their life that bariatric surgery was cheating or that they could have lost weight through more conventional means if they had just exerted more willpower.

Cindi, whom Sarah met during the first month of fieldwork when Cindi was already two years postsurgery, talked about the conundrums she had faced at her previous job. Part of her motivation for undergoing the surgery in the first place, she said, was to lose weight so that she could change professions, since she had felt that people would be prejudiced about hiring her if she was "super obese." However, she also felt that her old place of employment, where she had worked for over a decade, did not appreciate her until she lost weight, and that bothered her. She said that she was really good at her job, but she never heard positive feedback until she started losing weight. The compliments about how good she looked then rolled in constantly.

Cindi later mentioned that her son had recently told her that she had gotten meaner postsurgery. Cindi responded that he had also gotten more rebellious as he got older and so they had "both changed." Her other son just said he appreciated that they went to the park more and were more active; he told his brother not to rock the boat. When asked, Cindi said "of course" she had changed emotionally since the surgery, especially in having more confidence and feeling, "I look good again." Many participants attributed the occasional negative reaction from others to their own increased confidence and resulting willingness to say no. This made it easier for patients to overlook the negativity and frustrations and focus instead on the positive developments during that first year after surgery.

Other participants who experienced increased self-confidence connected to their weight loss, followed by positive social and career developments, were left wondering which change precipitated the other. Both Ava and Sofia were recommended for work promotions a year or two postsurgery, and both did a similar internal analysis: was it the weight loss, or was it the increase in self-confidence that led to the recommendation for promotion? Both women ultimately felt that it was the combination of thinner body and increased confidence that made the difference in their career success.

Anne, who was already two years postsurgery when first interviewed, retroactively described the changes that affected her in that initial period after surgery. Most of them were positive: she loved her increased confidence and the compliments she received. Some of the feedback was more off-putting. In an interview, Anne related the following stories:

> I still shop at Dillard's because I guess it's my happy place. You know, I shop other places too, but I always know they have the brands, I know what sizes I wear, I know what fits well. So I go back there on their sales and stuff. But the gal there was pretty much the one that got me feeling good about myself. . . . I got two dresses, and I bought a dress for this wedding we went to. . . . And I wore the dress to the wedding, and everybody was nutso because some of the people hadn't seen me, some of the family hadn't seen me in a long time. . . . The funny thing is that people that . . . I worked with for years don't know who I am at all. So I've gone up to a couple of them and gone, "Hi." And, "Do I know you?" And I'll say, "Yeah, it's Anne." "Oh my God. Oh my God." That type of thing. But it's always extremely positive. You know, "You look amazing. You look twenty years younger. How did you do it?" And I'm very open. And my husband will say, "Why do you have to tell people that?" And I say, "Because I think I'm so proud of what I've done that I don't care if people know that my crutch was surgery." I had one person say to me, "Well, you

did it the easy way." . . . He will never say that again. I lashed out at him. He got it full force, and he will never say that again. I mean, if you think having surgery and going through what I went through is easy, I said, "You've got a lot to learn." And so he never will say that again.

There are a lot of ideas to unpack in this narrative. Positive experiences and developments for Anne included better shopping options, increased confidence and feelings of achievement over her successful weight loss, and a stream of excited feedback and compliments from others. She did, however, note that one person accused her of taking the "easy way" to weight loss by opting for bariatric surgery. Perhaps more tellingly, she also related that her husband wished she would not be so public about the surgery and she herself referred to her bypass as a "crutch."

We discussed this notion of the "work of weight loss" and the idea that people are somehow cheating at this work if they opt for bariatric surgery in chapters 1 and 2.[18] Certainly, participants did confront social judgment for going through bariatric surgery, but overall most participants during the honeymoon period echoed Anne's feelings of excitement and accomplishment.

## The New Normal?

Underlying all of the stories of fitting better, feeling better, receiving more positive and less negative attention, and successfully self-monitoring consumption and compliance was a powerful new relationship with notions of "normal." Participants entered the program with a designation of morbid obesity, and this meant that their bodies—and their presumed personal habits—were considered abnormal by American mainstream social mores. The precipitous and profound weight loss and the abrupt cessation of symptoms from diseases like diabetes during patients' first year after surgery meant that for the first time in many years, patients could occupy bodies that were casually identified as normal. Normalcy had suddenly become attainable. Normal, however, meant slightly different things to different people.

Sofia, for example, focused on her new relationship with food in her third interview, because the surgery and associated counseling had "retrained" her habits and allowed her to get out of her lifelong tendency to overeat when stressed. For her, this was as important as the weight loss itself. She said,

> I know for me, the desire to just feel normal about food intake, about my weight, it shouldn't be something that it takes up so much time and space in my life. So I even would say that I would rather be just where I am at fifty pounds [lighter] even for a while then try to get to eighty or so, which I think is probably where my goal is, by being hypervigilant about it. Like particularly for me, I feel like I'm at this comfortable place. I'm not skinny, I'm not fat. I'm enjoying my medium size.

Sofia pointed out in the interview that (like Luke, quoted earlier) she wanted the surgery to help her reset her attitudes toward food to be more normal, which she identified as less obsessive and more effective in eating enough for sustenance but not more. Through this more normal eating, she had achieved a medium-sized, more normal body.

Clara explicitly focused on the ways in which her body was starting to look more normal and the complex interaction between her physical body and her interactions with others. In her third interview, she explained,

> I'm getting back to where I need to be, like back into Clara again, you know what I mean? . . . Like my chubby cheeks and stuff, I'm starting to get thinned out—face back, and that's nice. . . . Yeah, I'm still fat, but it's . . . better than who I was, and I'm willing to accept that and keep progressing and moving forward. Yeah, I can fit in [an] airplane seat. . . . It [being smaller] just makes you more functionable in life, and you get to live your life a little bit more, be more active in it. . . . People just treat you differently when you look better. When you carry yourself a certain way, you get treated better. That's just the way it is. That's society for you. But yeah, I think when you physically feel better, you drop that weight, and you can do those things, and it makes you feel good, you know? It just does.

Here again the reflection on weight loss identified easier "fitting" into spaces and seats, increased confidence, better treatment from others— and, thus, yet more increased confidence. Clara also underlined that for her, she felt she was getting her true self back again, as it emerged via her weight loss.

Shannon also focused on the iterative feedback loops between a more normal appearance, more confidence, and more normal interactions with others. In her third and final interview, she talked about this extensively. Sitting outside a coffee shop in the sunshine over coffee (Sarah) and unsweetened tea (Shannon), Shannon said,

> I feel different, yeah. I feel like a different person. Like, when we came here, normally I would go to someplace to get a drink or something, and I would stand there waiting for my order thinking, "These people are all judging me because of my size. They're all thinking, 'What did she order?'" Those sorts of things. And I would be so self-conscious. And I'd just be fidgety all over the place and things like that and just want to blend in and not stand out at all. And now, I don't feel that. . . . I feel normal, you know?

When asked if she thought people were judging her before or whether her perceptions had changed, Shannon replied, "I think sometimes they were. But I think probably sometimes when I thought they were, they weren't necessarily. . . . I feel better in my skin than I used to."

The physical shift toward a more normal body is mirrored in discursive constructions of normative identities.[19] Put more simply, this is the idea that people lost weight in order to fit societal notions about what a normal body and weight looks like and, at the same time, participants talked about the fact that they were responsible, healthy citizens who behaved in ways that fit these same standards and expectations. In other words, they worked hard to move from a social/medical category of abnormal and diseased to one of normalcy or "being normal" both through actions that changed their physical bodies and via what they said and how they acted.[20]

In both these activities, bariatric surgery patients unequivocally echo attitudes and practices in which most Americans today constantly engage. In other words, their pursuit of normalcy through weight-loss efforts makes them very normal within the US in the twenty-first century. We said this in the introduction. The vast majority of Americans engage at least occasionally in diet and exercise behaviors for the express purpose of weight loss or to prevent weight gain; some do it constantly. For participants who had, for the most part, suffered a lifetime of failure at these normative weight-loss efforts, it was a relief to attain a normative body. Of course, the huge irony here is that failure at weight-loss efforts is the actual norm in the US today; that is, most Americans either do not lose the weight they want to lose in the first place or else they cannot maintain weight loss. As we remarked at the beginning of this book, ideas about weight, fat, and the body in the twenty-first-century United States display a remarkable discrepancy between an idealized, aspirational norm of thinness and successful weight loss and the average daily experience of most people, who are heavier than they articulate wanting to be and display less control and discipline over their consumption than they say they would wish. What is so very ironic here, then, is that in the pursuit of normalcy through weight loss, people who opted for bariatric surgery in the program we studied were not at all normal precisely because they were so successful at it. Instead, they achieved an aspirational norm.

## When the Honeymoon Is Over

All of the bariatric patients we met during fieldwork experienced some form of a honeymoon period after their surgery, a time filled with excitement over fitting better and feeling more normal, alongside experienced reductions in chronic illnesses. However, the length of the honeymoon varied from person to person. Some people were still losing weight consistently a year and a half after surgery, whereas others found the honeymoon ground to a halt well within the first year.

After the excitement and optimism of the honeymoon period, when weight drops off visibly from week to week and anything seems possible, the longer-term outlook is necessarily more complex. Weight loss is fairly negligible for most people after the first year, and they have become more accustomed to, and less excited by, their improved health status. Other people have also become more accustomed to their new appearance and dole out fewer compliments.

New chronic body issues and annoyances also begin to emerge in the months and years after bariatric surgery. These are the focus of chapter 4. All of these issues are sources of stress in the years after surgery and come to the fore after the buzz of the honeymoon period has ended.

# 4

## Weight, Worry, and Surveillance

It's the third class of this cycle, which means the student-patients had the first week of information and introductions taught by one of the nurses, had the second week taught by one of the dieticians, and now are back with a nurse again. She began with the topic of "Why am I overweight." She went through all of the causes of weight gain, including thyroid issues, a "crummy" metabolism, "just genetics," sex, the environment, and family upbringing and cultural background, asking for thoughts from people as she went through the items. . . . The nurse then asked if people thought there is such a thing as weight-related stigma. Emily said, "Yes, across all different levels. . . . For example, when hiring—even for just stocking shelves—they are going to hire the person who is healthier and can move better." The nurse said, "There certainly is that perception that healthy and lower weight go together, especially with insurance mandating that." A discussion then ensued about self-image and stigma experiences relating to weight. . . . The nurse pulled up a PowerPoint slide that demanded, "So why don't we just do it?" She asked, "Is it that we don't know better?" "No, we know better. . . . It's just hard to avoid things in society," said Jim. "It's also about time," said Emily. "I get home, and I can throw a pizza in the oven . . . or really take a lot of time and plan a meal." More discussion ensued about the ubiquity of food at all social occasions and the process of learning how to be happy and engaged when there is no food, as well as learning not to eat when not hungry and being able to leave food on your plate. . . . The nurse talked about the importance of establishing a healthier relationship with food long term after surgery and then drew an arc, showing extreme weight loss in the first year. She then said, "It's perfectly normal to gain some weight after that." She went through the different types of hunger, ranging from physical hunger to emotional hunger, stressing again that people needed to be able to distinguish between these before going into surgery, or they would have trouble both adjusting to the surgery's physical effects and in dealing with the return of hunger and cravings after many of those effects end and people "are on their own." . . . The nurse detailed all of the improvements in health, social stigma, and self-image that improve in the wake of surgery.

However, she also talked about the "magical thinking" that some people have, believing that surgery will cure everything that they don't like about themselves and their lives. "You will still be you after the surgery," she said. "Losing weight will not fix everything in your life."
—Sarah's field notes, spring 2015

The preceding excerpt from Sarah's field notes illustrates some of the complex issues that patients must navigate in the months and years after bariatric surgery. In this chapter, we consider how people negotiate these various stressors and the specific role that weight plays in how they cope (or fail to). We focus our analysis on a relatively underexplored area of anthropological concern, the meanings and implications of excess skin, as well as offering new perspectives on more-often-discussed topics such as self-surveillance of eating.

## Health Remains a Balancing Act

A relatively large literature, mostly medical, documents the many health improvements that result from bariatric surgery, both indirectly due to weight loss and more directly because of the surgery itself changing hormone levels, gut microbiomes, and other processes.[1] Many conditions continue to show maintained improvement relative to before surgery five, ten, and even twenty years post-op, especially if people maintain the eating and exercise habits advocated by the bariatric program.[2] These improvements are especially apparent with respect to hypertension, type 2 diabetes, and dyslipidemia, but broader measures assessing quality of life also show sustained improvements.[3]

In contrast, other medical and social science literature has documented the health problems that can result from going through bariatric surgery. Although relatively rare (especially if the surgeries are performed in an accredited institution), these can initially include surgical complications such as strictures, difficulty swallowing, and infections, among others.[4] More common side effects stem not from the surgery itself but from the effect of the surgery on the gut's ability to process and absorb nutrients. Frequent long-term health problems reported in the literature include persistent nausea and fatigue, the development of food sensitivities and intolerances (especially lactose intolerance), and the development of nutritional deficiencies.[5] As one set of authors observed, "Bariatric operations result in permanent alteration of a patient's anatomy, which can lead to complications at any time during the course of a patient's life."[6]

We listened to countless stories of miraculous cures and long-term improvements in health during our years of ethnographic research with this particular bariatric population. Participants in the ethnographic part of the study, other patients in the program, and various members of the bariatric medical staff enthusiastically recounted the many ways health improved after the weight loss of the first year and how it remained substantially better years later. Type 2 diabetes and joint pain were the most common conditions that patients said had previously caused a great deal of daily suffering and that improved significantly after surgery. For example, Brad felt that his Roux-en-Y gastric bypass cured both his diabetes and his joint pain, and despite some weight gain in the second year, his health remained significantly improved. Brad gave Sarah his perspectives in a third and final interview over three years after his bypass:

> And you say, wow, when everything is that complex and the body is that complex, exactly why did my diabetes go away? Why has it all of a sudden got insulin? We're not really sure, but we know it works. That's good enough for me, but still you don't know, right? It's all complex. And it all comes down to one question. Somebody gave me a second shot at life, wow. I mean, how many people get that, you know. There again, I'm also one of the luckiest people to ever walk the face of the earth.

Quoted in chapter 3, Brad had said that his experience after bariatric surgery felt like a near miracle cure. This theme of a miraculous change again threaded its way through his narrative here. He did point out that scientists are still trying to understand the precise mechanics underlying bariatric surgery's effects on diabetes and other diseases. Unlike health-care providers, who point to the lack of evidence as part of their cautions about regarding the surgery as a "cure" or "fix," Brad's perspective in this quote was that the mystery actually deepens the miracle, giving him a second chance at life. Not everyone experiences long-term life after surgery quite so positively, however.

Survey respondents, for example, were equally clear about the dramatic improvements in their health after surgery, but they too reported chronic struggles with problems like the effects of vitamin deficiencies (36 percent) and food intolerances (47 percent). As noted in chapter 3, underconsumption of the daily recommended caloric intake due to meal skipping was not uncommon. Underconsumption of micronutrients was also a problem. Failure to follow the program guidelines for supplements and minimum protein and water thresholds led to symptoms such as severe fatigue, cramping, dizziness, and exacerbated hair loss. These symptoms escalated if the deficiencies were not addressed. Nevertheless, because the physical feedback was not as immediate as an episode of dumping (for example, skipping iron supplements did not lead to same-day fatigue), people often had a difficult time remembering to meet their thresholds, take their pills, and so on. It is not uncommon to forget to take vitamins from time to time, but it is not something that individuals who have undergone bariatric surgery can afford to forget very often without potentially serious physical consequences.

For example, a longterm, severe B12 deficiency has serious cognitive effects—in fact, in the nineteenth-century US, sufferers used to be put in insane asylums, which gives some idea of how bad the consequences can be. A deficiency is unavoidable in an individual who has had bariatric surgery if they do not take a particular type of supplement, no matter how much B12 they get in their diet, because the bypassed intestine and reduced stomach pouch malabsorb B12. A gastric bypass patient must therefore take a sublingual or injection supplement of B12 every month. Such supplements are particularly annoying to remember because they require extra steps. The recommended regular B12 injection was explained by the patients as problematic to remember because it required a trip to a pharmacy or clinic or the extra unpleasantness of a self-administered shot. The alternative, a B12 supplement that had to be administered sublingually, also caused confusion: the "sublingual" administration was not at all the same as popping a regular vitamin supplement pill in one's mouth.

One of the most striking trends to emerge from our survey and ethnographic data is that patients overwhelmingly indicated that they did not regret undergoing bariatric surgery even when the surgery resulted in constant demands and serious health complications. Almost everyone we spoke with said that the trade-offs, which sometimes involved exchanging one set of health concerns for another, were worth it. Shannon was a case in point. Sarah saw Shannon frequently outside of the arranged interviews, including at support group meetings, and watched with concern over time as she developed some serious health complications. In the months after her surgery, she looked increasingly gaunt and gray. In the formal second interview five months postsurgery, when she was finally feeling better again, she told Sarah in more detail about what had happened:

> I got a stricture at the site. . . . I think that in the beginning, I probably was exhibiting some of it and just didn't realize it. I thought, "Oh, I can't eat that much because my stomach is smaller," that sort of thing. But then it got to a point where even fluids were not moving very quickly. I had eight or nine dilations. It was hard. And they kept trying to stretch out the time between, so they'd pretty much wait until I couldn't keep stuff down, and then I'd go in for another dilation. Then they decided that the scar tissue was probably hardening before they got back in to do another dilation. . . . So they started doing them closer, and that's what really broke up the scar tissue. . . . I mean, it's one of the complications that can happen. I knew going into it that it could happen.

As Shannon pointed out, the program not only warns would-be patients that there could be complications after surgery but specifically identified a stricture (also known as stenosis, or narrowing) as a not uncommon result.[7] Warnings and preparation help, and a stricture is treatable; but the experience is still deeply unpleasant.

Shannon gave a detailed picture of the ordeal she had been through but also remained philosophical, saying that she knew the complications were possible and that it was important to remain positive. When asked if she had experienced a great deal of nausea and pain, she replied, "It was more the deficiencies than anything. My protein was really low. My potassium was low. You know, I wasn't necessarily nauseated, but I felt this tightness. And even if I would drink something, it felt like the fluid wasn't going anywhere. So I would go a long time before I would drink again, so I was definitely dehydrated and just in bad shape." Imagine trying to get through a workday and function within a family while unable to eat or drink in any quantity, while plagued with fatigue, dizziness, and vitamin and protein deficiencies.

At the time of the interview from which we just quoted, Shannon had recently emerged from several months of being extremely ill. She had been forced to take two five-week periods off work, maxing out her paid vacation time. She still felt that the surgery was worth it. She had lost eighty-eight pounds and was ecstatic about her weight loss and how much less self-conscious and more confident she felt. Sarah left the interview feeling relieved on Shannon's behalf. Subsequently, however, Shannon developed a hernia, her intestines looped themselves around the hernia, and she ended up needing another surgery to repair everything. Still, when Sarah saw her several months later, in passing at the clinic, Shannon told her that although it had been a terrible year, she was almost at her "goal weight" and had high hopes for the following year.

Most of the men and women in the study similarly felt that losing the pathologized, socially unacceptable fat body was worth trade-offs of this kind. Their reasoning tended to be twofold. First, medical issues such as nutrient deficiencies often seemed less serious to people than their previous problems with type 2 diabetes and hypertension. Moreover, the deficiencies seemed more malleable and easily fixed compared with their struggles to control their blood-sugar levels or resolve their knee pain. Various practitioners tried to change this attitude, including through presentations at the support group about the serious long-term impacts of certain deficiencies, but the attitude persisted, reinforced by all the public attention in the US today centered on obesity as a diseased state.

Second, people also preferred the problems associated with bariatric surgery because they were less obviously stigmatized. The surgery could be socially hidden, after all, whereas the fat could not. This meant that when patients discussed knee pain or diabetes with others, they tended to receive a curt admonition to lose weight, whereas when they discussed their tiredness and malnutrition, their audience tended to be more sympathetic.

## Lifelong Consequence #1: Self-Surveillance of Eating

Postsurgery patients may not always have hewed as closely to nutritional guidelines and supplement recommendations as their clinicians wished, but they were all hyperaware of the food they put into their mouths. To put this in context, consider that monitoring of food and eating has become a major preoccupation across US societies more generally, reflecting important cultural ideas about health, responsibility, morality, consumption, and control.[8]

Careful surveillance of eating is increasingly normalized in the United States as key to maintaining a kind of belonging called moral citizenship, whereby ideas about personal responsibility feed into ideals about morality and being a good and selfless member of a community.[9] Strategies of external surveillance and self-surveillance are supposed to produce docile "good bodies" through practices of "watching what we eat."[10] The power of this surveillance depends on the act of watching and also on the accompanying processes of normalization. Thus, we make judgments about what is and is not normal food-related behavior, and then we rewrite this practice and process itself as also normal—a cultural norm, in fact.

In the US, surveillance of the eating practices of people who are considered fat is especially rife with judgments, usually centered on notions that such individuals overconsume and undermonitor their own food intake.[11] By contrast, we observed a great deal of surveillance and self-monitoring among participants *before* their surgeries. However, we were also struck by how this self-monitoring was continually dismissed by both the participants themselves and the people around them because it failed; in other words, it did not result in long-term, sustained weight loss.[12]

Coupled with surveillance and notions of control is the theme of risk. To be at risk is popularly conceived as being out of control, with regard both to habits and to the way these habits have become physically embodied, with assumed repercussions for future health.[13] This idea forms the bedrock for popular portrayals of eating disorders. To be fat is perceived not only as aesthetically undesirable but also as inherently risky and out of control, but to be anorexic is perceived as too controlling and overregulated.[14] Our interest was where bariatric patients fit along this spectrum. They were once perceived to be out of control, fat, and risky overconsumers, but their eating habits after surgery were necessarily rigid and regulated.

Control, especially self-control, is threaded through the qualitative bariatric literature.[15] Self-monitoring, self-control, and mindfulness around eating after bariatric surgery are practices imposed by the surgery itself: the reduction in stomach size and bypassing of much of the intestine means that only well-chewed portions of food are tolerated; fats and sugars may become indigestible; and incautious eating or drinking may result in vomiting, diarrhea, or dumping. However, postoperative patients report that this imposed control subsequently became linked with increased self-esteem and self-efficacy, especially when accompanied by visible weight loss.[16] In other words, people who undergo bariatric surgery and its associated extreme internal disruptions develop new daily habits and practices as a result of the altered physical body.[17] They also imbue these new habits with moral significance.

Several studies also have shown that if individuals postsurgery make mistakes in their food intake and self-monitoring, they may experience not only physical sickness but also self-blame, doubt, and feelings of failure.[18] These feelings may be heightened if patients are not satisfied with their weight loss after surgery. We certainly observed this in our own research.

Among the participants we interviewed, constant self-surveillance of eating had to become the "new normal" after bariatric surgery. To prevent weight regain, lifelong attention to what they ate was expected long after their physical tolerance of fats and sugars and higher quantities of food had increased. The degree of self-monitoring in participants' daily lives was therefore sometimes extraordinary. Anne, who at two years after her gastric bypass had lost over one hundred pounds, described her daily negotiations with food in this way:

> I do MyFitnessPal [an online fitness application]. . . . Oh yes, religiously. . . . Yes, especially when I had to balance things so closely. I don't want too much protein. . . . I used the powdered unflavored [protein powder] because I found you can add it to more things. You can add it to applesauce, you can add it to soup, and you can add it to whatever. There's no flavor. . . . And a lot of things have tons of protein, but they're also high

in sugar, and I can't have that. Or they're okay with one, but it's only five grams of protein, which really isn't enough. . . . I usually have a smoothie for breakfast every morning. I find that that starts me out with a good protein hit. And it's just Chobani yogurt with fresh fruit. That's it. And that works to get me going.

Anne's approach had been the same for years, and she planned to stay the course for the rest of her life. Although overall very happy with the results of her weight loss and new regime, she did note that her extensive tracking of food took a substantial amount of time.

It is interesting in this context to consider that much of the participants' self-monitoring was influenced by cultural conceptions of "healthy" food monitoring, and therefore it did not necessarily agree with the program guidelines. For example, the program dieticians often tried to get people to focus on portion sizes rather than counting calories. Participants would tell us that they had been to see one of the dieticians for a checkup, and often, the advice was to eat good meals, watch portion sizes, "and stop counting calories!" All of the apps people liked, however, did count calories for them. Food labels, of course, also provided them. Thus, the common ways people across the US are encouraged to monitor their food typically held sway over the bariatric experts' medical advice in this area.

Similarly, avoiding (complex) carbohydrates entirely was not recommended by the program dieticians. "You could end up starving your body of necessary nutrients!" said one dietician to a group of patients. Participants—who usually entered the program having heard some of the current diet-industry messages about the evils of carbs—consistently tried to do so anyway. One woman, Caroline, said that she had joined a social-media-based group for people who had undergone bariatric surgery and were trying to follow a Paleo diet. When she went for her check-in, the dietician she saw strongly recommended she not adopt such a diet. Caroline heeded the dietician's advice to the extent that she was not strictly following a Paleo diet, but she still tried to avoid carbs when possible. She also stayed in the online group, although she mentioned during her third interview that the group's approach to eating bothered her a great deal—and that no one else from "our" program was a part of the group.

Not everyone felt that they were exerting enough self-control. The survey data certainly highlighted this feeling. In the sections of the survey that focused on diet specifically, people were asked to self-evaluate how well they stuck to the recommended diet plan after surgery on a scale of 1 (not very well) to 10 (very well). In the first wave of the survey, 192 respondents were fairly critical of themselves: the mean was 6.27, and few people rated themselves as particularly adherent or particularly nonadherent. However, in the second wave of the survey that was sent out to the same patients a year later, the mean had dropped to 3.01, a statistically significant decline. In other words, people on the survey perceived themselves to be less adherent over time.

Research on such dietary adherence and dieting in general indicates that self-monitoring of food intake, coupled with the perception that one should be limiting food intake to a greater extent, leads to intense frustration and stress.[19] Many people in this particular bariatric population had experienced intense degrees of self-stigma, shame, and blame over perceived failure at dieting in the long years before bariatric surgery. This personal history meant that people's perceptions of failure in the years after surgery were also keenly felt.

The ethnographic data also highlighted the worry many people felt as they got further from surgery, felt increasingly less adherent, and continued self-monitoring their increased consumption. A decline in adherence was virtually unavoidable, since it would have been difficult to continue to eat as little as patients did during the first six to nine months after a bypass, when their stomachs were the size of walnuts and a spoonful of cookie dough could result in hours of vomiting. Thus, people watched themselves consume more (relative to that first year post-op), even counting the calories as they disappeared into their mouths, but felt unable to stop. The fact that postsurgery this "overconsumption" might equal only a couple hundred extra calories did not lessen the feelings of self-blame that often accompanied the (self-identified) uncontrolled eating. The self-monitoring therefore added a huge side helping of stress and shame to people's plates, without being at all effective in halting self-identified bad habits. People would report that they knew when they began eating outside the parameters of their diet (for example, "cheating" via slider foods, alcoholic drinks, and so on), but once they perceived that they were starting to spiral out of control, it was very difficult for them to stop. If this sounds familiar to anyone reading this book, we are not surprised—this sort of moralizing, hyperaware framework is pervasive across US society in the twenty-first century.

Consider the following situation described by Natalie in her first interview when she was several years postsurgery:

> I'm very competitive is what I found out, so I'll count out like twelve M&Ms. I'll sit them on my desk, and I'll be like—"It's ten o'clock in the morning," I'll say. "I need an M&M." And then I look at it and think, "Oh, but if I have them now and then if I get frustrated at four, then I don't have any more today." So most days, I put them away. . . . And then I think with the stress and the traveling, I discovered jelly beans. And I could just throw a handful in, thirty of them, 140 calories. And so I would count out thirty and throw them in my mouth at the airport, then that would get me another eight-hour flight. I'm like, "Okay, I have to get off jelly beans."

Natalie lost significant weight during her first year after her bypass but struggled with weight fluctuations thereafter, despite a militant approach to food monitoring. Since her surgery was two years prior, she could tolerate junk food if she limited the amount she ate at a time, but she was counting out her jelly beans and M&Ms to track calories, not to prevent sickness. Natalie also knew how many jelly beans or M&Ms equaled a serving size and how many calories were in that serving. Nevertheless, despite all of her counting and calculating and hedging, she could not quite stop herself from eating them. Instead, she used them as a treat to get through difficult workdays. Does this also sound familiar? Again, it should: Americans engage in eating behaviors like this often.

Participants like Natalie spent a considerable portion of their already busy days thinking about food, counting grams of protein and calories, measuring portion sizes (often with a kitchen scale), and weighing themselves. This represented not only a substantial investment of time but also emotional energy. Moreover, the sticking point for many patients was whether this surveillance translated into "successful" control of eating and therefore weight.

## Lifelong Consequence #2: Self-Surveillance of Weight

Self-surveillance of weight went hand in hand with self-surveillance of eating. Like self-surveillance of eating, self-surveillance of weight tended to be both extreme and normalized as a key to successful weight loss and long-term weight-loss maintenance. Underlying the policing and surveillance was a deep-seated fear of regain. Even in the midst of massive weight loss, people voiced their fear that they would regain weight, especially if they did not practice self-surveillance.

As one participant named Golti said several months after her bypass, "I don't feel super confident, like I beat this. Every day, every day I have to think about it, every day. I think it's going to be a lifelong thing." Indeed, many bariatric patients do regain weight in the years following surgery,[20] and although exact numbers are difficult to ascertain, all our participants had heard horror stories of dramatic boomerang weight regains. Fears of weight regain also became fears of moral failure, and weight surveillance was not always effective in the ways that people wished. In other words, extreme monitoring did not inevitably lead to control of weight.

Over 80 percent of the survey respondents, for example, reported that they weighed themselves at least every week, which reflected a substantial amount of self-monitoring. Moreover, fewer than 20 percent of these respondents said they felt their current weight was ideal. On average, respondents said that their ideal weight was about twenty-five pounds below their actual weight at the time of the survey. However, when asked to distinguish between when they felt they were at their "healthiest weight" and when they felt they were at their "ideal weight," most respondents reported an ideal weight that was significantly lower than their healthiest weight. In other words, self-monitoring of weight in the years after bariatric surgery was rooted in continued dissatisfaction with the current body and current weight. Furthermore, this dissatisfaction appeared to be more closely related to aesthetic cultural ideals of thinness than to medically healthy weights. Finally, people were able to make this distinction (most Americans tend to conflate aesthetic ideals with health), but the dissatisfaction remained.

The following interview excerpt nicely sums up the balancing act of long-term weight-loss monitoring. Anne considered herself to be one of the program's major success stories. As we already noted, she began participating in our project when she was almost two years postsurgery, and over the course of the following year, she provided many insights into what it means to be successful at bariatric surgery and weight loss over the longer term. This excerpt is from the second interview, when she was two years and two months postsurgery. Anne told Sarah, "[I'm currently at] 130 pounds. . . . I weigh myself every morning. . . . MyFitnessPal and the scale [are key]. And there was one gal, she was very hesitant at the [support group] meetings. . . . We were talking, and I said, 'I have to weigh myself every day.' And her comment was, 'If I did that, I'd go crazy.'" Extreme self-surveillance of weight and eating habits appeared to work well for Anne; she had kept her weight off and was not going crazy. Nonetheless, it did require a level of self-monitoring that was difficult for many participants to sustain long term.

Olivia was another participant who, at a year and a half after surgery, was doing very well by both clinic standards and her own estimation. At the time of her third interview, she was at a weight she had not seen in forty years. When asked how often (if ever) she got on a scale, she said, "Probably every three days, yeah. I used to try to weigh every day, and that was maddening. . . . But weighing about three times a week. I don't weigh in Monday morning because after a weekend, I know I'm up. But I'll weigh in tomorrow [Tuesday] morning, and I'll weigh on Thursday. Maybe Thursday, Friday. You know, whenever I think to do it and timing, yeah." Three times a week still represents quite a bit of self-monitoring. It is certainly far more than Olivia was doing presurgery, when she told Sarah that she recalled seeing the scale as the enemy and hated it so much that she rarely weighed herself outside of the doctor's office.

Of course, as with eating surveillance, weight surveillance is common in the US today. Many people weigh themselves every week or even every day. Weight surveillance is also normalized as key to what is considered successful self-management.[21] Also like eating surveillance, weight surveillance is accepted as cultural fact even though it has proven absolutely ineffective as a weight-management technique in the general population, while effectively increasing shame and blame.[22] This last point is counterintuitive for many Americans today, but a great deal of research substantiates that weight surveillance does not help maintain body weight. A bariatric population is indisputably different from the general population. Nonetheless, many participants ended up veering away from frequent weigh-ins after their first postsurgical year precisely because the numbers no longer decreased in reassuring and exciting ways.

If patients' attempts to maintain postsurgical weight loss derailed and they started regaining weight, that could mean very different things to different people. Everyone we spoke with knew anecdotal stories of bariatric patients who regained all of their presurgery weight. Usually, these were coworkers, relatives, neighbors, or people who appeared on weight-loss TV shows. Various participants recounted tales of people they knew (usually not well) who opted for bariatric surgery, lost a lot of weight in the first year, and then put it all back on in the next couple of years.

These stories were incredibly scary for people, and they mitigated their fear, in interviews, by telling Sarah about their own surveillance practices and greater preparation at the clinic, while also arguing that their surgeries were more effective than the ones that other "failed" patients had. Many of these others had opted for gastric bands, for example, which can be adjusted or removed upon request. Many of the patients in these weight-regain stories also did not have counseling and nutrition training before surgery, which meant, according to participants, that they did not substantively change their lifestyles after surgery. Brad told a story of meeting a man fresh from a bariatric surgery who was counting the days until he could resume eating doughnuts. "We never spoke again," said Brad.

There were, however, patients within this clinic who also derailed from their careful eating and exercise regimes—and who then stopped coming to the clinic because they were ashamed of their weight regain. Cindi, for example, began interviews when she was over two years postsurgery and doing very well by her own estimation. At the time of her first interview, she was extremely active in the support group meetings. At the time of her third and final interview, she was over three years postsurgery and experiencing a difficult period in her life, reflected in some weight gain. In this third interview, she said,

> I mean, back when I had my surgery, I knew what I was eating, meal to meal. That first year was a walk in the park and . . . [laughs] . . . You

know, my niche [professionally], what I'm marketing to, we're all about healthy and obesity awareness, and here I am not being a model citizen. I recognize that this is going to impact—although I'm only seeing things that a good amount of people who go through this . . . I'm not ashamed that it's happened to me. I'm not hugely—I've regained twenty pounds in the past year.

Despite saying that she was not ashamed, Cindi had not been back to the clinic since she began regaining weight, even though she herself pointed out that twenty pounds was not a massive weight regain. Like Natalie, she "rewarded" herself with food when life (employment, children, parents) became stressful, fully aware of the extra calories she put in her mouth, usually in the form of candy.

Again, this coupling of awareness of her own eating habits, close tracking of her weight regain, and frustration over her inability to bring her eating and exercise habits under control resulted in a great deal of self-blame. In Cindi's case, she had read enough of the obesity literature to know that self-blame was emotionally damaging and ineffective as a weight-loss technique, and as a result she then became frustrated over her self-blame habits as well.

## Lifelong Consequence #3: Oh, the Skin!

Over the course of our fieldwork, we found that skin emerged as a defining feature of many bariatric patients' postsurgical lives. Skin is a pivotal trait on which people build identity and shape their reactions to others, at a time when skin-care products, regimes, and advertising proliferate and expectations for perfect, poreless, taut skin have never been higher. There has been surprisingly little social science research into skin to date (aside from a rich literature on race and skin color). We say "surprisingly" both because skin is a pivotal component of people's identity (extending far beyond the meanings and implications of color) and because it can be the source of a great deal of daily suffering.

Almost two decades ago, Sarah Ahmed and Jackie Stacey argued that skin studies are an important extension of embodiment work because the skin is the "fleshy interface between bodies and worlds."[23] While relatively few scholars have built on this insight, a 2018 special issue of *Body & Society* did focus on skin.[24] Although none of the articles in the journal issue explored the challenge of excess skin after weight loss—the primary issue of concern to the bariatric patients we knew—several scholars did examine skin ailments more generally as undignified "petty form[s] of suffering" that are seen as not serious enough to be considered real suffering.[25] The insights offered about "undignified" and "petty" forms of suffering go a long way, we think, toward explaining why issues like loose skin have not been taken seriously by many social scientists and clinicians.

Almost all adults develop loose skin after bariatric surgery, precisely because the surgery causes rapid and massive shrinking of the body; that "fleshy interface" cannot shrink fast or comprehensively enough to match the weight loss occurring underneath it. An adult who loses one hundred pounds in a year, therefore, will probably be left with a lot of loose, stretched-out skin. This stretched skin can be embarrassing and uncomfortable and may even cause problems like rashes and yeast infections or hamper mobility.

Prior research shows that patients express high rates of dissatisfaction with this new excess, but many live chronically with it because skin-removal surgery is expensive and often needs to be self-funded.[26] Even skin-removal surgery does not always fix all the problems: some research indicates that after skin-removal surgery, certain individuals still feel their "problem areas" are unsightly.[27] A recent meta-analysis of existing research, however, argued that higher rates of physical functioning, psychological well-being, and social functioning were found in bariatric patients who had undergone subsequent body-contouring surgery.[28]

Both weight-loss and bariatric research has accorded relatively little space to date for discussions around excess skin or relatedly about attitudes and experiences with perceived excess skin versus excess fat. As we noted earlier, one of the challenges of being fat is that it is hard to hide that status from others. Loose skin, however, can be hidden within clothing to some extent (consider, for example, the advertising around shapewear). Interestingly, there is some evidence to suggest that excess skin might be experienced differently by men versus women.[29] Many questions, however, remain unanswered. Moreover, most of the data are based on post-operative patient self-reporting, which may mean some degree of bias since a post-operative patient may be more likely to respond to a survey about excess skin if she is experiencing difficulties with skin.

Although both bariatric surgery and skin removal surgeries are "elective" technological interventions upon the body, they tend to be treated differently by insurance companies. This produces a profound disjuncture in who can afford bariatric surgery versus skin removal. Most of the people interviewed, for example, had their bariatric surgeries covered by insurance. In contrast, skin removal is typically treated as a cosmetic surgery and tends to be self-funded.[30] Many of the clinic patients we encountered were aware of this gap and worried even before bariatric surgery that they would be stuck with excess skin that they would grow to hate.

Satisfaction in the years immediately after bariatric surgery, however, remained generally high, even as people articulated ongoing problems with excess skin. People routinely said that they learned to acknowledge but also to negotiate their embodied changes, including "undesired" alterations.[31] One participant summarized this attitude by saying, "Do I like the skin? No. But I didn't like my body before. This is still so much better." Patients overwhelmingly reported that they felt the trade-off of fat for loose skin had been worth it, and they voiced this opinion in support group meetings, conversations with one another, discussions with health-care providers, and conversations with us. Loose skin was more manageable than fat, more easily hidden, and less of a health and mobility hazard, said participants.

For example, Natalie talked extensively about her exercise routine in her first conversation with Sarah, as well as in support group meetings. As a result, Sarah was startled when Natalie remarked in her first interview that she was intentionally exercising less. When Sarah asked why she had changed her habits, Natalie responded, "I felt like I was getting too thin and my skin hurt. . . . The skin [on] my arm and legs was so loose. And my abdomen skin just burned. . . . I would wrap myself in . . . saran wrap to hold my skin tighter. Then I would put yoga pants over it and another pair of pants over it." This sounded unimaginably uncomfortable to Sarah—and yet many women of all sizes (not just from this study but in US societies more generally) routinely wear tight shapewear (like Spanx) under their regular clothes, even on trips to the gym and when out and about in summertime heat. In other words, saran wrap and yoga pants is not a particularly unusual beauty-containment practice among the many women in the US who seek to hide their bodies from scrutiny.

One of the standard pieces of medical advice for people with loose skin after weight loss is to exercise; we heard this proffered repeatedly in our fieldwork. Ironically, though, Natalie perceived exercise as exacerbating her excess skin. She had always been an avid walker, but she told Sarah that she felt exercise made her lose too much weight. This was not in response to her actual size but rather to the looseness of her skin. She explained that she could tolerate excess skin but not past a certain point. Significantly, neither the loose skin nor the reduction in daily exercise was an issue that Natalie raised with bariatric staff or other patients.

Natalie had resumed daily walking by the time of the second interview, because her weight was beginning to creep higher than she wanted. She had also rediscovered her love for shapewear. Sometimes, she said, she would wear two sets, one on top of the other. At the time, Natalie was traveling extensively for work while juggling the demands of her family and her frantically busy work schedule. She had no plans to get skin-removal surgery, since she was able to manage her outward appearance with clothes, and Spanx. She had no desire to go through the pain and recovery time associated with skin-removal surgery, especially since she had loose skin in many areas of her body and felt that her age would limit her skin resiliency.

Luke was a very different personality than Natalie. Extremely quiet in large groups, Luke was nonetheless far more forthcoming about personal quandaries during interviews. Although Sarah and Luke met in the preoperative classes, Luke only contacted us about participating in our study a few months after his surgery. His first interview occurred soon thereafter, which meant that although Luke was losing weight at the time of the first interview, his appearance had not had time to change visibly from before surgery, at least to a casual outside observer. When Sarah first saw Luke walking into his second interview, however, she was shocked at his physical changes less than a year postsurgery even compared to all the other patients. He was exercising one to two hours a day, and he had lost a dramatic amount of weight. Despite or perhaps because of these changes, he was more somber than he had been earlier in his weight-loss trajectory, describing continued struggles with identity, fear of weight regain, and self-consciousness about his current body.

The conversation with Luke veered into a discussion of how other people he knew were doing after bariatric surgery. Sarah asked if he knew anyone who was contemplating skin-removal surgery, and he told her,

> I know some others, like females, that have had the surgery. And they've had a lot of excess skin, so some of them have. . . . They've gotten like tummy tucks. . . . Yeah, out of pocket. It's a lot of money. They'll save up for that. Yeah, if you lose enough weight, and you have skin—I have skin too. . . . So that's another thing. I was thinking about that too. You lose all the weight, and you feel great, and, you know, almost all your comorbidities are gone, but then you have still this body image thing. . . . Yeah, so it doesn't look that great. It feels good, but you don't look that great. So I think people idealize it, the whole procedure. They think, "Oh yeah, I'm going to be a stud" or "I'm going to be bikini ready, and I'll go out to the beach." And it's just not true sometimes, you know? Most of the time, they're talking about—because, I mean, that skin is not going to go away for a long time probably.

Here, Luke contrasted his more straightforwardly positive changes with respect to health and weight with the more complex issues that continued (or erupted) around body image.

Luke talked a bit more about his own loose skin. When Sarah asked if he would ever have it removed, he was unequivocal:

> I'm not sure if it's not that bad, but I just don't think it's worth all the torture to go through that [skin-removal surgery]. I hear that's more painful than the [bariatric] surgery itself. And the [bariatric] surgery was pretty painful for me, so I don't want to go through that again. . . . So I can be fine with a T-shirt and shorts. I don't need to be—I'm not at that age. I saw some people online that they're younger, they're twenties and thirties, so it's more of an issue for them maybe. So it's not really a big issue for me. I'm going to go at it just a slow approach. I know there's ways to do it naturally just with time. So I'm patient. I'll just take my time. But it is kind of disturbing because you don't just shrink. Some parts shrink more than

others, like more of my neck area, excess skin. . . . And then under my armpits and stuff. And it doesn't look good at all because it's kind of weird looking with excess skin more in one area than the other. . . . You can't tell when you're wearing clothes. Yeah, so I just leave it alone for now.

Luke downplayed his feelings about his loose skin when talking directly about it, alluding to his gender and age as reasons for why the excess skin did not matter as much to him. However, as the conversation later circled back to the topic, it became clear that he did in fact mind his skin, but he did not think skin-removal surgery was for him, mostly because it seemed such a painful and expensive surgery.

Luke and Natalie are illustrative of many other stories we heard within the bariatric program. The loose skin, people agreed, was easier to hide than their fat had been, and it did not have the accompanying health concerns (although we see from Natalie's narrative that it could impact mobility). Thus, even with excess skin, patients could look "normal," as they could not when they were fat.[32] They also felt physically better, which made the negotiations of undesired bodily changes more palatable.[33] Ava, for example, who had a great deal of loose skin on her stomach, did not opt for skin-removal surgery during the time we knew her and was fairly philosophical about it. Still, she complained about it on a number of occasions, saying that it looked "unnatural" and that she did not at all care for the way it spread out when she took her clothes off.

Similarly, although most of the survey respondents reported that excess skin posed a problem for them postsurgery, only seven people (of 189 responses) actually had proceeded to the point of getting skin-removal surgery. When we surveyed the same group a year later, only four additional respondents had gone through the procedure. This meant nearly 95 percent of the respondents were living chronically with the loose skin that was a major side effect of surgery.

As we noted earlier, most of the men and women who responded to the survey or who participated in some aspect of the ethnographic research reported that life had improved after surgery and weight loss—and so had their physical bodies. Moreover, many of the older participants, especially, pointed out that sagging, loose skin was a natural part of the aging process. Accordingly, they did not register their loose skin as that far outside the norm—and they tended to consider it age inappropriate to have surgery to remove the loose skin. Only about half of our ethnographic participants—all women—said they even contemplated cosmetic surgery to fix loose, excess, or sagging skin. More probably entertained the idea but pushed it aside, perhaps because they thought it seemed vain and inappropriate (the result of its status as a cosmetic procedure), because skin removal is a painful and invasive surgery, because their sagging skin was widespread, or because of the expense. We suspect that, given gender norms that discourage men (especially those in older age cohorts) from expressing body worries, men in particular may have felt constrained from telling us about sagging skin issues and considerations of cosmetic surgery.

Erica, in her late twenties at the time she had surgery, was one of the youngest participants in the study. During our final interview, Erica mentioned that she was not strictly following the dietary guidelines recommended by the program, but she nevertheless had lost a huge amount of weight (seventy-five pounds at that stage) and was still on a downward weight trajectory. Not every aspect of her current, smaller body thrilled Erica, however. She mentioned that she had loose skin, then pointed at her upper arms and said,

> This is really the biggest . . . I say wings. Oh my God, Alex [her boyfriend] and I had the funniest little thing because I said—I was telling him, "I feel like a flying squirrel." And I said, "Oh my gosh, that's what I should go for Halloween as, flying squirrel." And he thought that was really funny. . . . It's pretty much just the arms, . . . but it's a lot. Like, it's extreme in my arms. . . . And so, I have a little bit in the tummy right here. I used to put my arms [stretching upward] like this to make myself look skinnier, and it looked nice. Now when I do that . . . when I put my arms up, you can see the wrinkled stuff. And I'm pretty sure I'll have some more loose skin problems on my stomach with another twenty pounds or so. But so far, it's not too bad. . . . And I just don't have taut skin. I don't. Like, it's always been soft. And so I just don't think it's going to happen [the skin tightening on its own]. I'm pretty sure that I will get my arms fixed. . . . And I looked it up, and I think it runs like $4,000 or $5,000, so I think I can figure that out. It's worth it for my comfort. If they weren't so bad, but they're bad. It's not just . . . I don't wear tank tops. I wear them around the house, but that's it. . . . I'll wear tank tops around him [Alex], but

when I'm cooking and stuff and I'm doing this, there is a part of me that's like, "Eh," right? And he's noticed. Like not unprompted. I said something about my arms, and he was like, "Yeah, I've noticed you got a little bit of loose skin going on there in your arms." But that's okay. It's worth it for sure. . . . Oh yeah, definitely, definitely, of course.

In this narrative, Erica started with humor, comparing herself and the loose skin on her arms to a flying squirrel. Nonetheless, she was entirely serious about the issue and the fact that she thought it was unsightly and uncomfortable and she was going to get the excess skin removed. Even though insurance probably would not cover the skin-removal surgery and Erica and Alex had a relatively tight budget within which they operated, the surgery was "worth it for sure."

Sarah asked Erica if she would still think bariatric surgery was worth it if she could not get her arms "fixed." Erica replied,

Yeah, even then. I mean, it would suck. I would still be like, "It sucks to lose all this weight and still have to deal with that," that kind of self-conscious thing. But no, it would be worth it still for sure. . . . I think she [the nurse] told me that six months after I stop losing weight or that my weight is stable, that they'll refer me to somebody [for the skin-removal surgery]. And then I'm sure it's probably more time. And there's some navigating my future plans with having kids if I ended up getting the stomach done too. I don't want to do that before I have kids.

Erica's main worry at this time was eventual weight regain, and she had developed several strategies to combat this. Her desire to have children had even been factored into this long-term plan. Although she did not like her loose skin, she was willing to wait on skin-removal surgery to try to lose more weight. Avoiding fat was more important to her than dealing with loose, excess skin.

Tiffany provided an interesting foil to Erica's story in many respects. The two women ended up echoing some of the same themes even though they were very different people. Tiffany, as mentioned in chapter 1, was in her early forties at the time of her gastric bypass, worked as a nurse, and was single for most of the study period. By the time Sarah sat down with Tiffany for a third interview, Tiffany had made up her mind to undergo skin-removal surgery. She was still processing this decision, however, which is obvious in that interview. Tiffany said,

> I'm down 132, 134-ish pounds. But I was told I have probably about 20, 25 pounds of skin. . . . Just in my abdomen. My arms did good. I barely have any. . . . Legs just went. . . . It's probably right now the only thing that— I'm not going to say unhappy with, but it's the only thing that's eating at me because it's just uncomfortable. And I know that if it wasn't there, I'd be so much thinner. I mean, visually, you know? So it's coming off. . . . I met yesterday with [the nurse], and I have to see her for my one year in August, late August. And at that time, we're going to set a consult up with the plastic surgeon. But we talked a great deal about it. But I need to wait. It'll be February or March before I can have it done. . . . And I understand that, you know . . . I'm still losing. It's really slow, but the weight's still coming off, and they want you to be, you know, fluctuating a few pounds here and there, but they want you at a steady weight for so long before they'll do that. You know, why remove it and keep losing and then have to do it again? And from what I hear, it's a pretty harsh surgery. . . . Because I guess they take from hip to hip and just pull and stretch, up and down, and sew you right up.

As with her vivid description of dumping in chapter 3, Tiffany once again provided us with a detailed, graphic description of skin-removal surgery, leaving us in no doubt that it is a painful, difficult experience. She was unequivocal that she wanted that surgery, however, and was impatient that she had to wait to undergo it, given how uncomfortable the twenty pounds of excess, loose skin on her abdomen felt.

When Sarah asked her about insurance coverage for the skin removal, Tiffany replied,

> Hygiene is not my issue. I'm a very clean person, but there's skin discoloration now, I'm prone to yeast. You know, it's skin infections, so it's a medical issue. . . . I've already seen my primary care because of itching and discomfort and needing topical medication and stuff like that. I mean, it is what it is. I was a, for lack of better words, huge girl. So I mean, it's expected. And it just makes it all the more exciting to look forward to. . . . Am I excited to be down four to six weeks [after skin-removal

surgery]? No, not again, but . . . I lay on my back and everything just flattens out. Like yesterday, [the nurse] was like, "Oh my God, you have ribs, you have hip bones. Look at you." And I mean, well, that feels good, but once I sit up, here it all comes back up, you know? So I think it's just a personal thing. But I think my journey that I've gone on, I think I deserve to get it taken off. . . . I'm excited to see me for who I really am. So right now, I'm looking forward to it. But after my conversation with [the nurse] yesterday on how extreme this procedure is, I think I'm going to be scared crapless. I really do, as it gets closer. But like I said, I deserve it. I feel I deserve it. I've got to see me for who I really am physically. So it's not an option. I'm going to get it done. . . . I mean, I can't remember being anything but heavy, big. I can't remember anything. I've seen pictures of me as a little girl, and I was cute and had these big green eyes and these big locks of curls and, you know, just a cute little kid. And then as I see older pictures of me getting older, everything just kind of fills out. And adolescence set in, and boom, there was a big girl. I can't remember seeing, for lack of better words, seeing me how I would like to see me. And now I'm so close.

Tiffany articulated several interesting points here. First, there are the physical factors: she was relatively young (early forties), she had already lost over 130 pounds in less than a year postsurgery, all of her loose skin was in her stomach, and she was getting skin irritation and infections in her loose skin. These factors combined to make her a good candidate for skin-removal surgery, as well as to have it covered by insurance. However, these combined factors also made her feel that her skin was a burden. She was not old enough for loose skin to feel normal, it was all concentrated in her belly, and there was considerably more of it than some other participants experienced. Her close association at work with other health-care professionals, in combination with all of these other things, meant that she viewed the loose skin as a medicalized condition.

Even more telling is Tiffany's repetition of "I deserve this" and her description of her true self as buried for most of her life, first under fat and then under loose skin. Other social scientists have noted that bariatric patients may experience their true selves as "buried,"[34] but given the dearth of research into skin-removal surgery, we had not seen enough analysis of this interesting coupling of fat and loose skin in impeding and burying identity. The moral justification underlying "I deserve this" also counters the common criticism (often directed inward) that cosmetic surgery is vain. In Tiffany's narrative, she not only gave medicalized reasons for cosmetic surgery but also portrayed herself as achieving a moral high ground as a result of past suffering related to her intractable physical body.

Tiffany went on in the interview to contrast her current loose skin with her previous fat, and in the following excerpt, she reiterated themes that were near universal among participants. She told Sarah,

> I think a year ago, I was thinking, "Okay, I'm going to do whatever it takes because I want to lose some more weight. I want to see the result. I want to see me. I want to look in the mirror and see me, not see fat." I look now, I see my clavicle, I see shoulder bones, I see tendons in my neck that were never there. I mean, they were there, but I never saw them. I see that stuff now. So I think in a year, I want to see all this skin gone. I want to see this. And so I think it's kind of like a snowball effect. . . . I think my journey that lies ahead is going to be just as much if not greater than what my journey was prior to this and getting to where I am now. So I think the fact of staying on track, keeping the weight off, and continuing, I think you learn it in the classes that it's a lifelong commitment. And in August of last year, I made that commitment. And there's no reason to take it away, so I'm good with it. I'm excited. See, I get all excited now talking to you. . . . I mean, I think the only negative or any type of criticism that I'm getting is I'm giving it to myself about the skin right now, you know? And I went through it before my surgery. I would give it to myself about the fat, you know? I mean, it's me. I'm my biggest critic.

Again, we hear the repetition of wanting to see herself in the mirror, not just her fat or her loose skin. Coupled with this, we hear Tiffany state that she is her own worst critic and that she wants to silence that critic once and for all by maintaining her weight loss, getting her excess skin removed, and adhering to the "lifelong commitment" imposed by bariatric surgery.

When asked if the self-critique over the excess skin felt the same as the previous self-critique over her weight, Tiffany said,

No, I mean, it's different. I feel better, and I know the fat was just there. I mean, you couldn't—it was just there. The skin, it's movable. I mean, it's rearrangeable, if you will. I mean, it's more of an annoyance. I think the fat was just—there was a lot of words to describe it: gross, disgusting, just there, huge, big, I mean, just all of those bad, terrible words. The skin is just there. I mean, you can push it in. I was in a size 32 jeans. I'm in an 18 now. I mean, it's just crazy. It's crazy. So that skin is movable. The fat, it wasn't. I mean, I couldn't squeeze into a pair of jeans when I had the fat. Now I can squeeze into something if I need to.

Like Erica, Tiffany categorized fat as far worse than loose skin, which unlike fat could be disguised, flattened, and covered. Moreover, Tiffany's success at weight loss somewhat dampened her internal critical voice, which she found to be a huge relief. Nevertheless, Tiffany was adamant that the skin was coming off. In fact, she was quite clear that she would be pretty miserable if she did have to keep the excess skin.

It is this misery stemming from skin that we want to analyze briefly in closing here, because it is both theoretically interesting and very relevant to everyday life experiences. In particular, we return to the supposedly "petty" nature of this misery. Naomi Segal, for example, quotes André Gide (1954), who argued that problems with one's skin can be infuriating and impossible to ignore and can cause huge amounts of suffering but, at the same time, are "undignified" and not given the weight that "real" pain is afforded by others.[35] Thus, pain and itching and discomfort situated in the skin can be harrowing for the afflicted person but actually look amusing and/or repellent to an outsider. This is very clearly a thread both in bariatric patients' perspectives about themselves and their loose skin and in wider conversations occurring in the US. Take, for instance, the slew of popular articles and social media pieces that have been produced in the past ten years that have highlighted the loose skin resulting from massive, bariatric-surgery-induced weight loss. Most of these pieces have presented loose skin as fundamentally undignified and even repellant rather than knowable and sympathetic.[36]

## Lifelong Consequence #4: A Daunting Timeline

In our discussions of surveillance of eating and weight after bariatric surgery earlier in this chapter, we mentioned that the timeframe for maintaining change—forever—is difficult for many people. Once the honeymoon months immediately after surgery are over, the expected management of one's body rolls out across the years without a break or a pause for the rest of one's life.

As we have also already mentioned, chronic diseases generally have been tricky for health-care systems and the people in them to manage precisely because they are often set within a "forever timeline." In other words, among the general population, an individual may successfully manage hypertension and high blood pressure diagnosed in their forties for thirty years—but success in this instance may include regular trips to the doctor, medication, food restriction, and worry throughout those decades. There is no finite period of illness followed by an equally finite cure.

As we have already observed, a bariatric population is not normal, and many do experience the surgery as a cure, especially in the short term. Longer term, however, the preceding sections on "lifelong consequences" should have made it obvious that the surgery precipitates a series of health trade-offs and lifelong management. Moreover, most of our conclusions about this long term are based on information (gathered via participant observation, interviews, and surveys) from people who were less than a decade postsurgery at the time of our research. Our research design allowed us to follow people across an arc of time starting at different points pre- and post-op. Some moved from presurgery to postsurgery during the years we spent in the clinic, and some, whom we met when they were already post-op, simply moved a couple of years further out from the operation. Regardless, we seldom encountered individuals in the clinical spaces we frequented who had been living with a gastric bypass or sleeve for more than five years and met exceedingly few who had been living with these modifications for a decade or more. A clinical ethnography such as ours benefits in many respects from the institutional context but faces some of the same restrictions and limitations that the clinic does. We felt these limitations particularly acutely when it came to the issue of long-term patient follow-up.

The clinic itself offered support to postoperative patients in the short term but ideally also hoped to maintain such supportive connections for years afterward. For example, the dieticians always ended the final presurgery class by telling the group that if they felt they were having problems after surgery to "please, please just make an appointment" with them. The nurses echoed this and included strongly worded advice to try to attend bariatric support group meetings. One critique leveled against many bariatric surgery programs worldwide is a persistent lack of support and care after surgery.[37] In "our" clinic's explicit focus on providing postoperative medical care and emotional support and on retaining patients, it attempted to address this important gap and meet established (US-based) best practices.

Some patients did seek this help from the providers. We saw many of these patients. Others returned to the monthly support group meetings. We encountered them as well. Then there were the patients who stopped coming to support group meetings and follow-up appointments with the clinicians. A few of these patients stayed in touch with us separately. Cindi, whom we quoted extensively earlier in this chapter, is one such example. Broadly speaking, however, our clinic-based research faced the same issue that clinics themselves do: if an individual wanted to become invisible and drop out of sight after bariatric surgery, that individual did so.

Research on bariatric surgery indicates that *most* bariatric patients—looking across high-income countries all over the world—do not remain engaged with the clinic where they obtained surgery in the years and even decades after surgery.[38] In saying this, we do not want to blame persistent gaps in support and care on the patients themselves; structural and cultural issues abound in bariatric clinics worldwide, including negative stigmatizing experiences felt by patients, gaps in the care provided by a particular clinic, and changes in patients' insurance coverage, places of employment, and living situations. Moreover, patients who experience life in the long term after surgery as characterized by uneventful and unremarkable maintenance work *and* patients who experience massive weight regain after surgery tend not to be highly motivated to take themselves off to the clinic to be weighed, measured, prodded, and tracked. Patients who do inevitably end up getting tracked are those who experience multiple adverse medical events, including serious gastrointestinal and nutritional disorders, revisional surgeries, and the like.[39]

In the course of fieldwork, Sarah once met a woman who had bariatric surgery in the 1970s. The woman faced many health challenges as a result of this surgery, but it was difficult to draw conclusions from these that could have been applicable to the patients undergoing surgery at the time of our project. Firstly, the woman could not remember precisely what type of surgery she had undergone (this was not uncommon among people we met who underwent bariatric surgery in programs that were not accredited, i.e., that did not provide educational and support programs), saying only that she had had her "stomach stapled." Secondly, the science has changed in the intervening years, and the surgeries themselves have gotten more sophisticated. Nutrient deficiencies are still common in bariatric patients, but they were much more severe in earlier surgeries, as was the possibility of sepsis. Earlier surgeries were not laproscopic either, which results in a different recovery trajectory. Lastly, the patients getting bariatric surgery have changed, inasmuch as the pool of candidates has gotten larger and more diverse. Bariatric surgery is now being recommended for certain adolescents, for example, and although some studies show positive outcomes for this,[40] we do not actually know at the time of this writing what life will be like for a sixty-five-year-old who underwent gastric bypass at age nineteen.

The result is that when we look to the larger literature to try to address the questions remaining in our own work, we most often encounter more questions. Overall, there are relatively few studies that track patients more than five years postsurgery,[41] and the field itself has changed so dramatically that conclusions can be tenuous. We said at the outset of this section that the timeline is daunting; this is true from both a patient perspective and from a data-gathering one. This is an important caveat to keep in mind.

## Reflections on What It Means to Be Normal

*Am I normal now? If so, will I lose it? What is normal anyway? How does normal act? Do people think I'm normal?* These questions, and an intense fear of losing the new normal body once eating habits become less restrictive, often underlie many of the long-term issues people grapple with after bariatric surgery. For the people with whom we spoke, a normal body meant maintaining their new weight and not returning to formerly felt out-of-control eating habits, while at the same time being able to eat in a more normal manner, less circumscribed by the restrictions imposed by the surgery during the first months. For the people with whom we spoke, normal also meant being able to participate in mainstream US consumerism: fitting in airline seats and restaurant booths, buying new wardrobes, and so on. This is important, because many markers of normalcy in contemporary US society center (to an unusual extent, viewed globally) on being able to casually consume a seemingly endless supply of products.

People with very different experiences before and after surgery still voiced similar fears about losing all of the benefits that had manifested themselves in the immediate wake of surgery. Olivia, for example, in her third interview, was engaging in eating and weight surveillance that she identified as effective at a time when she had whittled her body down to a very petite size. She had also seen her joint pain and cardiovascular issues improve dramatically. Yet she still had reservations about the future. She said,

> I haven't been to a support group meeting yet. . . . And I'd like to just pop in some day to see what that's like because, yeah, after that weekend of celebration, I went up [in weight], and that bothered me. Because it's in the back of your mind that if you aren't vigilant about this, it will come back. I know a woman who had the surgery done, and she's big, as big [as] she was or bigger. And I know she likes her wine, and she likes her sugar. . . . But I'm wondering too if this is one of those things where, as time goes on, if I can [keep the weight off and if] . . . the change can be more permanent. I'm hoping so.

For Olivia, normal was her new body, plus her new habits maintaining that body. Abnormal, for Olivia, was her familial predisposition toward fat. Yet she worried that she would revert back, following that predisposition.

Anita had a slightly different perspective on what it meant to be normal. At the time of her third interview, she had not seen dramatic weight loss or a dramatic reduction in her blood sugar. But she felt she was doing everything she could and should, and her numbers (both on the scale and in her bloodwork) were slowly heading in the direction she wanted. She too expressed nervousness about how she would adjust long term, after her body stopped placing such severe limitations on her eating. She also expressed impatience with others who she thought had unrealistic and irresponsible expectations for life after surgery. Anita said,

It's like you've got to make those changes. And I sat through those "Change" classes, and I listened to what some of the people say. And when they're asking questions about "Well, when will I be able to eat normal?" kind of thing, I'm thinking, "Are you really ready for this?" Because your normal in your mind right now can never be the normal ever again, or you're going to put your weight back on. I mean, they say one thousand to twelve hundred calories. Once you get back to what they [the other patients asking the questions] deem normal, you're going to gain your weight back. And you can't go back to eating like you did before. And when they're asking those questions, I'm thinking, "What are you thinking here?" Because they're [the providers] trying to retrain you to say, even when your hunger does come back, your appetite does come back, that you still have to keep track and you still can only eat one thousand to twelve hundred calories a day, which isn't a lot.

According to Anita, in order to have a normal body and normal blood-sugar levels, her eating habits could never be normal again. In her view, no one who undergoes bariatric surgery can afford to be normal.

This is one of the central ironies of the surgery. In order to look more normal in US society and to register as more medically normal with regard to certain disease risks that medical providers commonly track, a massive surgical intervention restructures patients' stomachs, guts, and eating habits so that they will never again be "normal," when compared to most other Americans.

# Conclusion

A recurring theme throughout this book is the symbolic power of the body, embedded in cultural norms defining what normal bodies look like and do. Anthropologists and other scholars have spilled a lot of ink analyzing the ways in which norms are culturally constructed, so that "normal" is conflated with "moral" and "respectable" and contrasted with "abnormal" and "immoral."[1] This book has delved in detail into one specific case study, focusing on bodies defined medically as morbidly obese that are then "fixed" via bariatric surgery. We have shown how stigma accrues to weight deemed excessive and how people internalize it. We have also shown that stigma and related self-doubt can persist even once the weight is lost. Finally, we have described the ways in which notions of success at weight loss are a complex ongoing balancing act that cannot be described in simple terms of noncompliance versus compliance.

Attempts to fit in and be normal are part of our fundamental human efforts to be accepted and acceptable to others. Perhaps because of the fear that health issues evoke, many of the most illustrative cases of colossal social failures to be normal or to fit into particular social circles have occurred around medically defined issues. Well-known examples from the literature include the fear that mental health conditions inspire across many sociocultural contexts, the deep-seated stigma that developed around the HIV/AIDS epidemic beginning in the 1980s, and centuries of disgust and fear of leprosy in medieval Europe. Specific medically defined conditions can become stigmatized when they are perceived by the state, medical bureaucracies, society, and the individuals themselves as abnormal and disorderly. Once a condition is seen as deviating from the norm and causing social disorder and chaos, then it is a small step to see people with those conditions as inherently abnormal and disorderly.[2] As we said at the beginning of this book, obesity has recently been reclassified as a medical disease in its own right (at least within the United States) but also triggers strong associations of social abnormality and social burden. These associations then stick to the people who are medically classified as obese and/or socially categorized as fat.

Bodies have particular power within these paradigms, perhaps because they are commonly assumed to be the most obvious manifestation and indicator of normalcy versus abnormality. We are interested in the fact that now, in this moment, certain bodies are ascribed certain kinds of power. Thin body ideals, especially when coupled with not-fat body norms, push individuals to pursue ever-elusive body sizes in order not to be judged abnormal. Stigma is a specific dynamic that only emerges as a result of the construction of and widespread social agreement over certain norms. In other words, both norms and stigma lie at the crux of culturally shared knowledge. In this ethnographic study, the experience of fat stigma—and the distress it causes—emerges as a result of body norms in a particular place and time that enshrine not-fatness.

As we wrote this book, we asked ourselves again and again why people struggle so hard to be not-fat even now that most adults in the US are technically overweight. How do these contradictions fit with ideas about what is normal? Why is there such increasingly singular consensus in the current world that normal is not-fat? Even as average body weights have gone up everywhere and social media attention increasingly focuses on self-congratulatory stories of a supposed expansion and diversification of body ideals, people in the world are relentlessly engaging in efforts to be not fat. We have seen this very clearly in our other earlier research on culture and body weight in places as diverse as Paraguay, Samoa, and the United Arab Emirates. Our sense now, based on comparison, is that people in the US (including American media and social media) might talk body tolerance, but ultimately, most people still revert back to what they "truly" believe: that fat bodies signal social, emotional, and physical abnormality. Consider the fact that, at the time of this writing (the first half of 2020), people in the US are still going to the gym "for their health" in the midst of widespread attempts by public health authorities to get populations to practice social distancing to prevent the spread of COVID-19. That discrepancy highlights something very profound about how Americans understand the "work" individuals are supposed to put into maintaining their own health.

The expansion of body norms is very narrow compared to the expansion of physical bodies that has occurred across the US in recent decades, and thus, we see swathes of the population rendered abnormal, even pathological. This harmful dynamic is intensified by the extra burdens placed on women and people of color to conform to White-dominated norms in a male-dominated world. Why, then, do people struggle so hard to be a particular type of normal, one that does not correspond with either the average body or an espoused commitment to diverse bodies? The payoff with regard to freedom from judgment and social condemnation appears worth the effort and setbacks, or at least that is what we have heard across the broad range of our team's various research projects, including this bariatric ethnography.

Struggles to achieve social norms, at their core, rely on hope—but hope is tricky. People who choose to undergo bariatric surgery are impelled by hope. On the one hand, they hope to reduce their medical conditions and to move from a pathological state into one that is more closely identified as "normal healthy." On the other hand, they also hope to reduce their socially stigmatized fat body and to morph into a "normal sized" body. The people we met through the program worked extremely hard in their journeys toward this dual ideal, and the program itself worked extremely hard to provide them with adequate medical and social support on these often difficult and highly fraught journeys. The sacrifices are indisputable: people removed sections of their stomachs, bypassed parts of their intestines, endured horrible nausea and dumping, coped with the lifelong threat of micronutrient deficiencies and dehydration, and restructured their entire habitus and habits around that most basic of human activities—eating.

The great irony here is that to meet our current social (and medical) body norms in an overarching environment that paradoxically encourages constant consumption, people permanently restructure their guts into a very abnormal arrangement. Or, at least, it is abnormal when contextualized against the entire evolution of our species, in which we see the slow evolution of stomach and intestines in conditions of chronic scarcity. Perhaps, however, this new intestinal arrangement will become the new US ideal?

Admittedly, a surgically altered stomach and gut will never be the average. The success stories of bariatric patients who lose massive weight rapidly and then keep it off are a tiny sliver of the overall phenomenon covered in this book, one that we condense to the observation that weight is a burden, with a multiplicity of consequences. In many respects, these are stories about people at the pinnacle of privilege, who have access to the surgery and also to unparalleled high-quality medical and emotional caregiving within a comprehensive and competent health system. In this, we ourselves are somewhat atypical for our subfield, given that an enduring focus within medical anthropology has been on embodied suffering and inequalities in health and the ways in which these become manifest as a result of *lack* of access to health care. Here, in a context of very good health care, we still hear stories of suffering, stigma, blocked socioeconomic opportunities, and enduring long-term anxiety. More interesting still, these stories echo, albeit in an acute form, those of many other people worldwide.

The vast majority of people around the world who are struggling with obesity or fatness (and the resulting negative impacts of their nonconformity to social norms) are never going to have access to the kind of "success" that this particular program gave the participants in this study. What we continue to find fascinating, however, is that very few people feel this way. As a result of a barrage of public health messaging and weight-loss-oriented advertising campaigns, successful long-term weight loss is constantly portrayed to be within anyone's grasp. Again, it comes back to hope, a hope that is founded neither in actual scientific data nor in anecdotal experiences, since across almost all contexts, people do not lose substantial amounts of weight and maintain that weight loss. This, almost more than anything else, illustrates the immense power of the sociocultural norms that currently inform how we think about weight and bodies.

Thin ideals and not-fat norms are very much a social construct rooted in modern practices and perceptions. Often, people view social constructs as soft, mutable, arbitrary, culturally specific, and not necessarily (or even often) rational; "they can be easily changed," goes this kind of thinking. We wish to stress that a social construct may be invisible and flexible, but it is neither easily breakable nor changeable. Norms have immense power, in that no matter how hard people push against them—using their own bodies, rhetoric, and positions in society—they cannot make much individual progress dispelling the norms in the absence of broader sociocultural change.

Most exasperating perhaps is that the lack of progress is both internalized and externalized in a vicious blame-shame loop. In chapter 4, we quoted a bariatric participant who blamed herself for gaining weight after surgery, then blamed herself for blaming herself. Self-awareness and reflection did not help her escape the blame-shame cycle but rather locked her into it even more firmly. She blamed herself not only for gaining weight but also for self-stigmatizing and stressing herself out. This particular tangle of awareness leading to more self-induced pressure, not less, is not limited to bariatric patient populations.

In this way, we revert to our original point: the case study of individual Americans going through weight-loss surgery is not especially out of step with mainstream cultural mores—and it is actually this alignment that makes the case study so interesting and powerful. The themes that emerged as significant for the bariatric patients with whom we interacted are themes that reverberate increasingly across diverse communities within the United States and beyond. The stories of the bariatric patients from the clinical program we studied are therefore stories that are widely characteristic of our time. These bariatric patients are perhaps simply more aware and more articulate about the issues at play that are affecting us all.

# Epilogue

I had a long conversation with Emily today—which I am still processing. Emily has cancer. Has actually had cancer for a while, I just didn't
know about it, since we hadn't kept in touch after our final interview.
She suspected it, went in, got diagnosed, already had the tumor out, and
is now going through radiation/chemo (I was so flustered during the
conversation, I remain unclear whether she was opting for radiation or
chemo). She is determined to beat this—pointed out that this is just the
latest challenge in a lifetime of them—but worried about the effects on
the family. She had a very specific message for me. Emily said, "I thought
of you when I first suspected cancer because I don't think I would have
ever been able to track the tumor or cope with some of the symptoms
that have hit me if I hadn't had the bypass and lost weight. I think that's
important for me to say—that losing weight and feeling better because
of it are now helping me in ways I couldn't have predicted." I hope Emily
is going to be OK. Prognosis is good right now, but there's obviously no
certainty. I hope Emily beats cancer. She's already survived so much.
—Sarah's field notes, winter 2017

# ACKNOWLEDGMENTS

We acknowledge first and foremost all of the participants, patients, and providers who generously gave of their time and who made this study possible. Hopefully, you know how grateful we are.

Our work was supported by the Virginia Piper Charitable Trust through an award to Arizona State University President Michael Crow, for the Obesity Solutions Initiative. We thank the core Obesity Solutions team, including James Levine, Deborah Williams, Gabriel Koebb, Seung Yong Han, and the late Elizabeth Capaldi Phillips, for their crucial support of the larger project that resulted in this book. Senior ASU administrators, particularly Sethuraman Panchanathan and William Petusky in ASU's Office of Knowledge Enterprise Development, also generously provided assistance and support for our relationship building with the hospital administration and leadership. Drs. Cindi SturtzSreetharan and Melissa Beresford helped us think through a number of key ethnographic interpretations, and we thank them for their unwavering collegiality and intellectual support. Lastly, we thank Dr. Jodi O'Brien for helping us to disentangle the world of book publishing.

# APPENDIX A

*Ethnographic Methods*

BACKGROUND

The ethnographic research for this project primarily took place in the medical facilities of a large health-care provider with several locations in the continental United States. Ethnographic activities focused on documenting and analyzing the bariatric program within this particular medical system, and to do this, fieldwork occurred in two clinical spaces firmly rooted in one city in the western US: the large, in-patient hospital complex in a northern suburb of the city and an outpatient clinic and research facility in an outlying area to the northeast. Both sites housed components of the specific bariatric program that was the target of our inquiry. As such, this work follows other studies that are based on ethnographic fieldwork conducted within clinic spaces.[1]

For twenty-four months, we conducted participant observation in the clinic and hospital facilities, with Sarah particularly active in attending the preoperative behavioral change classes (held once a week for eight-week cycles and required for all patients), as well as in the monthly postsurgery bariatric support group meetings. This bariatric program, which conducted 80–120 surgeries a year at the time of our study, is a comprehensive program that meets the guidelines established by the Metabolic and Bariatric Surgery Accreditation and Quality Improvement Program.

For reasons stemming from issues of patient privacy and confidentiality, none of the authors observed the individual clinic encounters, but we spoke frequently with both patients and providers within the bariatric program. Mutual discussions of observed themes in patient narratives and observed behaviors were thus key in moving the findings discussed here forward. Significantly, Alex spent two years discussing and negotiating with hospital physicians and administrators higher up in the medical hierarchy before the research described in this text could even be approved. Moreover, her efforts were ultimately successful only because senior Arizona State University administrators also invested time and effort in cultivating relationships and in articulating for hospital leadership the role that social scientists play in major ongoing cross-institution collaborations. As others have pointed out, ethnographic work within hospital contexts requires considerable translation and constant justification to hospital staff, administrators, and patients, all of whom may frequently be confused by the exact role and purpose of in-depth, small-scale research-gathering activities that do not have an immediate, overt "life-saving" function.[2] Without such multilevel support and careful articulation of our relevance from senior administrators, the project would simply never have happened.

Lastly, it is worth noting that in order to work with the bariatric patients, we needed approval from our university and from the appropriate office of oversight within the clinic itself. In the clinic's Human Subjects office, the gold standard for research was a clinical trial (large sample sizes, the collection of biomarkers, limited researcher-participant interactions, etc.) or an anonymized survey (again, big sample sizes and standardized sets of questions), and our ethnographic study with its emphasis on personal relationship building and "messy" qualitative data confused them. Because the clinic deeply cared about the quality of its patient-driven care and, indeed, had made its reputation on its articulated patient-centered focus, the clinic's Human Subjects office was also concerned that we would be annoying to patients (a legitimate concern: social scientists can be very annoying in many settings) at a very sensitive time in their lives. The approval process was therefore labyrinthine: multiple explanations to staff in the office itself, multiple revisions to the language of our application, and multiple visits to our clinic contacts ensued. The process took months. If Alex had not built solid clinic contacts in the first place—and had not developed a nuanced understanding of human-subjects review and approval processes as a result of a decade spent serving on a variety of institutional boards herself—we do not know if we would have been approved.

We also had to make some substantial compromises to fit the project with the clinic's mores. One of the biggest for us was an agreement that once clinic data collection ended, we could not reach out to reconnect with participants. In practice, this meant we lost touch with people we cared about and liked very much (unless they made an effort to track us down in order to send us updates about themselves, entirely on their own initiative). From a clinical standpoint, this stipulation certainly makes sense: why would a professional relationship between a patient and a researcher/provider continue after the formal, medicalized basis of the relationship has ended? Any anthropologist who has invested time in a community and become close with the people there and who reads the preceding stipulation, however, probably winced. Indeed, one of our least favorite aspects of the project was having to explain to the many wonderful people who gave freely of their time and energy over the course of this project why we could not actively stay in touch. Furthermore, it would have greatly helped our writing process if we could have gotten feedback from participants as we wrote. We have benefited from the critical insights of many scholars and colleagues during the writing of this book but remain aware that feedback from the audience about whom we care most— the patient-participants—is missing.

## PARTICIPANT INTERVIEWS: A PANEL DESIGN

In addition to participant observation throughout the clinic spaces, we conducted interviews with bariatric patients. Recruitment occurred primarily in person and at the clinic. We were interested in tracking changing experiences across time, as people lost weight during the behavioral change classes before surgery and then after undergoing surgery, but we faced the conundrum that most long-term, longitudinal, qualitative studies do: not enough time and not enough resources to truly capture the scope of change that occurs in the year before surgery and the decade after it. Our compromise—which still had the advantage of being analytically rigorous, thanks to Amber—was a qualitative panel design, including a sample of interviews by purposively selected participants, was interviewed up to three times over a period of thirty-six months. Key to this design was the fact that we spoke with participants at a variety of different points in their trajectories through the presurgery preparation and postsurgery experience.

The result was thirty-five initial interviews with thirty-five individuals who were either in the throes of preparing for bariatric surgery or negotiating the aftermath of the surgery. Individuals under age twenty-one were excluded. We followed participants for two years after the initial interview, conducting second and third interviews with roughly half of the original sample. Due to the fact that the presurgical program was one of our main sites of recruitment, an overwhelming preponderance of the initial interviews were conducted presurgery: twenty-six individuals allowed us to interview them in the three- to nine-month period before surgery, while they waited for surgery dates. Of these twenty-six, nineteen people participated in a second interview, which took place in the one- to six-month period postsurgery, and then again in a third interview, which took place in the four- to twelve-month period postsurgery. Our aim was to space the postsurgery interviews three to six months apart.

As we pointed out in the introduction, prior research indicates that some of the most profound changes associated with bariatric surgery and weight loss occur in the first twelve to eighteen months after surgery. However, due to the fact that most prior research has been quantitative, cross-sectional, or based on extremely small sample sizes, the further from surgery individuals progress, the less is known about their experiences. In this regard, the fact that our panel design also allowed us to follow individuals through a longer arc postsurgery was also important. Thus, our interview sample also included nine people whose initial interview took place postsurgery, somewhere between three and thirty-six months after surgery. Out of these nine people, eight people consented to be interviewed four to six months after the first interview, and seven of them then consented to be interviewed a third time, four to six months after the second interview.

SEMISTRUCTURED INTERVIEWS

In the book chapters, we talk in more detail about the participants who enriched and informed our ethnographic work and, in particular, their own articulated views and experiences. Here, we provide only the broad outlines of the group, which was overwhelmingly female and White, reflecting both the clinic population as a whole and possibly the fact that the three of us are also White women.

The total bariatric population at the medical facilities we studied is recorded (based on self-identified ethnicity and gender) as about 35 percent "ethnic minorities" (this was the clinic's designation and language) and about 30 percent male. Eight out of the thirty-five participants in our ethnographic "panel design" identified as people of color (Asian American, Black, and Latinx); the remaining twenty-seven participants either identified as White or did not talk about racial identity. Ultimately, eight of the participants in the interviews were men, aged thirty to sixty-six years, all of whom opted for a gastric bypass. The twenty-seven women participants ranged in age from twenty-nine to seventy-five years of age, and all but two of them opted for the gastric bypass.[3] The remaining two women had sleeve gastrectomies. Self-reported BMIs before surgery ranged from 39 to 65, with most people reporting BMIs between 45 and 55.

The interview protocols were organized around five meta-themes, which we developed deductively, based on the existing literature. These themes were as follows:

1. Body Work

   *Sample questions*: What made you decide to get surgery?
2. Food, Eating, Self, and the Body

   *Sample questions*: Do you count calories, and if so, for how long have you been doing so? What about portion sizes? Do you measure fat, protein, vitamin, sugar, salt content? If so, for how long have you been doing so?
3. Social Interactions

   *Sample questions*: Do you feel like you are going into this surgery with solid support from your family and/or friends? Has that made a difference in your experience? How?
4. Body Capital

   *Sample questions*: Given the fact that US society tends to talk about being thin in order to be attractive, do you feel like this attitude impacts your life day to day?
5. Body and Self in the Clinical Encounter

   *Sample questions*: What has been your experience with medical professionals up to this point?

## CODING AND ANALYSIS OF ETHNOGRAPHIC DATA

Codebook development and thematic analysis of the field notes and transcribed interviews followed the approach recommended by H. Russell Bernard, Amber Wutich, and Gery W. Ryan in *Analyzing*

*Qualitative Data.*[4] Codes were developed deductively,[5] based on the relevant literature—partially mirroring our interview protocols. During the analysis process, however, we also added inductive codes. These were codes that emerged as powerful themes in the data after we began interviewing.

The final codebook was organized around six themes, each of which was further broken down into subthemes. These were as follows:

1. Stigma
   *Subthemes*: social/external stigma, internalized stigma, structural stigma, clinical stigma, visibility, external locus of control, scapegoating fat
2. Outer Body Work
   *Subthemes*: food restriction, exercise, new clothes/haircuts/makeovers, bariatric surgery for weight loss, bariatric surgery for health, bariatric surgery for mobility, other surgeries for health, comorbidities
3. Inner Body Work
   *Subthemes*: emotional work focused externally, emotional work focused internally, history of obesity, history of emotional distress, actively ignoring emotional engagement, positive coping
4. Social Interactions
   *Subthemes*: social distance, positive clinical encounter, new alliances, romance, negative judgment from family, nonnegative family interactions, negative judgment from friends, nonnegative friend interactions, negative judgments from strangers, nonnegative stranger interactions, negative judgment from coworkers, nonnegative coworker interactions
5. Body Capital
   *Subthemes*: increased body capital, decreased body capital, upward mobility through surgery–projected, upward mobility through surgery–achieved, ideal body, relative body capital
6. Food and Eating
   *Subthemes*: emotional food consumption, watching what I eat in public, watching what others eat in public, private surveillance, adverse reactions to food

The codebook included detailed definitions, typical exemplars, atypical exemplars, and marginal/irrelevant examples from the texts[6] to illustrate the range of meanings assigned to each subtheme. All elicited data was systematically coded in MaxQDA, based on the established codebook. Core analytic tools include thematic comparison[7] and constant comparison.[8] For the analysis portion of the research specifically, interrater reliability was assessed using a random sample of forty segments from our preliminary interviews.[9] Final code definitions reached a high level of interrater agreement (kappa > 0.7), as measured by Cohen's kappa.[10]

*The Survey*

Roughly a year after we began our ethnographic research, we added a quantitative component to the research to assess changing experiences over time among bariatric patients within the particular medical system our fieldwork was situated within. Unlike the ethnographic research, which was situated on one particular medical campus, our survey captured data from patients at multiple campuses. Working across such widely disparate locations was greatly facilitated by our position as investigators within a cohesive medical system with concurrently high levels of patient contact, follow-up, and care at all of the sites. The survey was mailed to all patients who underwent bariatric surgery within the health-care system in two different cities (one of them the same city as where we did our ethnographic research) in the previous sixty months.

The first wave of the survey was sent out in June 2015. We were told it was one of the longest surveys sent through that particular system, and we waited somewhat nervously to see if anyone would respond. To our relief, returned surveys began to trickle in almost immediately. The final sample size of those who participated in the survey was three hundred (40 percent of the total clinical population). About 23 percent of respondents were male, and only 7 percent identified as an "ethnic minority." The average age at the time of bariatric surgery was fifty-two years old. The demographics roughly match that of the total clinical population with regard to age and gender, although "ethnic minorities" were underrepresented among survey respondents.

The second wave of the survey was sent out a year later, in June 2016. Although shorter than the first wave, it was still a lengthy questionnaire, since the purpose of it was to attempt to assess reported changes in health, well-being, daily life, and interactions with others over time.

To do this, we needed to be able to compare responses in the first wave with those in the second, to ascertain if patients reported differences as they moved further away from the date of their actual surgery. Also as a consequence of this purpose, the second wave of the survey was sent only to the three hundred individuals who responded to the first wave (along with a fervent thank-you note).

We know there was some overlap between the interview participants and the survey respondents, if for no other reason than that several interviewees complained about the length of the survey to us. We have no way, however, of correlating interview data with survey data, given the completely anonymous nature of the latter.

The remainder of this appendix consists of a lengthy excerpt from the survey. The original survey was over three hundred questions. Here, we include only those questions that are important to the discussions and data with which this book has engaged. Questions that reference the clinic by name or identifying descriptions have also been omitted. Analyses of survey data can also be found in some of our other publications.[1]

SURVEY EXCERPT

*Part 1: Surgical & Weight History Questions*
The first several questions are about your weight loss surgery experiences and your health since surgery.

1. What is today's date? _____
2. What type of weight loss surgery did you have?
   _____ Roux-en-Y gastric bypass
   _____ Laparoscopic adjustable gastric banding
   _____ Sleeve gastrectomy
   _____ Duodenal switch with biliopancreatic diversion
   _____ Other: _____
   _____ Unsure
3. How important were each of the following in your initial decision to have weight loss surgery?

Health concerns

| Not important | Somewhat important | Very important |

Mobility issues

    Not important           Somewhat important        Very important

Your own feelings about your weight

    Not important           Somewhat important        Very important

The reactions of others to your weight

    Not important           Somewhat important        Very important

4. Please answer for your health *now* and your health *before surgery.* Did a doctor ever tell you that you have any of the following? (check all that apply)

TABLE A.1. Health Information

|  | Now | Before surgery |
|---|---|---|
| High blood pressure (hypertension) |  |  |
| High cholesterol or high lipids |  |  |
| Heart disease, angina, or stroke |  |  |
| Type 2 diabetes (adult onset) |  |  |
| Metabolic syndrome |  |  |
| Cancer |  |  |
| Asthma |  |  |
| Sleep apnea |  |  |
| Other breathing problems such as obesity hypoventilation syndrome (OHS) |  |  |
| Infertility |  |  |
| Depression |  |  |
| Anxiety or panic disorder |  |  |
| Degenerative arthritis |  |  |
| Gastroesophageal reflux disease (GERD) |  |  |
| Non-alcoholic fatty liver disease |  |  |
| Kidney disease |  |  |
| Gallstones |  |  |
| Other conditions as a result of excess weight _____ |  |  |
| None of the above |  |  |

5. Which of the following best describes how bariatric surgery has impacted your overall medical conditions? (check one)

    _____ I am less healthy because my pre-existing conditions didn't improve or got worse

    _____ I am less healthy because the surgery or weight loss created new health problems

_____ My health conditions stayed pretty much the same

_____ Surgery improved my health conditions a little

_____ Surgery improved my health conditions a lot

Please describe: _____

6. Did your weight loss surgery cause any of the following complications? For each complication related to surgery, please let us know if you suffer from it now or suffered from it at any time since surgery.

TABLE A.2. Surgery Complications

| Complication | Now | | At any time since surgery | |
|---|---|---|---|---|
| Dumping | Yes | No | Yes | No |
| Vomiting or extreme nausea | Yes | No | Yes | No |
| Food intolerances, such as to milk or pasta | Yes | No | Yes | No |
| Vitamin deficiencies, such as vitamin B12, vitamin D, calcium, or iron | Yes | No | Yes | No |
| Extreme tiredness | Yes | No | Yes | No |
| Hair loss | Yes | No | Yes | No |
| Excess skin | Yes | No | Yes | No |
| Trouble healing skin or growing nails | Yes | No | Yes | No |
| Chronic pain | Yes | No | Yes | No |
| Bacterial overgrowth | Yes | No | Yes | No |
| Osteomalacia or osteoporosis (weak bones) | Yes | No | Yes | No |
| Hypoglycemia (low blood sugar) | Yes | No | Yes | No |
| Hypotension or tachycardia (low blood pressure or irregular heart beat) | Yes | No | Yes | No |

7. What is your height, in feet and inches?

_____ feet and _____ inches

8. What was your starting weight at the time you *first* had weight loss surgery?

_____ pounds

9. What is your *current* weight in pounds?

_____ pounds

10. How often do you weigh yourself?

Daily          Weekly          Monthly          Occasionally          Never

11. Have you lost or gained weight in the last 3 months?

_____ Lost

How many pounds did you lose? _____ pounds

_____ Gained

How many pounds did you gain? _____ pounds

_____ Stayed the same

12. What do you think is the main reason why you lost/gained/stayed the same weight in the last 3 months? Please check one of the following:

_____ Results of surgery

_____ Complications from surgery

_____ Support from friends and/or family

_____ Lack of support from friends and/or family

_____ My own efforts in diet and exercise

_____ Lack of my own efforts in diet and exercise

_____ Medical support or advice

_____ Lack of medical support or advice

_____ Current medication use (please specify): _____

_____ Other (please describe): _____

13. What was your weight *6 months* after your first surgery?

_____ pounds OR

_____ I had surgery less than 6 months ago

14. What was your weight *12 months* after your first surgery?

_____ pounds OR

_____ I had surgery less than 12 months ago

15. What was your weight *18 months* after your first surgery?

_____ pounds OR

_____ I had surgery less than 18 months ago

16. Have you ever had skin removal or body contouring surgery?

_____ No

_____ Yes

1. Month _____ year _____ of most recent procedure

2. Was this procedure done at the clinic?

_____ Yes

_____ No

3. Did you have the procedure overseas?

_____ Yes

_____ No

17. Whom have you told that you had weight loss surgery? (check one)

_____ No one

_____ Close family and friends

_____ All family and friends

_____ Everyone I know

*Part 2: Health-Related Quality of Life Questions*

The next several questions are about your quality of life and feelings now, and how they have changed since your first weight loss surgery.

1. Would you say your life in general is better, worse, or the same because of your initial decision to have weight loss surgery? Please explain your answer.

_____ Better

_____ Worse

_____ Same

Why?

2. Currently, would you say you are . . . ?

_____ Extremely overweight

_____ Somewhat overweight

_____ Healthy weight

_____ Underweight

3. In general, would you say your current health is . . . ?

_____ Excellent

_____ Very good

_____ Good

_____ Fair

_____ Poor

4. Does your current health limit you in moderate activities, such as moving a table, pushing a vacuum cleaner, bowling, or playing golf?

_____ Yes—Limited a lot

_____ Yes—Limited a little

_____ No—Not limited at all

5. Does your current health limit you in walking more than a mile?

_____ Yes—Limited a lot

_____ Yes—Limited a little

_____ No—Not limited at all

6. Does your current health limit you in going about your usual activities, like working, going to the grocery, or spending time with family or friends?

_____ Yes—Limited a lot

_____ Yes—Limited a little

_____ No—Not limited at all

7. What would you say would be the healthiest weight for you to be at this stage of your life?

_____ pounds

_____ My current weight

8. Thinking about how you would like to look, what weight would be your personal ideal?

_____ pounds

_____ My current weight

*Part 3: Daily Activity Questions*

The next set of questions is about your activity levels *in the last 7 days.* Please answer each question even if you do not consider yourself to be an active person. Please think about the activities you do at work, as part of your house and yard work, to get from place to place, and in your spare time for recreation, exercise, or sport.

1. During the last 7 days, on how many days did you do vigorous physical activities? Here, when we say, "vigorous physical activities," we mean activities that take hard physical effort and make you breathe harder than normal. Think only about those physical activities that you did for at least 10 minutes at a time.

_____ days per week (*write in the number of days, 0–7*)

2. How much time did you usually spend doing vigorous physical activities on any one of those days?

_____ hours per day

_____ minutes per day

_____ I did no vigorous physical activities in the last 7 days.

3. During the last 7 days, on how many days did you do moderate physical activities? Moderate activities refer to activities that take moderate physical effort and make you breathe somewhat harder than normal. Think only about those physical activities that you did for at least 10 minutes at a time. Omit walking.

_____ days per week (*write in the number of days, 0–7*)

4. How much time did you usually spend doing moderate physical activities on any one of those days?

_____ hours per day

_____ minutes per day

_____ I did no moderate physical activities in the last 7 days

5. During the last 7 days, on how many days did you walk for at least 10 minutes at a time? This includes at work and at home, walking to travel from place to place, and any other walking that you might do solely for recreation, sport, exercise, or leisure.

_____ days per week (*write in the number of days, 0–7*)

6. How much time did you usually spend walking on one of those days?

_____ hours per day

_____ minutes per day

_____ I did not walk for at least 10 minutes at a time in the last 7 days

7. During the last 7 days, how much time did you spend sitting on a weekday? Include time spent at work, at home, while doing course work, and during leisure time. This may include time spent sitting at a desk, visiting friends, reading, or sitting or lying down to watch television. Do not include sleeping.

_____ hours per day

_____ minutes per day

8. How has bariatric surgery impacted your overall activity level? Check the best response.

_____ Typically now I am more active than I was before surgery.

_____ Typically now I am less active than I was before surgery.

_____ My activity level has not changed much since my surgery.

9. Thinking of the last month, have you done any of the following either alone or with family/friends? (check all that apply)

a. Done a workout at a gym or recreation center

_____ No

_____ Yes, on my own

_____ Yes, with others

b. Participated in any leisure sports, such as skiing, golf, swimming, or basketball

_____ No

_____ Yes, on my own

_____ Yes, with others

c. Ran, bicycled, walked, or hiked in order to get exercise

_____ No

_____ Yes, on my own

_____ Yes, with others

*Part 4. Diet and Eating Questions*

Next are a few questions about your current eating patterns.

1. On a typical day, how many times do you eat a snack or have a meal? (A snack is something eaten between meals or after dinner and contains 150 calories or more.)

_____ times

2. In the last month, how often would you estimate that you ate or drank the following foods/drinks? Please mark your response for each food or drink with an "X."

TABLE A.3. Food/Drink Frequency

| | Daily | | | | Weekly | | | Monthly or less | |
|---|---|---|---|---|---|---|---|---|---|
| | 6+ times per day | 4–5 times per day | 2–3 times per day | Once per day | 5–6 times per week | 2–4 times per week | Once per week | 1–3 times per month | Less than once per month |
| Lean meats | | | | | | | | | |
| Fish or shellfish | | | | | | | | | |
| Beans, lentils, or other legumes | | | | | | | | | |
| Eggs | | | | | | | | | |
| Tofu or other vegetable protein | | | | | | | | | |
| Low-fat or fat-free dairy products | | | | | | | | | |

TABLE A.3. (*cont.*)

| | Daily | | | | Weekly | | | Monthly or less | |
|---|---|---|---|---|---|---|---|---|---|
| | 6+ times per day | 4–5 times per day | 2–3 times per day | Once per day | 5–6 times per week | 2–4 times per week | Once per week | 1–3 times per month | Less than once per month |
| Fresh fruits | | | | | | | | | |
| Fresh vegetables | | | | | | | | | |
| Whole grains | | | | | | | | | |
| Refined grains | | | | | | | | | |
| Olive oil | | | | | | | | | |
| Sunflower oil or other vegetable oil (except olive oil) | | | | | | | | | |
| Butter | | | | | | | | | |
| Salty snacks like chips | | | | | | | | | |
| Sweets like cookies or ice cream | | | | | | | | | |
| Sweetened drinks like juice, soda, sweet tea, or energy drinks | | | | | | | | | |
| Alcoholic drinks* | | | | | | | | | |

* One drink is equivalent to a 12-ounce beer, a 5-ounce glass of wine, or a drink with one shot of liquor.

3. How well would you say you are following the diet plan given to you by the dietitian? Please circle the best response for you.

Not well at all                                                        Very well

1      2      3      4      5      6      7      8      9      10

4. Please explain your answer to the question above. What aspects of the diet plan are hardest to follow?

_____

_____

_____.

*Part 5: Treatment by Others Questions*

The following statements describe reactions that many people have when they experience negative situations related to their weight. Using the following scale, please indicate the extent to which each response is true of you in those circumstances at this point in your life AND before you had bariatric surgery.

1. Please indicate how often you have felt stigmatized or discriminated against by each of the following types of people because of your weight. For each type of person, mark your response with an "X." Answer for experiences within the last 3 months as well as before your weight loss surgery.

TABLE A.4. Stigma

|  | In the last 3 months | | | | At any time before my surgery | | | |
|---|---|---|---|---|---|---|---|---|
|  | Never | Once | A few times | Several times | Never | Once | A few times | Several times |
| Spouse/partner |  |  |  |  |  |  |  |  |
| Other family members |  |  |  |  |  |  |  |  |
| Friends |  |  |  |  |  |  |  |  |
| Coworkers, classmates, or colleagues at school and work |  |  |  |  |  |  |  |  |
| Employers, supervisors |  |  |  |  |  |  |  |  |
| Teachers, professors |  |  |  |  |  |  |  |  |
| Doctors |  |  |  |  |  |  |  |  |
| Nurses |  |  |  |  |  |  |  |  |
| Dieticians, nutritionists |  |  |  |  |  |  |  |  |
| Mental health professionals such as psychologists or social workers |  |  |  |  |  |  |  |  |
| Neighbors and other acquaintances |  |  |  |  |  |  |  |  |
| Someone else you know besides the people listed above |  |  |  |  |  |  |  |  |
| Servers at restaurants |  |  |  |  |  |  |  |  |
| Sales clerks at stores |  |  |  |  |  |  |  |  |
| Strangers in public places |  |  |  |  |  |  |  |  |
| Strangers online/ on social media |  |  |  |  |  |  |  |  |

Please indicate how often you have experienced each of the following situations, both in the last 3 months and at any time before your surgery.

2. A spouse/partner calling you names because of your weight.

| In the last 3 months | | | | | At any time before your surgery | | | | |
|---|---|---|---|---|---|---|---|---|---|
| Never | Once | A few times | Several times | N/A | Never | Once | A few times | Several times | N/A |

3. A spouse/partner telling you to lose weight in order to be more attractive.

| In the last 3 months | | | | | At any time before your surgery | | | | |
|---|---|---|---|---|---|---|---|---|---|
| Never | Once | A few times | Several times | N/A | Never | Once | A few times | Several times | N/A |

4. Having your children tease or insult you because of your weight.

| In the last 3 months | | | | | At any time before your surgery | | | | |
|---|---|---|---|---|---|---|---|---|---|
| Never | Once | A few times | Several times | N/A | Never | Once | A few times | Several times | N/A |

5. Being hit, beaten up, or physically attacked because of your weight.

| In the last 3 months | | | | At any time before your surgery | | | |
|---|---|---|---|---|---|---|---|
| Never | Once | A few times | Several times | Never | Once | A few times | Several times |

6. Being offered fashion advice by strangers.

| In the last 3 months | | | | At any time before your surgery | | | |
|---|---|---|---|---|---|---|---|
| Never | Once | A few times | Several times | Never | Once | A few times | Several times |

7. Being sexually harassed (cat-calls, wolf-whistles, etc.) because of your weight.

| In the last 3 months | | | | At any time before your surgery | | | |
|---|---|---|---|---|---|---|---|
| Never | Once | A few times | Several times | Never | Once | A few times | Several times |

8. Being stared at in public because of your size.

| In the last 3 months | | | | At any time before your surgery | | | |
|---|---|---|---|---|---|---|---|
| Never | Once | A few times | Several times | Never | Once | A few times | Several times |

9. Being told, "All you really need is a little willpower."

| In the last 3 months | | | | At any time before your surgery | | | |
|---|---|---|---|---|---|---|---|
| Never | Once | A few times | Several times | Never | Once | A few times | Several times |

10. Being unable to get a date because of your size.

| In the last 3 months | | | | At any time before your surgery | | | |
|---|---|---|---|---|---|---|---|
| Never | Once | A few times | Several times | Never | Once | A few times | Several times |

11. Friends, acquaintances, coworkers, etc. making fun of your appearance.

| In the last 3 months | | | | At any time before your surgery | | | |
|---|---|---|---|---|---|---|---|
| Never | Once | A few times | Several times | Never | Once | A few times | Several times |

12. Having a doctor make cruel remarks, ridicule you, or call you names.

| In the last 3 months | | | | At any time before your surgery | | | |
|---|---|---|---|---|---|---|---|
| Never | Once | A few times | Several times | Never | Once | A few times | Several times |

13. Having a doctor recommend a diet even if you did not come in to discuss weight loss.

| In the last 3 months | | | | At any time before your surgery | | | |
|---|---|---|---|---|---|---|---|
| Never | Once | A few times | Several times | Never | Once | A few times | Several times |

14. Having a romantic partner exploit you, because s/he assumed you were "desperate" and would put up with it.

| In the last 3 months | | | | At any time before your surgery | | | |
|---|---|---|---|---|---|---|---|
| Never | Once | A few times | Several times | Never | Once | A few times | Several times |

15. Having family members feel embarrassed by you or ashamed of you.

| In the last 3 months | | | | At any time before your surgery | | | |
|---|---|---|---|---|---|---|---|
| Never | Once | A few times | Several times | Never | Once | A few times | Several times |

16. Having people assume that you overeat or binge-eat because you are overweight.

| In the last 3 months | | | | At any time before your surgery | | | |
|---|---|---|---|---|---|---|---|
| Never | Once | A few times | Several times | Never | Once | A few times | Several times |

17. Having people assume you have emotional problems because you are overweight.

| In the last 3 months | | | | At any time before your surgery | | | |
|---|---|---|---|---|---|---|---|
| Never | Once | A few times | Several times | Never | Once | A few times | Several times |

18. Having strangers suggest diets to you.

| In the last 3 months | | | | At any time before your surgery | | | |
|---|---|---|---|---|---|---|---|
| Never | Once | A few times | Several times | Never | Once | A few times | Several times |

19. In the supermarket, having people criticize or make comments about your food choices.

| In the last 3 months | | | | At any time before your surgery | | | |
|---|---|---|---|---|---|---|---|
| Never | Once | A few times | Several times | Never | Once | A few times | Several times |

20. Losing a job or a promotion because of your size.

| In the last 3 months | | | | At any time before your surgery | | | |
|---|---|---|---|---|---|---|---|
| Never | Once | A few times | Several times | Never | Once | A few times | Several times |

21. Not being able to find clothes that fit.

| In the last 3 months | | | | At any time before your surgery | | | |
|---|---|---|---|---|---|---|---|
| Never | Once | A few times | Several times | Never | Once | A few times | Several times |

22. Not being able to find medical equipment in a size that works for you.

| In the last 3 months | | | | At any time before your surgery | | | |
|---|---|---|---|---|---|---|---|
| Never | Once | A few times | Several times | Never | Once | A few times | Several times |

23. Not being able to fit comfortably into seats on airplanes or in public places.

| In the last 3 months | | | | At any time before your surgery | | | |
|---|---|---|---|---|---|---|---|
| Never | Once | A few times | Several times | Never | Once | A few times | Several times |

24. Not being hired because of your weight, shape, or size.

| In the last 3 months | | | | At any time before your surgery | | | |
|---|---|---|---|---|---|---|---|
| Never | Once | A few times | Several times | Never | Once | A few times | Several times |

25. Other people having low expectations of you because of your weight.

| In the last 3 months | | | | At any time before your surgery | | | |
|---|---|---|---|---|---|---|---|
| Never | Once | A few times | Several times | Never | Once | A few times | Several times |

26. Overhearing other people making rude remarks about you in public.

| In the last 3 months | | | | At any time before your surgery | | | |
|---|---|---|---|---|---|---|---|
| Never | Once | A few times | Several times | Never | Once | A few times | Several times |

27. Parents or other relatives telling you how attractive you would be, if you lost weight.

| In the last 3 months | | | | At any time before your surgery | | | |
|---|---|---|---|---|---|---|---|
| Never | Once | A few times | Several times | Never | Once | A few times | Several times |

28. Seeing bumper stickers, T-shirts, advertising, etc. that ridicule fat people.

| In the last 3 months | | | | At any time before your surgery | | | |
|---|---|---|---|---|---|---|---|
| Never | Once | A few times | Several times | Never | Once | A few times | Several times |

29. When eating in public, being told, "You really shouldn't be eating that because of your size."

| In the last 3 months | | | | At any time before your surgery | | | |
|---|---|---|---|---|---|---|---|
| Never | Once | A few times | Several times | Never | Once | A few times | Several times |

30. When walking outside, having people drive by and laugh or shout insults.

| In the last 3 months | | | | At any time before your surgery | | | |
|---|---|---|---|---|---|---|---|
| Never | Once | A few times | Several times | Never | Once | A few times | Several times |

31. Being told you have "such a pretty face."

| In the last 3 months | | | | At any time before your surgery | | | |
|---|---|---|---|---|---|---|---|
| Never | Once | A few times | Several times | Never | Once | A few times | Several times |

Please indicate how often you have experienced each of the following situations related to your decision to have surgery.

32. A spouse/partner telling you that he/she doesn't like you as much since surgery.

| Never | Once | A few times | Several times |
|---|---|---|---|

33. A family member or friend saying that he/she doesn't like you as much since surgery.

      Never             Once           A few times        Several times

34. Being told, "All you really need is a little willpower to lose weight— why did you have surgery? Surgery is cheating!"

      Never             Once           A few times        Several times

35. When eating with family or friends, being told, "You really shouldn't be eating that because of your surgery."

      Never             Once           A few times        Several times

36. In the last three months, have you heard the following types of stories about other people being judged or mistreated because of their weight? For each type of story, circle "yes" or "no" for people you know and people you don't know.

TABLE A.5. Stories

|  | People you know | | People you don't know | |
|---|---|---|---|---|
| a. Being called names, laughed at, teased, or verbally harassed because of their weight. | Yes | No | Yes | No |
| b. Being hit, beaten up, or physically attacked because of their weight. | Yes | No | Yes | No |
| c. Being stared at because of their weight. | Yes | No | Yes | No |
| d. Being ignored by public service workers, such as in restaurants, stores, or airlines, because of their weight. | Yes | No | Yes | No |
| e. Not being promoted, being fired, or having difficulty getting a job because of their weight. | Yes | No | Yes | No |
| f. Having a doctor make rude remarks or fail to provide proper and thoughtful care because of their weight. | Yes | No | Yes | No |
| g. Having family members feel embarrassed by or ashamed of them. | Yes | No | Yes | No |
| h. Having trouble getting a date or being dumped because of their weight. | Yes | No | Yes | No |
| i. Not being able to find clothes that fit. | Yes | No | Yes | No |
| j. Not being able to sit comfortably, such as in seats on airplanes or in offices. | Yes | No | Yes | No |

Please rate how strongly you agree with each statement below. Circle the response that best represents your experience.

37. It's my fault if I am overweight: I can lose weight if I just work hard at it.

Strongly disagree          Disagree          Agree          Strongly agree

38. An overweight person is just as good as anyone else.

Strongly disagree          Disagree          Agree          Strongly agree

39. I am less attractive than most other people if I am overweight.

Strongly disagree          Disagree          Agree          Strongly agree

40. I feel anxious when I am overweight because of what people might think of me.

Strongly disagree          Disagree          Agree          Strongly agree

41. Whenever I think a lot about being overweight, I feel depressed.

Strongly disagree          Disagree          Agree          Strongly agree

42. I feel that being overweight has never interfered with my ability to be a good and decent person.

Strongly disagree          Disagree          Agree          Strongly agree

43. I hate myself when I am overweight.

Strongly disagree          Disagree          Agree          Strongly agree

44. My weight is a major way that I judge my value as a person.

Strongly disagree          Disagree          Agree          Strongly agree

45. As an overweight person, I feel that I am just as deserving of respect as anyone.

Strongly disagree          Disagree          Agree          Strongly agree

46. It really bothers me that people look down on overweight people.

Strongly disagree          Disagree          Agree          Strongly agree

47. When I'm overweight, I don't feel like my true self.

Strongly disagree          Disagree          Agree          Strongly agree

48. When I am overweight, I don't understand how anyone attractive would want to date me.

Strongly disagree          Disagree          Agree          Strongly agree

49. I believe that society's prejudice against overweight people is unfair.

Strongly disagree          Disagree                 Agree              Strongly agree

Please indicate how often you have used the following strategies to cope with negative experiences related to your weight. Please answer for strategies you use at this time in your life AND at any time before you had surgery:

50. I act(ed) politely to everyone, even if they are not polite to me.

| At this point in my life | | | Before my surgery | | |
|---|---|---|---|---|---|
| Never | Sometimes | Often | Never | Sometimes | Often |

51. I love(d) myself, even when it seems like other people don't.

| At this point in my life | | | Before my surgery | | |
|---|---|---|---|---|---|
| Never | Sometimes | Often | Never | Sometimes | Often |

52. I make/made a point of not hiding my body.

| At this point in my life | | | Before my surgery | | |
|---|---|---|---|---|---|
| Never | Sometimes | Often | Never | Sometimes | Often |

53. I think/thought, "I don't care what others think of me; it only matters that I like myself."

| At this point in my life | | | Before my surgery | | |
|---|---|---|---|---|---|
| Never | Sometimes | Often | Never | Sometimes | Often |

54. I tell/told people it's not right to make remarks about my size and shape.

| At this point in my life | | | Before my surgery | | |
|---|---|---|---|---|---|
| Never | Sometimes | Often | Never | Sometimes | Often |

55. I think/thought that no one will ever love me because of my appearance.

| At this point in my life | | | Before my surgery | | |
|---|---|---|---|---|---|
| Never | Sometimes | Often | Never | Sometimes | Often |

56. I yell(ed) at people who try to humiliate me.

| At this point in my life | | | Before my surgery | | |
|---|---|---|---|---|---|
| Never | Sometimes | Often | Never | Sometimes | Often |

57. If someone tries to make me feel inferior, I remind(ed) myself that I do not deserve this.

|                | At this point in my life |       |                | Before my surgery |       |
|----------------|--------------------------|-------|----------------|-------------------|-------|
| Never          | Sometimes                | Often | Never          | Sometimes         | Often |

58. I avoid(ed) going out in public because I am afraid people will make comments about my size.

|                | At this point in my life |       |                | Before my surgery |       |
|----------------|--------------------------|-------|----------------|-------------------|-------|
| Never          | Sometimes                | Often | Never          | Sometimes         | Often |

59. I avoid(ed) looking in the mirror so that I don't have to think about my weight.

|                | At this point in my life |       |                | Before my surgery |       |
|----------------|--------------------------|-------|----------------|-------------------|-------|
| Never          | Sometimes                | Often | Never          | Sometimes         | Often |

60. I avoid(ed) places where I might have a hard time finding a place to sit because of my size.

|                | At this point in my life |       |                | Before my surgery |       |
|----------------|--------------------------|-------|----------------|-------------------|-------|
| Never          | Sometimes                | Often | Never          | Sometimes         | Often |

61. I often cry/cried about my weight, but then I get over it.

|                | At this point in my life |       |                | Before my surgery |       |
|----------------|--------------------------|-------|----------------|-------------------|-------|
| Never          | Sometimes                | Often | Never          | Sometimes         | Often |

62. I have quit jobs where I encountered stigma or discrimination.

|                | At this point in my life |       |                | Before my surgery |       |
|----------------|--------------------------|-------|----------------|-------------------|-------|
| Never          | Sometimes                | Often | Never          | Sometimes         | Often |

63. I refuse(d) to restrict my activities even though I might not fit in or might attract attention.

|                | At this point in my life |       |                | Before my surgery |       |
|----------------|--------------------------|-------|----------------|-------------------|-------|
| Never          | Sometimes                | Often | Never          | Sometimes         | Often |

64. I have changed doctors in order to find one who is more sensitive to my needs.

|                | At this point in my life |       |                | Before my surgery |       |
|----------------|--------------------------|-------|----------------|-------------------|-------|
| Never          | Sometimes                | Often | Never          | Sometimes         | Often |

65. I have divorced/broken up with spouses/partners who are critical of my size.

| At this point in my life | | | Before my surgery | | |
|---|---|---|---|---|---|
| Never | Sometimes | Often | Never | Sometimes | Often |

66. I do/did physical activity in order to feel more comfortable in my body.

| At this point in my life | | | Before my surgery | | |
|---|---|---|---|---|---|
| Never | Sometimes | Often | Never | Sometimes | Often |

67. I do/did nice things for myself to make me feel better when I am down.

| At this point in my life | | | Before my surgery | | |
|---|---|---|---|---|---|
| Never | Sometimes | Often | Never | Sometimes | Often |

68. I feel/felt really bad about myself.

| At this point in my life | | | Before my surgery | | |
|---|---|---|---|---|---|
| Never | Sometimes | Often | Never | Sometimes | Often |

69. I get/got depressed and isolate myself.

| At this point in my life | | | Before my surgery | | |
|---|---|---|---|---|---|
| Never | Sometimes | Often | Never | Sometimes | Often |

70. I rely/relied on friends and family to support me when I get upset.

| At this point in my life | | | Before my surgery | | |
|---|---|---|---|---|---|
| Never | Sometimes | Often | Never | Sometimes | Often |

71. I go/went to therapy to get help dealing with situations where I feel I experience trouble or emotional pain.

| At this point in my life | | | Before my surgery | | |
|---|---|---|---|---|---|
| Never | Sometimes | Often | Never | Sometimes | Often |

72. I pray(ed) and rely/relied on my faith to get help dealing with situations where I experience trouble or emotional pain.

| At this point in my life | | | Before my surgery | | |
|---|---|---|---|---|---|
| Never | Sometimes | Often | Never | Sometimes | Often |

73. I eat/ate and rely/relied on food in order to feel better after experiencing trouble or emotional pain.

| At this point in my life | | | Before my surgery | | |
|---|---|---|---|---|---|
| Never | Sometimes | Often | Never | Sometimes | Often |

74. I diet(ed) and restrict(ed) my food intake in order to feel better after experiencing trouble or emotional pain.

| At this point in my life | | | Before my surgery | | |
|---|---|---|---|---|---|
| Never | Sometimes | Often | Never | Sometimes | Often |

75. I put myself and my needs before other people's.

| At this point in my life | | | Before my surgery | | |
|---|---|---|---|---|---|
| Never | Sometimes | Often | Never | Sometimes | Often |

76. I treat(ed) myself to new clothes that look good on me.

| At this point in my life | | | Before my surgery | | |
|---|---|---|---|---|---|
| Never | Sometimes | Often | Never | Sometimes | Often |

# NOTES

INTRODUCTION

1. Braziel and LeBesco 2001; Farrell 2011; Lee and Pause 2016; McCullough and Hardin 2013; Puhl and Heuer 2009, 2010; Rogge 2004.
2. Beck 1992; Bell, McNaughton, and Salmon 2011; Elliott 2010; Farrell 2011; LeBesco 2011; Lupton 1993, 1995, 2012; McNaughton 2013; Monaghan 2008; Ogden 1995; Petersen and Bunton 1997; Solomon 2016; Vaz and Bruno 2003.
3. CDC 2019a, 2019b, 2019g, 2019h; WHO 2019.
4. Mann et al. 2007; Pietiläinen et al. 2012; Rothblum 2018.
5. CDC 2019c, 2019e, 2019f, 2019g; WHO 2019.
6. Adams 2016; Jutel 2006; Trainer, Brewis, Hruschka, and Williams 2015; Yates-Doerr 2014.
7. Baker 2011; Buchwald 2014; Celio and Pories 2016; Umemura et al. 2015.
8. Baker 2011; Buchwald 2014; Celio and Pories 2016; Umemura et al. 2015.
9. Ahmed and Stacey 2001; Davis 2014; Lafrance 2018; Lee and Pause 2016; McCullough and Hardin 2013.
10. CDC 2019a, 2019d, 2019g. We use the terms "Black" and "Latinx" because at the time of this writing, in 2020, they are aligned with social justice and antiracism. While we expect language to change and evolve over time (and these terms may come to seem dated years from now), we want readers to know that our support for social justice and antiracism remains firm.
11. Gao et al. 2019; Kim and Daly 2019; Soto et al. 2019.
12. Andersen and Collins 2001; Nakayama and Martin 1999.
13. McMillan Cottom 2019; Patterson-Faye 2014, 2016.
14. Berg 2019.
15. ASMBS 2019.
16. English 1993; Hiller 1992.
17. Goffman 1963.
18. Brewis et al. 2011.
19. Becker 1995, 2004; Brewis 2011; Brewis et al. 2011; Edmonds 2010; Nichter 2000; Popenoe 2004; Solomon 2016; Talukdar 2012; Trainer 2012; Yates-Doerr 2015.
20. Bernard, Wutich, and Ryan 2016; Boeije 2002; Guest, Bunce, and Johnson 2006; Krippendorff 2012; MacQueen et al. 1998; McLellan, MacQueen, and Neidig 2003; Wutich and Gravlee 2010.

21. Adams et al. 2017; Andersen et al. 2015; Chevallier 2010; Evers, Sandoval, and Seeley 2017; Gribsholt et al. 2016; Hiorth et al. 2019; Inge et al. 2019; Meleo-Erwin 2019a, 2019b; O'Brien et al. 2013; Thereau et al. 2019.

22. Le Guin 1998, 62.

23. CDC 2019a, 2019b, 2019h.

24. Adams 2016; Hruschka and Hadley 2016; Jutel 2006; Trainer, Brewis, Hruschka, and Williams 2015; Yates-Doerr 2014.

25. Trainer, Brewis, Williams, and Rosales Chavez 2015.

## 1. WEIGHT AS PATHOLOGY

1. Bell, McNaughton, and Salmon 2011; Elliott 2010; Farrell 2011; LeBesco 2011; McNaughton 2013; Monaghan 2008.

2. Flegal et al. 2012, 2016.

3. Pollack 2013.

4. Boero 2012; Bordo 1993; Braziel and LeBesco 2001; Brewis 2014; Farrell 2011; Fikken and Rothblum 2012; Gard and Wright 2005; Hardin 2019; Howard 2018; Kulick and Meneley 2005; LeBesco 2011; Lee and Pause 2016; Lupton 2012; McCullough and Hardin 2013; Orbach 1978; Puhl and Heuer 2009, 2010; Rogge 2004; Rothblum 2018; Rothblum and Solovay 2009; Saguy 2014; Spitzack 1990; Solomon 2016; Stoll 2019; Wolf 1990.

5. Beck 1992; Bell, McNaughton, and Salmon 2011; Elliott 2010; Farrell 2011; Hardin, McLennan, and Brewis 2018; LeBesco 2011; Lupton 1993, 1995, 2012; McNaughton 2013; Monaghan 2008; Mrig and Spencer 2018; Ogden 1995; Petersen and Bunton 1997; Vaz and Bruno 2003.

6. Bell, McNaughton, and Salmon 2011; Elliott 2010; Farrell 2011; LeBesco 2011; McNaughton 2013; Monaghan 2008.

7. Gard and Wright 2005; Spitzack 1990.

8. Foucault 1994; Lilleleht 2002; Shildrick and Price 1998; Waitzkin 1989; Willis, Waddington, and Marsden 2013.

9. Lee and Pause 2016; Puhl and Heuer 2009, 2010; Sabin, Marini, and Nosek 2012; Stoll 2019.

10. ASMBS 2019.

11. ASMBS 2019.

12. Adams et al. 2017; Andersen et al. 2015; Chevallier 2010; Evers, Sandoval, and Seeley 2017; Gribsholt et al. 2016; Hiorth et al. 2019; Inge et al. 2019; Meleo-Erwin 2019a, 2019b; O'Brien et al. 2013; Thereau et al. 2019.

13. Trainer, Brewis, Hruschka, and Williams 2015.

14. Cassell 2005; Edmonds and Sanabria 2014; Hunter et al. 2008; Hunter, Spence, and Scheinberg 2008; Jain and Jadhav 2009; Long, Hunter, and Van der Geest 2008; Mrig and Spencer 2018; Rapp 1999; Warin 2003; Wind 2008.

15. Lee and Pause 2016; McCullough and Hardin 2013; Raves et al. 2016; Rogge 2004.

16. Whitesel and Shuman 2016.

17. Gay 2018; Kinzel 2018; Tait and Sugden 2018.

18. Horswill, Scott, and Voorhees 2017; Leung et al. 2018; Levine 2007; SWNS 2019.

19. Bordo 1993; Fikken and Rothblum 2012; Lee and Pause 2016; Orbach 1978; Shildrick and Price 1998; Spitzack 1990; Stoll 2019; Wolf 1990.

20. Bordo 1993; Nichter 2000; Spitzack 1990.

21. Atkinson 2014; Birbeck and Drummond 2006; Bordo 1993; Crawshaw 2007; Gill, Henwood, and McClean 2005; Grogan and Richards 2002; Hebl and Turchin 2005; McCreary and Sasse 2000; Monaghan 2007, 2008; Murray and Touyz 2012; Norman 2013; Parasecoli 2013; Watson 2000.

22. Boston University School of Medicine 2018; Bruff et al. 2018; Dotinga 2017; McLean et al. 2018; Ng et al. 2015; Stanford et al. 2015; Wee et al. 2013; Wood et al. 2019.

23. Boston University School of Medicine 2018.

24. Hsu et al. 2015; Huang 2013; Medaris Miller 2016; WHO Expert Consultation 2004; Yi et al. 2015.

25. CDC 2019a, 2019g.

26. Hsu et al. 2015; Huang 2013; Medaris Miller 2016; WHO Expert Consultation 2004; Yi et al. 2015.

27. Gladwell 2000; Pollan 2008; Smith-Morris 2005, 2006.

28. CDC 2019i; Howard 2018; Smith-Morris 2005, 2006.

29. Bell, McNaughton, and Salmon 2011.

30. Boero 2010, 2012.

31. Mayo Clinic 2019a.

32. Mayo Clinic 2019b.

33. CDC 2019e.

34. CDC 2019c.

35. Stanford Health Care 2019.

36. CDC 2019f.

37. CDC 2019a, 2019b, 2019c, 2019d, 2019e, 2019f, 2019g, 2019h.

38. Beck 1992; Bell, McNaughton, and Salmon 2011; Elliott 2010; Farrell 2011; Howard 2018; LeBesco 2011; Lupton 1995, 2012; McNaughton 2013; Monaghan 2008; Ogden 1995; Petersen and Bunton 1997; Rothblum 2018; Vaz and Bruno 2003.

39. Boero 2012; Bordo 1993; Braziel and LeBesco 2001; Brewis 2014; Farrell 2011; Fikken and Rothblum 2012; Gard and Wright 2005; Kulick and Meneley 2005; LeBesco 2011; Lee and Pause 2016; Lupton 2012; McCullough and Hardin 2013; Orbach 1978; Puhl and Heuer 2009, 2010; Rogge 2004; Rothblum 2018; Rothblum and Solovay 2009; Saguy 2014; Spitzack 1990; Wolf 1990.

40. Campo-Engelstein 2010a, 2010b.

41. NIDDK 2016.

42. Trainer and Benjamin 2017.

43. Rubino et al. 2020.

## 2. WEIGHT AS JUDGMENT

1. Burnham 2019; Kirkland 2008.

2. Boero 2012; Bordo 1993, 2013; Braziel and LeBesco 2001; Brewis 2014; Farrell 2011; Fikken and Rothblum 2012; Gard and Wright 2005; Kulick and Meneley

2005; LeBesco 2011; Lee and Pause 2016; Lupton 2012; McCullough and Hardin 2013; Orbach 1978; Puhl and Heuer 2009, 2010; Rogge 2004; Rothblum and Solovay 2009; Saguy 2014; Spitzack 1990; Stoll 2019; Wolf 1990.

3. Metraux 2019; Mull 2018.

4. Muttarak 2018.

5. CDC 2019d, 2019g, 2019h; Robinson, Webb, and Butler-Ajibade 2012; Springfield et al. 2015.

6. Nichter 2000.

7. Denee 2019; Gay 2017; Granberg et al. 2008; Granberg, Simons, and Simons 2009; Gregg 2017; McClure 2013; McMillan Cottom 2019; Patterson-Faye 2014, 2016; Ristovski-Slijepcevic et al. 2010.

8. Becker 1995; Bordo 1993; Bourdieu 1984, 1992, 1997; Featherstone 1982; Foucault 1994; Lock and Kaufert 2001; Merleau-Ponty 1962; Scheper-Hughes and Lock 1987; Turner 1982, 1984.

9. Becker 1995, 2004; Brewis 2011; Brewis, Hruschka, and Wutich 2011; Edmonds 2010; Hardin, McLennan, and Brewis 2018; Nichter 2000; Popenoe 2004; Reischer and Koo 2004; Sobal and Maurer 1999; Talukdar 2012; Taylor 2015; Trainer 2012; Yates-Doerr 2015.

10. Bordo 2013; Gimlin 2002; Greenhalgh and Carney 2014; Monaghan 2008.

11. Becker 1995; Bordo 1993; Counihan 1999; Gimlin 2002; Nichter 2000.

12. Groven, Ahlsen, and Robertson 2018.

13. Braziel and LeBesco 2001; Brewis 2011, 2014; Brewis et al. 2011, 2017; Farrell 2011; Gimlin 2002; Lee and Pause 2016; McCullough and Hardin 2013; Puhl and Heuer 2009, 2010; Rogge 2004; Rothblum and Solovay 2009; Stoll 2019.

14. Granberg et al. 2008; Granberg, Simons, and Simons 2009; McClure 2013; Ristovski-Slijepcevic et al. 2010; Taylor 2015.

15. Metraux 2019; Mull 2018; White 2016.

16. CDC 2019a, 2019b, 2019c, 2019d.

17. Bailey 2016.

18. Patterson-Faye 2016.

19. McMillan Cottom 2019.

20. Shange 1975.

21. Lorde 1999.

22. Nash 2011.

23. Agyemang and Powell-Wiley 2013; Fitzgibbon et al. 2012; Kyryliuk, Baruth, and Wilcox 2015; Robinson, Webb, and Butler-Ajibade 2012; Springfield et al. 2015.

24. Braziel and LeBesco 2001; Brewis 2014; Brewis et al. 2017; Farrell 2011; Hong et al. 2019; Lee and Pause 2016; Lupton 2012; McCullough and Hardin 2013; Orbach 1978; Puhl and Heuer 2009, 2010; Rogge 2004; Rothblum and Solovay 2009; Sabin, Marini, and Nosek 2012; Stoll 2019.

25. Bourdieu 1984, 1992, 1997; Edmonds and Mears 2017; Hakim 2010.

26. Bordo 1993; Granberg et al. 2008; Granberg, Simons, and Simons 2009; Greenhalgh and Carney 2014; McCullough and Hardin 2013; Monaghan 2008; Nichter 2000; Puhl and Heuer 2009, 2010.

27. Braziel and LeBesco 2001; Lee and Pause 2016; Rothblum and Solovay 2009.

28. Becker 1995; Bynum 2012; Counihan 1999; Martin 1992; Scheper-Hughes and Lock 1987; Townsend 2002; Weber 2002; Zigon 2008.

29. Becker 1995; Boero 2010, 2012; Bordo 1993; Carryer 1997; Featherstone 1982; Foucault 1994; Giddens 1991; Gimlin 2002; Nichter 2000; Trainer, Brewis, and Wutich 2017; Trainer, Wutich, and Brewis 2017; Turner 1982, 1984; Weber 2002.

30. Braziel and LeBesco 2001; Farrell 2011; McCullough and Hardin 2013; Puhl and Heuer 2009, 2010; Rogge 2004.

31. Goffman 1963.

32. Hatzenbuehler, Phelan, and Link 2013; Link and Phelan 2001, 2006; Martin, Lang, and Olafsdottir 2008; Pescosolido 2013.

33. Hatzenbuehler, Phelan, and Link 2013; Link and Phelan 2001, 2006; Martin, Lang, and Olafsdottir 2008; Pescosolido 2013.

34. Bell and McNaughton 2007; Bordo 2013; Monaghan 2008.

35. Brewis 2014; Puhl and Heuer 2009, 2010; Stoll 2019.

36. Lee and Pause 2016; Puhl and Heuer 2009, 2010: Stoll 2019.

37. WHO 2019.

38. Fardouly and Vartanian 2012; Mattingly, Stambush, and Hill 2009; Tucci et al. 2013; Vartanian and Fardouly 2013.

39. Brewis, Trainer, Han, and Wutich 2017; Bordo 2013; Carryer 1997; Dalley, Toffanin, and Pollet 2012; Gimlin 2002; Granberg et al. 2008; Nichter 2000; Trainer, Brewis, Hruschka, and Williams 2015.

40. Dalley, Toffanin, and Pollet 2012; Mann et al. 2007; Pietiläinen et al. 2012.

41. Becker 1995; Boero 2010, 2012; Throsby 2008; Townsend 2002; Weber 2002; Zigon 2008.

42. Trainer and Benjamin 2017; Trainer, Brewis, and Wutich 2017; Trainer, Wutich, and Brewis 2017.

43. Boero 2010; Groven 2014; Knutsen, Terragni, and Foss 2013; Meana and Ricciardi 2008; Ogden, Clementi, and Aylwin 2006; Throsby 2008.

44. Trainer and Benjamin 2017; Trainer, Brewis, and Wutich 2017; Trainer, Wutich, and Brewis 2017.

45. Butler 1993; Goffman 1963.

46. Christiansen, Borge, and Fagermoen 2012; Colls 2006.

47. Chouinard, Hall, and Wilton 2010; Colls and Evans 2014; Cooper 1997; Link and Phelan 2001; Livingston 2000; Garland-Thomson 2011.

48. Meleo-Erwin 2015.

49. Lewis et al. 2011; Brewis et al. 2017.

50. Foucault 1994; Gard and Wright 2005; Lupton 2012; Petersen and Bunton 1997.

51. Bell, McNaughton, and Salmon 2011; Greenhalgh and Carney 2014; LeBesco 2011; McCullough and Hardin 2013; Rose and Novas 2007.

52. Beck 1992; Lupton 1995; Ogden 1995; Vaz and Bruno 2003.

## 3. WEIGHT LOSS AS SUCCESS

1. Batsis, Romero-Corral, et al. 2008; Batsis, Sarr, et al. 2008; Buchwald and Williams 2004; Buchwald et al. 2004; Courcoulas et al. 2013; Gadiot et al. 2017.
2. Counihan 1999; Counihan and Van Esterik 2013.
3. Batsis et al. 2009; Bocchieri, Meana, and Fisher 2002; Boero 2010; Knutsen, Terragni, and Foss 2013; Ogden, Clementi, and Aylwin 2006; Throsby 2008; Vogel 2018.
4. Groven 2014; Groven, Engelsrud, and Råheim 2012; Groven, Råheim, and Engelsrud 2010, 2013.
5. Applbaum and Oldani 2010; Chakrabarti 2014; Greene 2004; Mykhalovskiy, Mccoy, and Bresalier 2004; Spencer 2018; Trostle 1997.
6. Ashrafian et al. 2015; Batsis, Romero-Corral, et al. 2008; Batsis, Sarr, et al. 2008; Buchwald et al. 2004; Courcoulas et al. 2013; Gadiot et al. 2017.
7. Batsis, Romero-Corral, et al. 2008; Batsis, Sarr, et al. 2008; Buchwald et al. 2004; Courcoulas et al. 2013; Gadiot et al. 2017; Koliaki et al. 2017; Uranga and Keller 2019.
8. Howard 2018.
9. Groven, Ahlsen, and Robertson 2018; Natvik et al. 2015; SturtzSreetharan et al. 2018.
10. Hardin 2016; Manderson and Smith-Morris 2010.
11. Estroff 1993; Manderson and Smith-Morris 2010; Weaver and Mendenhall 2014.
12. Ferzacca 2010; Smith-Morris 2005, 2006; Weaver and Mendenhall 2014.
13. Ferzacca 2010; Smith-Morris 2005, 2006, 2010; Weaver and Mendenhall 2014.
14. Ferzacca 2010.
15. Manderson and Warren 2016.
16. Meana and Ricciardi 2008.
17. Brewis et al. 2017.
18. Trainer and Benjamin 2017; Trainer, Brewis, and Wutich 2017; Trainer, Wutich, and Brewis 2017.
19. Gimlin 2002; Goffman 1963; Groven et al. 2015; Lupton 2012; Yates-Doerr 2015.
20. Foucault 1977; Gideonse 2015; Harris 2015; Lock and Nguyen 2010; Ong 2006; Warner 1999; Wolf-Meyer 2017.

## 4. WEIGHT, WORRY, AND SURVEILLANCE

1. Batsis, Romero-Corral, et al. 2008; Batsis, Sarr, et al. 2008; Buchwald et al. 2004; Courcoulas et al. 2013; Dixon et al. 2008; Gadiot et al. 2017; Koliaki et al. 2017; Uranga and Keller 2019.
2. Adams et al. 2017; Andersen et al. 2015; Batsis, Romero-Corral, et al. 2008; Batsis, Sarr, et al. 2008; Buchwald et al. 2004; Chevallier 2010; Courcoulas et al. 2013; Dixon et al. 2008; Evers, Sandoval, and Seeley 2017; Gadiot et al. 2017; Inge et al. 2019; O'Brien et al. 2013; Sjöström et al. 2004, 2014.
3. Andersen et al. 2015; Gribsholt et al. 2016.

4. Gribsholt et al. 2016; Groven 2014; Groven, Engelsrud, and Råheim 2012; Groven, Råheim, and Engelsrud 2010, 2013; Hiorth et al., 2019; Sjöström et al. 2004, 2014; Thereau et al. 2019.

5. Gribsholt et al. 2016; Groven 2014; Groven, Engelsrud, and Råheim 2012; Groven, Råheim, and Engelsrud 2010, 2013; Hiorth et al. 2019; Sjöström et al. 2004, 2014; Thereau et al. 2019.

6. Lim et al. 2018.

7. Lim et al. 2018.

8. Biltekoff 2013; Hayes-Conroy et al. 2014; Kimura et al. 2014; Trainer, Brewis, and Wutich 2017; Trainer, Wutich, and Brewis 2017.

9. LeBesco 2011; Lindsay 2010; Monaghan 2008; Nayar 2015; SturtzSreetharan et al. 2018.

10. Biltekoff 2013; Boero 2012; Bordo 1993; Foucault 1994, 2000; Hayes-Conroy et al. 2014; Kimura et al. 2014; Stover 2014; Vaz and Bruno 2003.

11. Biltekoff 2013; Boero 2012; Braziel and LeBesco 2001; Elliott 2010; Herndon 2005; LeBesco 2011; McCullough and Hardin 2013; Nichter 2000; Rogge 2004; Rothblum and Solovay 2009; Stover 2014; Tiggemann and Kuring 2004.

12. Trainer, Wutich, and Brewis 2017.

13. Beck 1992; Lupton 1993, 1995; Ogden 1995; Vaz and Bruno 2003.

14. Bell, McNaughton, and Salmon 2011; Elliott 2010; Farrell 2011; LeBesco 2011; McNaughton 2013; Monaghan 2008.

15. Batsis et al. 2009; Berg 2019; Bocchieri, Meana, and Fisher 2002; Boero 2010; Knutsen, Terragni, and Foss 2013; Meleo-Erwin 2019a, 2019b; Ogden, Clementi, and Aylwin 2006; SturtzSreetharan et al. 2018; Throsby 2008; Trainer, Brewis, and Wutich 2017.

16. Batsis et al. 2009; Bocchieri, Meana, and Fisher 2002; Boero 2010; Ogden, Clementi, and Aylwin 2006; Knutsen, Terragni, and Foss 2013; Throsby 2008; Trainer, Brewis, and Wutich 2017.

17. Bourdieu 1992, 1997; Manderson 2011.

18. Groven 2014; Groven, Engelsrud, and Råheim 2012; Groven, Råheim, and Engelsrud 2010, 2013.

19. Dalley, Toffanin, and Pollet 2012; Mann 2007; Pietiläinen et al. 2012.

20. Al-Khyatt et al. 2017; Burgmer et al. 2014; Sjöström et al. 2004, 2014.

21. Biltekoff 2013; Greenhalgh 2012; Hayes-Conroy et al. 2014; Kimura et al. 2014; LeBesco 2011; Lindsay 2010; Monaghan 2008; Nayar 2015.

22. Dalley, Toffanin, and Pollet 2012; Mann et al. 2007; Pietiläinen et al. 2012; Rothblum 2018.

23. Ahmed and Stacey 2001, 1.

24. Borgerson and Schroeder 2018; Hurst 2018; Lafrance 2018; Lafrance and Carey 2018; Le Breton 2018; Segal 2018; Skelly 2018.

25. Segal 2018, quoting Gide 1954, 263–264.

26. Aldaqal et al. 2013; Azin et al. 2014; Baillot et al. 2013; Giordano et al. 2013; Groven 2014; Groven, Engelsrud, and Råheim 2012; Groven, Råheim, and Engelsrud 2010, 2013; Gunnarson et al. 2015; Kitzinger et al. 2012; Meana and Ricciardi 2008;

Mitchell et al. 2008; Smith and Farrants 2013; Staalesen, Olsén, and Elander 2015; Throsby 2008, 2012; Wagenblast, Laessoe, and Printzlau 2014.

27. Mitchell et al. 2008.

28. Toma et al. 2018.

29. Aldaqal et al. 2013; Baillot et al. 2013; Giordano et al. 2013; Staalesen, Olsén, and Elander 2015; Wagenblast, Laessoe, and Printzlau 2014.

30. Aldaqal et al. 2013; Azin et al. 2014; Baillot et al. 2013; Giordano et al. 2013; Gunnarson et al. 2015; Kitzinger et al. 2012; Mitchell et al. 2008; Staalesen, Olsén, and Elander 2015; Wagenblast, Laessoe, and Printzlau 2014.

31. Manderson 2011.

32. Groven, Råheim, and Engelsrud 2013; Smith and Farrants 2013.

33. Manderson 2011.

34. Meana and Ricciardi 2008; Throsby 2008.

35. Segal 2018, quoting Gide 1954 [1931]: 263-264.

36. Almendrala 2017; Cocozza 2018; NBC News 2014.

37. Meleo-Erwin 2019a, 2019b; Thereau et al. 2019.

38. Meleo-Erwin 2019a, 2019b; Thereau et al. 2019.

39. Gribsholt et al. 2016; Hiorth et al. 2019; Inge et al. 2019; Thereau et al. 2019.

40. Inge et al. 2019.

41. For exceptions, see Adams et al. 2017; Andersen et al. 2015; Chevallier 2010; Gribsholt et al. 2016; Hiorth et al. 2019; O'Brien et al. 2013; Thereau et al. 2019.

CONCLUSION

1. Benedict 1934; Dressler 2017; Foucault 1977; Gideonse 2015; Harris 2015.

2. Foucault 1977; Gideonse 2015; Groven, Galdas, and Solbraekke 2015; Harris 2015; Lock and Nguyen 2010; Ong 2006; Warner 1999; Wolf-Meyer 2017.

APPENDIX A

1. Cassell 2005; Hunter et al. 2008; Hunter, Spence, and Scheinberg 2008; Jain and Jadhav 2009; Long, Hunter, and Van der Geest 2008; Rapp 1999; Warin 2003; Wind 2008.

2. Long, Hunter, and Van der Geest 2008.

3. No participants identified themselves to us as nonbinary.

4. Bernard, Wutich, and Ryan 2016.

5. Krippendorff 2012.

6. Following MacQueen et al. 1998; and Bernard, Wutich, and Ryan 2016.

7. Bernard, Wutich, and Ryan 2016.

8. Boeije 2002.

9. Wutich and Gravlee 2010.

10. Landis and Koch 1977.

APPENDIX B

1. Brewis et al. 2017; Raves et al. 2016.

# REFERENCES

Adams, T. D., L. E. Davidson, S. E. Litwin, J. Kim, R. L. Kolotkin, M. N. Nanjee, J. M. Gutierrez, S. J. Frogley, A. R. Ibele, E. A. Brinton, P. N. Hopkins, R. McKinlay, S. C. Simper, and S. C. Hunt. 2017. "Weight and Metabolic Outcomes 12 Years after Gastric Bypass." *New England Journal of Medicine* 377 (12): 1143–1155.

Adams, Vincanne. 2016. *Metrics: What Counts in Global Health.* Durham, NC: Duke University Press.

Agyemang, Priscilla, and Tiffany M. Powell-Wiley. 2013. "Obesity and Black Women: Special Considerations Related to Genesis and Therapeutic Approaches." *Current Cardiovascular Risk Reports* 7 (5): 378–386.

Ahmed, Sarah, and Jackie Stacey. 2001. *Thinking through the Skin.* New York: Routledge.

Aldaqal, Saleh M., Ahmad M. Makhdoum, Ali M. Turki, Basim A. Awan, Osama A. Samargandi, and Hytham Jamjom. 2013. "Post-Bariatric Surgery Satisfaction and Body-Contouring Consideration after Massive Weight Loss." *North American Journal of Medical Sciences* 5 (4): 301–305.

Al-Khyatt, Waleed, Rebecca Ryall, Paul Leeder, Javed Ahmed, and Sherif Awad. 2017. "Predictors of Inadequate Weight Loss after Laparoscopic Gastric Bypass for Morbid Obesity." *Obesity Surgery* 27 (6): 1446–1452.

Almendrala, Anna. 2017. "These Photos Show the Problem with Excess Skin after Extreme Weight Loss." *Huffington Post*, December 6, 2017. www.huffpost.com.

Andersen, J. R., A. Aasprang, T. I. Karlsen, G. K. Natvig, V. Vage, and R. L. Kolotkin. 2015. "Health Related Quality of Life after Bariatric Surgery: A Systematic Review of Prospective Long-Term Studies." *Surgery for Obesity and Related Diseases* 11 (2): 466–473.

Andersen, Margaret L., and Patricia Hill Collins, eds. 2001. *Race, Class, and Gender: An Anthology.* Blemont, CA: Wadsworth.

Applbaum, Kalman, and Michael Oldani. 2010. Introduction to "Towards an Era of Bureaucratically Controlled Medical Compliance?" Special issue. *Anthropology & Medicine* 17 (2): 113–127.

Ashrafian, Hutan, Tania Toma, Simon P. Rowland, Leanne Harling, Alan Tan, Evangelos Efthimiou, Ara Darzi, and Thanos Athanasiou. 2015. "Bariatric Surgery or Non-surgical Weight Loss for Obstructive Sleep Apnoea? A Systematic Review and Comparison of Meta-Analyses." *Obesity Surgery* 25 (7): 1239–1250.

ASMBS (American Society for Metabolic and Bariatric Surgery). 2019. "Estimate of Bariatric Surgery Numbers. 2011–2015." Accessed July 2019. https://asmbs.org.

Atkinson, Michael. 2014. "Masculinity on the Menu: Body Slimming and Self-Starvation as Physical Culture." In *Challenging Myths of Masculinity: Understanding Physical Cultures*, edited by L. Monaghan and M. Atkinson, 81–102. Aldershot, UK: Ashgate.

Azin, Arash, Carrol Zhou, Timothy Jackson, Stephanie Cassin, Sanjeev Sockalingam, and Raed Hawa. 2014. "Body Contouring Surgery after Bariatric Surgery: A Study of Cost as a Barrier and Impact on Psychological Well-Being." *Plastic and Reconstructive Surgery* 133 (6): 776e–782e.

Bailey, Moya. 2016. "Misogynoir in Medical Media: On Caster Semenya and R. Kelly." *Catalyst: Feminism, Theory, Technoscience* 2 (2). http://catalystjournal.org.

Baillot, A., M. Asselin, E. Comeau, A. Méziat-Burdin, and M.-F. Langlois. 2013. "Impact of Excess Skin from Massive Weight Loss on the Practice of Physical Activity in Women." *Obesity Surgery* 23 (11): 1826–1834.

Baker, M. T. 2011. "The History and Evolution of Bariatric Surgical Procedures." *Surgical Clinics of North America* 91 (6): 1181–1201.

Batsis, John A., Matthew M. Clark, Karen Grothe, Francisco Lopez-Jimenez, Maria L. Collazo-Clavell, Virend K. Somers, and Michael G. Sarr. 2009. "Self-Efficacy after Bariatric Surgery for Obesity: A Population-Based Cohort Study." *Appetite* 52 (3): 637–645.

Batsis, John A., Abel Romero-Corral, Maria L. Collazo-Clavell, Michael G. Sarr, Virend K. Somers, and Francisco Lopez-Jimenez. 2008. "Effect of Bariatric Surgery on the Metabolic Syndrome: A Population-Based, Long-Term Controlled Study." *Mayo Clinic Proceedings* 83 (8): 897–906.

Batsis, John A., Michael G. Sarr, Maria L. Collazo-Clavell, Randal J. Thomas, Abel Romero-Corral, Virend K. Somers, and Francisco Lopez-Jimenez. 2008. "Cardiovascular Risk after Bariatric Surgery for Obesity." *American Journal of Cardiology* 102 (7): 930–937.

Beck, Ulrich. 1992. *Risk Society*. London: Sage.

Becker, Anne E. 1995. *Body, Self, and Society: The View from Fiji*. Philadelphia: University of Pennsylvania Press.

———. 2004. "Television, Disordered Eating, and Young Women in Fiji: Negotiating Body Image and Identity during Rapid Social Change." *Culture, Medicine and Psychiatry* 28 (4): 533–559.

Bell, Kirsten, and Darlene McNaughton. 2007. "Feminism and the Invisible Fat Man." *Body & Society* 13 (1): 107–131.

Bell, Kirsten, Darlene McNaughton, and Amy Salmon, eds. 2011. *Alcohol, Tobacco, and Obesity: Morality, Mortality, and the New Public Health*. New York: Routledge.

Benedict, Ruth. 1934. "Anthropology and the Abnormal." *Journal of General Psychology* 10:59–82.

Bernard, H. Russell, Amber Wutich, and Gery W. Ryan. 2016. *Analyzing Qualitative Data: Systematic Approaches*. Thousand Oaks, CA: Sage.

Berg, Anita. 2019. "Untold Stories of Living with a Bariatric Body: Long-Term Experiences of Weight-Loss Surgery." *Sociology of Health and Illness* 42: 217–231.

Biltekoff, Charlotte. 2013. *Eating Right in America: The Cultural Politics of Food and Health*. Durham, NC: Duke University Press.

Birbeck, David, and Murray Drummond. 2006. "Understanding Boys' Bodies and Masculinity in Early Childhood." *International Journal of Men's Health* 5 (3): 238–250.

Bocchieri, Lindsey E., Marta Meana, and Barry L. Fisher. 2002. "Perceived Psychosocial Outcomes of Gastric Bypass Surgery: A Qualitative Study." *Obesity Surgery* 12 (6): 781–788.

Boeije, Hennie. 2002. "A Purposeful Approach to the Constant Comparative Method in the Analysis of Qualitative Interviews." *Quality and Quantity* 36 (4): 391–409.

Boero, Natalie. 2010. "Bypassing Blame: Bariatric Surgery and the Case of Biomedical Failure." In *Biomedicalization: Technoscience, Health and Illness in the U.S.*, edited by Laura Mamo, Adele E. Clarke, Jennifer R. Fosket, Jennifer R. Fishman, and Janet K. Shim, 307–330. Durham, NC: Duke University Press.

——. 2012. *Killer Fat: Media, Medicine, and Morals in the American "Obesity Epidemic."* New Brunswick, NJ: Rutgers University Press.

Bordo, Susan. 1993. *Unbearable Weight: Feminism, Western Culture, and the Body*. Berkeley: University of California Press.

——. 2013. "Not Just 'a White Girl's Thing': The Changing Face of Food and Body Image Problems." In *Food and Culture: A Reader*, 3rd ed., edited by C. Counihan and P. Van Esterik, 265–275. New York: Routledge.

Borgerson, Janet L., and Jonathan E. Schroeder. 2018. "Making Skin Visible: How Consumer Culture Imagery Commodifies Identity." *Body & Society* 24 (1–2): 103–136.

Boston University School of Medicine. 2018. "Race Plays Role in Regaining Weight after Gastric Bypass Surgery." *BU Medical Press*, November 15, 2018. https://medicalxpress.com.

Bourdieu, Pierre. 1984. *Distinction: A Social Critique of the Judgement of Taste*. Cambridge, MA: Harvard University Press.

——. 1992. "Structures, *Habitus*, Practices." In *The Logic of Practice*, translated by Richard Nice, 52–65. Stanford, CA: Stanford University Press.

——. 1997. "Bodily Knowledge." In *Pascalian Meditations*, translated by Richard Nice, 128–163. Stanford, CA: Stanford University Press.

Braziel, Jana E., and Kathleen LeBesco, eds. 2001. *Bodies Out of Bounds*. Berkeley: University of California Press.

Brewis, Alexandra. 2011. *Obesity: Cultural and Biocultural Perspectives*. New Brunswick, NJ: Rutgers University Press.

——. 2014. "Stigma and the Perpetuation of Obesity." *Social Science & Medicine* 118:152–158.

Brewis, Alexandra, Daniel Hruschka, and Amber Wutich. 2011. "Vulnerability to Fat-Stigma in Women's Everyday Relationships." *Social Science & Medicine* 73:491–497.

Brewis, Alexandra, Sarah Trainer, SeungYong Han, and Amber Wutich. 2017. "Publically Misfitting: Living with Extreme Weight and the Everyday Production and Reinforcement of Felt Stigma." *Medical Anthropology Quarterly* 31 (2): 257–276.

Brewis, Alexandra, Amber Wutich, Ashlan Falletta-Cowden, and Isa Rodriguez-Soto. 2011. "Body Norms and Fat Stigma in Global Perspective." *Current Anthropology* 52 (2): 269–276.

Bruff, Allison, Michael Mazzei, Satvajit Reddy, Rvaz Bashir, and Michael A. Edwards. 2018. "Contemporary Racial and Ethnic Disparities in Bariatric Surgery in the United States." *Surgery for Obesity and Related Diseases* 14 (11): S87.

Buchwald, Henry. 2014. "The Evolution of Metabolic/Bariatric Surgery." *Obesity Surgery* 24 (8): 1126–1135.

Buchwald, Henry, Yoav Avidor, Eugene Braunwald, Michael D. Jensen, Walter Pories, Kyle Fahrbach, and Karen Schoelles. 2004. "Bariatric Surgery: A Systematic Review and Meta-Analysis." *JAMA* 292 (14): 1724–1737.

Buchwald, Henry, and Stanley E. Williams. 2004. "Bariatric Surgery Worldwide 2003." *Obesity Surgery* 14 (9): 1157–1164.

Burgmer, R., T. Legenbauer, A. Muller, M. de Zwaan, C. Fischer, and S. Herpertz. 2014. "Psychological Outcomes 4 Years after Restrictive Bariatric Surgery." *Obesity Surgery* 24 (10): 1670–1678.

Burnham, Margaret. 2019. "Obesity Is a New Protected Class in Washington State." *SHRM*, July 16, 2019. www.shrm.org.

Butler, Judith. 1993. *Bodies That Matter: On the Discursive Limits of Sex*. New York: Routledge.

Bynum, Caroline Walker. 2012. "Fast, Feast, and Flesh: The Religious Significance of Food to Medieval Women." In *Food and Culture: A Reader*, 3rd ed., edited by C. Counihan and P. Van Esterik, 245–264. New York: Routledge.

Campo-Engelstein, Lisa. 2010a. "Consistency in Insurance Coverage for Iatrogenic Conditions Resulting from Cancer Treatment Including Fertility Preservation." *Journal of Clinic Oncology* 28 (8): 1284–1286.

———. 2010b. "For the Sake of Consistency and Fairness: Why Insurance Companies Should Cover Iatrogenic Infertility." *Oncofertility: Ethical, Legal, Social, and Medical Perspectives* 156:381–388.

Carryer, Jennifer B. 1997. "A Feminist Appraisal of the Experience of Embodied Largeness: A Challenge for Nursing." PhD diss., Massey University.

Cassell, Joan. 2005. *Life and Death in Intensive Care*. Philadelphia: Temple University Press.

CDC (Centers for Disease Control and Prevention). 2019a. "Adult Obesity Facts." Accessed July 2019. www.cdc.gov.

———. 2019b. "Defining Adult Overweight & Obesity." Accessed July 2019. www.cdc.gov.

———. 2019c. "Diabetes." Accessed July 2019. www.cdc.gov.

———. 2019d. "Health Disparities in Obesity." Accessed July 2019. www.cdc.gov.

———. 2019e. "Heart Disease." Accessed August 2019. www.cdc.gov/heartdisease.

———. 2019f. "High Blood Pressure." Accessed August 2019. www.cdc.gov.

———. 2019g. "Nutrition, Physical Activity, and Obesity: Data, Trends, and Maps." Accessed July 2019. www.cdc.gov.

————. 2019h. "Overweight & Obesity." Accessed July 2019. www.cdc.gov.

————. 2019i. "Tribal Health." Accessed August 2019. www.cdc.gov.

Celio, A. C., and W. J. Pories. 2016. "A History of Bariatric Surgery: The Maturation of a Medical Discipline." *Surgical Clinics of North America* 96 (4): 655–667.

Chakrabarti, Subho. 2014. "What's in a Name? Compliance, Adherence and Concordance in Chronic Psychiatric Disorders." *World Journal of Psychiatry* 4 (2): 30–36.

Chevallier, J. M. 2010. "From Bariatric to Metabolic Surgery: 15 Years Experience in a French University Hospital" (in French). *Bulletin de l'Academie Nationale de Medecine* 194 (1): 25–36.

Chouinard, Vera, Edward Hall, and Robert Wilton, eds. 2010. *Towards Enabling Geographies: 'Disabled' Bodies and Minds in Society and Space.* Farnham, UK: Ashgate.

Christiansen, Bjørg, Lisbet Borge, and May Solveig Fagermoen. 2012. "Understanding Everyday Life of Morbidly Obese Adults-Habits and Body Image." *International Journal of Qualitative Studies on Health and Well-Being* 7 (1): 17255.

Cocozza, Paula. 2018. "I Just Want to Cut it Off: The Weight-Loss Patients Who No Longer Fit Their Skin." *Guardian*, January 2, 2018. www.theguardian.com.

Colls, Rachel. 2006. "Outsize/Outside: Bodily Bignesses and the Emotional Experiences of British Women Shopping for Clothes." *Gender, Place and Culture* 13:529–545.

Colls, Rachel, and Bethan Evans. 2014. "Making Space for Fat Bodies? A Critical Account of 'the Obesogenic Environment.'" *Progress in Human Geography* 38 (6): 733–753.

Cooper, Charlotte. 1997. "Can a Fat Woman Call Herself Disabled?" *Disability and Society* 12 (1): 31–41.

Counihan, Carole. 1999. *The Anthropology of Food and Body: Gender, Meaning, and Power.* New York: Routledge.

Counihan, Carole, and Penny Van Esterik. 2013. *Food and Culture: A Reader.* 3rd ed. New York: Routledge.

Courcoulas, Anita P., Nicholas J. Christian, Steven H. Belle, Paul D. Berk, David R. Flum, Luis Garcia, Mary Horlick, Melissa A. Kalarchian, Wendy C. King, James E. Mitchell, Emma J. Patterson, John R. Pender, Alfons Pomp, Walter J. Pories, Richard C. Thirbly, Susan Z. Yanovski, and Bruce M. Wolfe. 2013. "Weight Change and Health Outcomes at 3 Years after Bariatric Surgery among Individuals with Severe Obesity." *JAMA* 310 (22): 2416–2425.

Crawshaw, Paul. 2007. "Governing the Healthy Male Citizen: Men, Masculinity, and Popular Health in *Men's Health* Magazine." *Social Science & Medicine* 65:1606–1618.

Dalley, Simon E., Paolo Toffanin, and Thomas V. Pollet. 2012. "Dietary Restraint in College Women: Fear of an Imperfect Fat Self Is Stronger than Hope of a Perfect Thin Self." *Body Image* 9 (4): 441–447.

Davis, Lennard. 2014. *The End of Normal: Identity in a Biocultural Era.* Ann Arbor: University of Michigan Press.

Denee, Marie. 2019. Home page. Accessed July 2019. www.mariedenee.com.

Dixon, John B., Paul E. O'Brien, Julie Playfair, Leon Chapman, Linda M. Schachter, Stewart Skinner, Joseph Proietto, Michael Bailey, and Margaret Anderson. 2008. "Adjustable Gastric Banding and Conventional Therapy for Type 2 Diabetes: A Randomized Controlled Trial." *JAMA* 299 (3): 316–323.

Dotinga, Randy. 2017. "Conference Coverage: Hispanics Trail Blacks, Whites in Bariatric Surgery Rates." *Clinical Endocrinology News*, November 22, 2017. www.mdedge.com/endocrinology.

Dressler, William W. 2017. *Culture and the Individual: Theory and Method of Cultural Consonance*. New York: Routledge.

Edmonds, Alexander. 2010. *Pretty Modern: Beauty, Sex, and Plastic Surgery in Brazil*. Durham, NC: Duke University Press.

Edmonds, Alexander, and Ashley Mears. 2017. "Managing Body Capital in the Fields of Labor, Sex, and Health." In *Fat Planet: Obesity, Culture, and Symbolic Body Capital*, edited by Eileen P. Anderson-Fye and Alexandra Brewis, 33–48. Albuquerque: University of New Mexico Press and SAR Press.

Edmonds, Alexander, and Emilia Sanabria. 2014. "Medical Borderlands: Engineering the Body with Plastic Surgery and Hormonal Therapies in Brazil." *Anthropology & Medicine* 21 (2): 202–216.

Elliott, C. D. 2010. "Kid Visible: Childhood Obesity, Body Surveillance, and the Techniques of Care." In *Surveillance: Power, Problems, and Politics*, edited by Sean P. Hier and Josh Greenberg, 33–45. Vancouver: UBC Press.

English, C. 1993. "Gaining and Losing Weight: Identity Transformations." *Deviant Behavior* 14 (3): 227–241.

Estroff, Susan. 1993. "Identity, Disability, and Schizophrenia: The Problem of Chronicity." In *Knowledge, Power, and Practice: The Anthropology of Medicine and Everyday Life*, edited by S. Lindenbaum and M. Lock, 247–286. Berkeley: University of California Press.

Evers, Simon S., Darleen A. Sandoval, and Randy J. Seeley. 2017. "The Physiology and Molecular Underpinnings of the Effects of Bariatric Surgery on Obesity and Diabetes." *Annual Review of Physiology* 79 (1): 313–334.

Fardouly, Jasmine, and Lenny R. Vartanian. 2012. "Changes in Weight Bias Following Weight Loss: The Impact of Weight-Loss Method." *International Journal of Obesity* 36 (2): 314–319.

Farrell, Amy E. 2011. *Fat Shame: Stigma and the Fat Body in American Culture*. New York: NYU Press.

Featherstone, Mike. 1982. "The Body in Consumer Culture." *Theory, Culture & Society* 1 (2): 18–33.

Ferzacca, Steve. 2010. "Chronic Illness and the Assemblages of Time in Multi-Sited Encounters." In *Chronic Conditions, Fluid States: Chronicity and the Anthropology of Illness*, edited by Lenore Manderson and Carolyn Smith-Morris, 157–174. New Brunswick, NJ: Rutgers University Press.

Fikken, Janna L., and Esther D. Rothblum. 2012. "Is Fat a Feminist Issue? Exploring the Gendered Nature of Weight Bias." *Sex Roles* 66 (9–10): 575–592.

Fitzgibbon, M. L., L. M. Tussing-Humphreys, J. S. Porter, I. K. Martin, A. Odoms-Young, and L. K. Sharp. 2012. "Weight Loss and African-American Women: A Systematic Review of the Behavioural Weight Loss Intervention Literature." *Obesity Reviews* 13 (3): 193–213.

Flegal, Katherine M., Margaret D. Carroll, Brian K. Kit, and Cynthia L. Ogden. 2012. "Prevalence of Obesity and Trends in the Distribution of Body Mass Index among US Adults, 1999–2010." *JAMA* 307 (5): 491–497.

Flegal, Katherine M., D. Kruszon-Moran, Margaret D. Carroll, C. D. Fryar, and Cynthia L. Ogden. 2016. "Trends in Obesity among Adults in the United States, 2005 to 2014." *JAMA* 315 (21): 2284–2291.

Foucault, Michel. 1977. *Discipline and Punish: The Birth of the Prison*. Translated by R. Sheridan. New York: Vintage Books.

———. 1994. *The Birth of the Clinic: An Archeology of Medical Perception*. Translated by R. Sheridan. New York: Vintage Books.

———. 2000. *The Essential Works of Michel Foucault, 1954–1984. Volume 3: Power*. Edited by J. Faubion, Translated by R. Hurley. New York: New Press.

Gadiot, Ralph P. M., L. Ulas Biter, Stefanie van Mil, Hans F. Zengerink, J. Apers, and Guido H. H. Mannaerts. 2017. "Long-Term Results of Laparoscopic Sleeve Gastrectomy for Morbid Obesity: 5 to 8-Year Results." *Obesity Surgery* 27 (1): 59–63.

Gao, Yan, DeMarc A. Hickson, Sameera Talegawkar, Arnita Ford Norwood, Katherine L. Tucker, Mario Sims, Ana V. Diez Roux, and Michael Griswold. 2019. "Influence of Individual Life Course and Neighbourhood Socioeconomic Position on Dietary Intake in African Americans: The Jackson Heart Study." *BMJ Open* 9:e025237.

Gard, Michael, and Jan Wright. 2005. *The Obesity Epidemic: Science, Morality, and Ideology*. New York: Routledge.

Garland-Thomson, Rosemarie. 2011. "Misfits: A Feminist Materialist Disability Concept." *Hypatia* 2 (3): 591–609.

Gay, Roxane. 2017. *Hunger: A Memoir of (My) Body*. New York: HarperCollins.

———. 2018. "What Fullness Is: On Getting Weigh Reduction Surgery." *Medium*, April 24, 2018. https://gay.medium.com.

Giddens, Anthony. 1991. *Modernity and Self Identity: Self and Society in the Late Modern Age*. Stanford, CA: Stanford University Press.

Gide, André. 1954. *Journal III: 1939–1949, Souvenirs*. Paris: Gallimard.

Gideonse, Theodore K. 2015. "Pride, Shame, and the Trouble with Trying to Be Normal." *Ethos* 43 (4): 332–352.

Gill, Rosalind, Karen Henwood, and Carl McLean. 2005. "Body Projects and the Regulation of Normative Masculinity." *Body and Society* 11 (1): 37–62.

Gimlin, Debra L. 2002. *Body Work: Beauty and Self-Image in American Culture*. Berkeley: University of California Press.

Giordano, Salvatore, Mikael Victorzon, Ilkka Koskivuo, and Erkki Suominen. 2013. "Physical Discomfort due to Redundant Skin in Post-Bariatric Surgery Patients." *Journal of Plastic, Reconstructive & Aesthetic Surgery* 66 (7): 950–955.

Gladwell, Malcolm. 2000. "The Pima Paradox." In *Nutritional Anthropology: Biocultural Perspectives on Food and Nutrition*, edited by Alan H. Goodman, Darna L. Dufour, and Gretel H. Pelto, 358–368. Mountain View, CA: Mayfield.

Goffman, Erving. 1963. *Stigma: Notes on the Management of Spoiled Identity*. New York: Simon and Schuster.

Granberg, Ellen M., Leslie G. Simons, and Ronald L. Simons. 2009. "Exploring a Body Image Paradox: The Impact of Family Racial Socialization on the Relationship between Body Size and Social Self Esteem among Adolescent African American Girls." *Youth and Society* 41 (2): 256–277.

Granberg, Ellen M., Ronald L. Simons, Frederick X. Gibbons, and Janet N. Melby. 2008. "The Relationship between Body Weight and Depressed Mood: Findings from a Sample of African American Middle School Girls." *Youth and Society* 39 (3): 294–315.

Greene, Jeremy A. 2004. "An Ethnography of Nonadherence: Culture, Poverty, and Tuberculosis in Urban Bolivia." *Culture, Medicine & Psychiatry* 28:401–425.

Greenhalgh, Susan. 2012. "Weighty Subjects: Biopolitics and the U.S. War on Fat." *American Ethnologist* 39 (3): 471–487.

Greenhalgh, Susan, and Megan Carney. 2014. "Bad Biocitizens? Latinos and the US 'Obesity Epidemic.'" *Human Organization* 73 (3): 267–276.

Gregg, Gabi. 2017. Home page. Accessed July 2017. http://gabifresh.com.

Gribsholt, S. B., A. M. Pedersen, E. Svensson, R. W. Thomsen, and B. Richelsen. 2016. "Prevalence of Self-Reported Symptoms after Gastric Bypass Surgery for Obesity." *JAMA Surgery* 151 (6): 504–511.

Grogan, Sarah, and Helen Richards. 2002. "Body Image: Focus Groups with Boys and Men." *Men and Masculinities* 4:219–232.

Groven, Karen Synne. 2014. "They Think Surgery Is Just a Quick Fix." *International Journal of Qualitative Studies on Health and Well-Being* 9 (1): 24378. www.tandfonline.com.

Groven, Karen Synne, Birgitte Ahlsen, and Steve Robertson. 2018. "Stories of Suffering and Success: Men's Embodied Narratives Following Bariatric Surgery." *Indo-Pacific Journal of Phenomenology* 18 (1): 1–14.

Groven, Karen Synne, Gunn Engelsrud, and Målfrid Råheim. 2012. "Living with Bodily Changes after Weight Loss Surgery: Women's Experiences of Food and 'Dumping.'" *Phenomenology & Practice* 6 (1): 36–54.

Groven, Karen Synne, Paul Galdas, and Kari Nyheim Solbraekke. 2015. "Becoming a Normal Guy: Men Making Sense of Long-Term Bodily Changes Following Bariatric Surgery." *Qualitative Studies on Health and Well-Being* 10:29923.

Groven, Karen Synne, Målfrid Råheim, and Gunn Engelsrud. 2010. "'My Quality of Life Is Worse Compared to My Earlier Life': Living with Chronic Problems after Weight Loss Surgery." *International Journal of Qualitative Studies on Health and Well-Being* 5 (4): 5553. www.tandfonline.com.

———. 2013. "Dis-Appearance and Dys-Appearance Anew: Living with Excess Skin and Intestinal Changes Following Weight Loss Surgery." *Medicine, Health Care and Philosophy* 16 (3): 507–523.

Guest, G., A. Bunce, and L. Johnson. 2006. "How Many Interviews Are Enough? An Experiment with Data Saturation and Variability." *Field Methods* 18 (1): 59–82.

Gunnarson, G. L., J. K. Frøyen, R. Sandbu, J. B. Thomsen, and J. Hjelmesæth. 2015. "Plastic Surgery after Bariatric Surgery." *Tidsskr Nor Laegeforen* 135 (11): 1044–1049.

Hakim, Catherine. 2010. "Erotic Capital." *European Sociological Review* 26 (5): 499–518.

Hardin, Jessica. 2016. "'Healing Is a Done Deal': Temporality and Metabolic Healing among Evangelical Christians in Samoa." *Medical Anthropology* 35 (2): 105–118.

———. 2019. *Faith and the Pursuit of Health: Cardiometabolic Disorders in Samoa*. New Brunswick, NJ: Rutgers University Press.

Hardin, Jessica, Amy K. McLennan, and Alexandra Brewis. 2018. "Body Size, Body Norms and Some Unintended Consequences of Obesity Intervention in the Pacific Islands." *Annals of Human Biology* 45 (3): 285–294.

Harris, Shana. 2015. "To Be Free and Normal: Addiction, Governance, and the Therapeutics of Buprenorphine." *Medical Anthropology Quarterly* 29 (4): 512–530.

Hatzenbuehler, Mark L., Jo C. Phelan, and Bruce G. Link. 2013. "Stigma as a Fundamental Cause of Population Health Inequalities." *American Journal of Public Health* 103 (5): 813–821.

Hayes-Conroy, Jessica, Adele Hite, Kendra Klein, Charlotte Biltekoff, and Aya H. Kimura. 2014. "Doing Nutrition Differently." *Gastronomica: The Journal of Critical Food Studies* 14 (3): 56–66.

Hebl, Michelle, and Julie Turchin. 2005. "The Stigma of Obesity: What About Men?" *Basic and Applied Social Psychology* 27 (3): 267–275.

Herndon, April Michelle. 2005. "Collateral Damage from Friendly Fire? Race, Nation, Class and the 'War against Obesity.'" *Social Semiotics* 15 (2): 127–141.

Hiller, D. V. 1982. "Overweight as Master Status: A Replication." *Journal of Psychology* 110 (1): 107–113.

Hiorth, S., I. Naslund, J.C. Andersson-Assarsson, P.A. Svensson, P. Jacobson, M. Peltonen, and L. M. S. Carlsson. 2019. "Reoperations after Bariatric Surgery in 26 Years of Follow-Up of the Swedish Obese Subjects Study." *JAMA Surgery* 154 (4): 319–326.

Hong, Young-Rock, Gregory Pavela, Alexandra M. Lee, Victoria G. Williamson, and Michelle I. Cardel. 2019. "Satisfaction with Health Care among Individuals with Overweight and Obesity: A Nationally Representative Cross-sectional Study." *Journal of General Internal Medicine* 34 (8): 1397–1399.

Horswill, C.A., H. M. Scott, and D. M. Voorhees. 2017. "Effect of a Novel Workstation Device on Promoting Non-Exercise Activity Thermogenesis (NEAT)." *Work* 58 (4): 273–287.

Howard, Heather A. 2018. "Settler Colonial Biogovernance and the Logic of a Surgical Cure for Diabetes." *American Anthropologist* 120 (4): 817–822.

Hruschka, D. J., and C. Hadley. 2016. "How Much Do Universal Anthropometric Standards Bias the Global Monitoring of Obesity and Undernutrition?" *Obesity Reviews* 17 (11): 1030–1039.

Hsu, William C., Maria Rosario G. Araneta, Alka M. Kanaya, Jane L. Chiang, and Wil-fred Fujimoto. 2015. "BMI Cut Points to Identify At-Risk Asian Americans for Type 2 Diabetes Screening." *Diabetes Care* 38 (1): 150–158.

Huang, Josie. 2013. "'Skinny Asian-American' Image Can Mask Obesity-Related Prob-lems, Physicians Say." *KPCC: Health*, October 28, 2013. www.scpr.org.

Hunter, Cynthia Louise, Kaye Spence, Kate McKenna, and Rick Iedema. 2008. "Learn-ing How We Learn: An Ethnographic Study in a Neonatal Intensive Care Unit." *Journal of Advanced Nursing* 62 (6): 657–664.

Hunter, Cynthia Louise, Kaye Spence, and Adam Scheinberg. 2008. "'Untangling the Web of Critical Incidents': Ethnography in a Paediatric Setting." *Anthropology & Medicine* 15 (2): 91–103.

Hurst, Rachel Alpha Johnston. 2018. "Collapsing the Surfaces of Skin and Photograph in Cosmetic Minimally-Invasive Procedures." *Body & Society* 24 (1–2): 175–192.

Inge, T. H., A. P. Courcoulas, T. M. Jenkins, M. P. Michalsky, M. L. Brandt, S. A. Xanthakos, J. B. Dixon, C. M. Harmon, M. K. Chen, C. Xie, M. E. Evans, M. A. Helmrath, and the Teen LABS Consortium. 2019. "Five-Year Outcomes of Gastric Bypass in Adolescents as Compared with Adults." *New England Journal of Medicine* 380 (22): 2136–2145.

Jain, Sumeet, and Sushrut Jadhav. 2009. "Pills That Swallow Policy: Clinical Ethnog-raphy of a Community Mental Health Program in Northern India." *Transcultural Psychiatry* 46 (1): 60–85.

Jutel, Annemarie. 2006. "The Emergence of Overweight as a Disease Entity: Measuring Up Normality." *Social Science & Medicine* 63:2268–2276.

Kim, Young-Joo, and Vincent Daly. 2019. "The Education Gradient in Health: The Case of Obesity in the UK and US." Economics Discussion Papers, School of Law, Social and Behavioural Sciences, Kingston University, Kingston upon Thames, UK.

Kimura, Aya H., Charlotte Biltekoff, Jessica Mudry, and Jessica Hayes-Conroy. 2014. "Nutrition as a Project." *Gastronomica: The Journal of Critical Food Studies* 14 (3): 34–45.

Kinzel, Lesley. 2018. "Nobody Owes You Fat Positivity: On Weight Loss Surgery as 'Betrayal.'" *Medium*, April 27, 2018. https://medium.com.

Kirkland, Anna. 2008. *Fat Rights: Dilemmas of Difference and Personhood*. New York: NYU Press.

Kitzinger, Hugo B., Sara Abayev, Anna Pittermann, Birgit Karle, Harald Kubiena, Arthur Bohdjalian, Felix B. Langer, Gerhard Prager, and Manfred Frey. 2012. "The Prevalence of Body Contouring Surgery after Gastric Bypass Surgery." *Obesity Surgery* 22 (1): 8–12.

Knutsen, Ingrid Ruud, Laura Terragni, and Christina Foss. 2013. "Empowerment and Bariatric Surgery: Negotiations of Credibility and Control." *Qualitative Health Research* 23 (1): 66–77.

Koliaki, Chrysi, Stavros Liatis, Carel W. le Roux, and Alexander Kokkinos. 2017. "The Role of Bariatric Surgery to Treat Diabetes: Current Challenges and Perspectives." *BMC Endocrine Disorders* 17 (1): art. 50.

Krippendorff, K. 2012. *Content Analysis: An Introduction to its Methodology.* Thousand Oaks, CA: Sage.

Kulick, Don, and Anne Meneley. 2005. *Fat: The Anthropology of Obsession.* New York: Penguin.

Kyryliuk, Rebecca, Meghan Baruth, and Sara Wilcox. 2015. "Predictors of Weight Loss for African American Women in the Faith, Activity, and Nutrition (FAN) Study." *Journal of Physical Activity & Health* 12 (5): 659–665.

Lafrance, Marc. 2018. "Skin Stories: Past, Present, and Future." *Body & Society* 24 (1–2): 3–32.

Lafrance, Marc, and R. Scott Carey. 2018. "Skin Work: Understanding the Embodied Experience of Acne." *Body & Society* 24 (1–2): 55–87.

Landis, J. R., and G. G. Koch. 1977. "An Application of Hierarchical Kappa-Type Statistics in the Assessment of Majority Agreement among Multiple Observers." *Biometrics* 33 (2): 363–374.

LeBesco, Kathleen. 2011. "Neoliberalism, Public Health, and the Moral Perils of Fatness." *Critical Public Health* 21 (2): 153–164.

Le Breton, David. 2018. "Understanding Skin-Cutting in Adolescence: Sacrificing a Part to Save the Whole." *Body & Society* 24 (1–2): 33–54.

Lee, Jennifer A., and Cat J. Pause. 2016. "Stigma in Practice: Barriers to Health for Fat Women." *Frontiers in Psychology* 7 (2063): 1–15.

Le Guin, Ursula K. 2015. *Steering the Craft: A 21st-Century Guide to Sailing the Sea of Story.* New York: HarperCollins.

Leung, S. L., J. A. Barber, A. Burger, and R. D. Barnes. 2018. "Factors Associated with Healthy and Unhealthy Workplace Eating Behaviours in Individuals with Overweight/Obesity with and without Binge Eating Disorder." *Obesity Science & Practice* 4 (2): 109–118.

Levine, James A. 2007. "Nonexercise Activity Thermogenesis—Liberating the Life-Force." *Journal of Internal Medicine* 262 (3): 273–287.

Lewis, Sophie, Samantha L. Thomas, R. Warwick Blood, David J. Castle, Jim Hyde, and Paul A. Komesaroff. 2011. "How Do Obese Individuals Perceive and Respond to the Different Types of Obesity Stigma That They Encounter in Their Daily Lives? A Qualitative Study." *Social Science & Medicine* 73 (9): 1349–1356.

Lilleleht, Erica. 2002. "Progress and Power: Exploring the Disciplinary Connections between Moral Treatment and Psychiatric Rehabilitation." *Philosophy, Psychiatry, and Psychology* 9 (2): 167–182.

Lim, Robert, Alec Beekley, Dirk C. Johnson, and Kimberly A. Davis. 2018. "Early and Late Complications of Bariatric Operation." *Trauma Surgery & Acute Care Open* 3:e000219.

Lindsay, Jo. 2010. "Healthy Living Guidelines and the Disconnect with Everyday Life." *Critical Public Health* 20 (4): 475–487.

Link, Bruce G., and Jo C. Phelan. 2001. "Conceptualizing Stigma." *Annual Review of Sociology* 27 (1): 363–385.

———. 2006. "Stigma and Its Public Health Implications." *Lancet* 367 (9509): 528–529.

Livingston, Kathy. 2000. "When Architecture Disables: Teaching Undergraduates to Perceive Ableism in the Built Environment." *Teaching Sociology* 28 (3): 182–191.

Lock, Margaret, and Patricia Kaufert. 2001. "Menopause, Local Biologies, and Cultures of Aging." *American Journal of Human Biology* 13 (4): 494–504.

Lock, Margaret, and Vinh-Kim Nguyen. 2010. *An Anthropology of Biomedicine.* Malden, MA: Blackwell.

Long, Debbi, Cynthia Hunter, and Sjaak Van der Geest. 2008. "When the Field Is a Ward or a Clinic: Hospital Ethnography." *Anthropology & Medicine* 15 (2): 71–78.

Lorde, Audre. 1999. "A Burst of Light: Living with Cancer." In *Feminist Theory and the Body: A Reader,* edited by Janet Price and Margrit Shildrek, 149–152. New York: Routledge.

Lupton, Deborah. 1993. "Risk as Moral Danger: The Social and Political Functions of Risk Discourse in Public Health." *International Journal of Health Services* 23 (3): 425–435.

———. 1995. *The Imperative of Health: Public Health and the Regulated Body.* London: Sage.

———. 2012. *Fat.* New York: Routledge.

MacQueen, Kathleen M., Eleanor McLellan, Kelly Kay, and Bobby Milstein. 1998. "Codebook Development for Team-Based Qualitative Analysis." *Cultural Anthropology Methods* 10 (2): 31–36.

Manderson, Lenore. 2011. *Surface Tensions: Surgery, Bodily Boundaries, and the Social Self.* San Francisco: Left Coast.

Manderson, Lenore, and Carolyn Smith-Morris, eds. 2010. *Chronic Conditions, Fluid States: Chronicity and the Anthropology of Illness.* New Brunswick, NJ: Rutgers University Press.

Manderson, Lenore, and Narelle Warren. 2016. "'Just One Thing after Another': Recursive Cascades and Chronic Conditions." *Medical Anthropology Quarterly* 30 (4): 479–497.

Mann, Traci, A. Janet Tomiyama, Erika Westling, Ann-Marie Lew, Barbra Samuels, and Jason Chatman. 2007. "Medicare's Search for Effective Obesity Treatments: Diets Are Not the Answer." *American Psychologist* 62 (3): 220–233.

Martin, Emily. 1992. *The Woman in the Body: A Cultural Analysis of Reproduction.* 2nd ed. Boston: Beacon.

Martin, Jack K., Annie Lang, and Sigrun Olafsdottir. 2008. "Rethinking Theoretical Approaches to Stigma: A Framework Integrating Normative Influences on Stigma (FINIS)." *Social Science & Medicine* 67 (3): 431–440.

Mattingly, Brent A., Mark A. Stambush, and Ashley E. Hill. 2009. "Shedding the Pounds but Not the Stigma: Negative Attributions as a Function of a Target's Method of Weight Loss." *Journal of Applied Biobehavioral Research* 14 (3): 128–144.

Mayo Clinic. 2019a. "Nonalcoholic Fatty Liver Disease." Accessed July 2019. www.mayoclinic.org.

———. 2019b. "Sleep Apnea." Accessed July 2019. www.mayoclinic.org.

McClure, Stephanie. 2013. "'It's Just Gym': Physicality and Identity among African American Adolescent Girls." PhD diss., Case Western Reserve University.

McCreary, Don, and Doris Sasse. 2000. "An Exploration of the Drive for Muscularity in Adolescent Boys and Girls." *Journal of American College Health* 48:197–304.

McCullough, Megan B., and Jessica A. Hardin, eds. 2013. *Reconstructing Obesity: The Meaning of Measures and the Measure of Meanings.* New York: Berghahn Books.

McLean, Kendall, Carolyn E. Moore, Derek C. Miketinas, and Catherine M. Champagne. 2018. "Comparison of Dietary Habits and Plans for Dietary Changes in Black and White Women Seeking Bariatric Surgery." *Surgery for Obesity and Related Diseases* 14 (1): 106–111.

McLellan, Eleanor, Kathleen M. MacQueen, and Judith L. Neidig. 2003. "Beyond the Qualitative Interview: Data Preparation and Transcription. *Field Methods* 15 (1): 63–84.

McMillan Cottom, Tressie. 2019. *Thick and Other Essays.* New York: New Press.

McNaughton, Darlene. 2013. "'Diabesity' Down Under: Overweight and Obesity as Cultural Signifiers for Type 2 Diabetes Mellitus." *Critical Public Health* 23 (3): 274–288.

Meana, Marta, and Lindsey Ricciardi. 2008. *Obesity Surgery: Stories of Altered Lives.* Reno: University of Nevada Press.

Medaris Miller, Anna. 2016. "Asians and Obesity: Looks Can Be Deceiving." *US News: Wellness*, March 11, 2016. https://health.usnews.com.

Meleo-Erwin, Zoë C. 2015. "'Shape Carries Story': Navigating the World as Fat." *Media/Culture Journal* 18 (3). http://journal.media-culture.org.au.

———. 2019a. "'No One Is as Invested in Your Continued Good Health as You Should Be': An Exploration of the Post-surgical Relationships between Weight-Loss Surgery Patients and Their Home Bariatric Clinics." *Sociology of Health and Illness* 41 (2): 285–302.

———. 2019b. "Risks and Responsibility: Navigating the Long-Term Care of Bariatric Patients." *Sociology Lens*, September 6, 2019. www.sociologylens.net.

Merleau-Ponty, Maurice. 1962. *Phenomenology of Perception.* Translated by Colin Smith. New York: Routledge.

Metraux, Julia. 2019. "The Body Positivity Movement Is Nothing without Fat Acceptance." *Tempest*, January 17, 2019.

Mitchell, James E., Ross D. Crosby, Troy W. Ertelt, Joanna M. Marino, David B. Sarwer, J. Kevin Thompson, Kathryn L. Lancaster, Heather Simonich, and L. Michael Howell. 2008. "The Desire for Body Contouring Surgery after Bariatric Surgery." *Obesity Surgery* 18 (10): art. 1308.

Monaghan, Lee. 2007. "Body Mass Index, Masculinities, and Moral Worth: Men's Critical Understandings of 'Appropriate' Weight-for-Height." *Sociology of Health and Illness* 29:584–609.

———. 2008. *Men and the War on Obesity: A Sociological Study.* New York: Routledge.

Mrig, Emily Hammad, and Karen Lutfey Spencer. 2018. "Political Economy of Hope as a Cultural Facet of Biomedicalization: A Qualitative Examination of Constraints to Hospice Utilization among U.S. Endstage Cancer Patients." *Social Science & Medicine* 200:107–113.

Mull, Amanda. 2018. "Body Positivity Is a Scam." *Vox*, June 5, 2018. www.vox.com.

Murray, Stuart, and Stephen Touyz. 2012. "Masculinity, Femininity and Male Body Image: A Recipe for Future Research." *International Journal of Men's Health* 11 (3): 227–239.

Muttarak, Raya. 2018. "Normalization of Plus Size and the Danger of Unseen Overweight and Obesity in England." *Obesity* 26 (7): 1125–1129.

Mykhalovskiy, Eric, Liza Mccoy, and Michael Bresalier. 2004. "Compliance/Adherence, HIV, and the Critique of Medical Power." *Social Theory & Health* 2:315–340.

Nakayama, Thomas K., and Judith N. Martin, eds. 1999. *Whiteness: The Communication of Social Identity*. Thousand Oaks, CA: Sage.

Nash, Jennifer C. 2011. "Practicing Love: Black Feminism, Love-Politics, and Post-Intersectionality." *Meridians* 11:1–24.

Natvik, Eli, Eva Gjengedal, Christian Moltu, and Målfrid Råheim. 2015. "Translating Weight Loss Surgery into Agency: Men's Experiences 5 Years after Bariatric Surgery." *International Journal of Qualitative Studies on Health and Well-Being* 10:27729.

Nayar, Pramod K. 2015. *Citizenship and Identity in the Age of Surveillance*. Delhi, India: Cambridge University Press.

NBC News. 2014. "After Huge Weight Loss, Sagging Skin Remains." March 6, 2014. www.nbcnews.com.

Ng, Janet, Richard Seip, Andrea Stone, Gualberto Ruano, Darren Tishler, and Pavlos Papasavas. 2015. "Ethnic Variation in Weight Loss, but Not Co-morbidity Remission, after Laparoscopic Gastric Banding and Roux-en-Y Gastric Bypass." *Surgery for Obesity and Related Diseases* 11 (1): 94–100.

Nichter, Mimi. 2000. *Fat Talk: What Girls and their Parents Say about Dieting*. Cambridge, MA: Harvard University Press.

NIDDK (National Institute of Diabetes and Digestive and Kidney Disorders). 2016. "Definition and Facts for Bariatric Surgery." www.niddk.nih.gov.

Norman, Moss. 2013. "'Dere's Not Just One Kind of Fat': Embodying the 'Skinny' Self through Constructions of the Fat Masculine Other." *Men and Masculinities* 16 (4): 407–431.

O'Brien, P. E., L. MacDonald, M. Anderson, L. Brennan, and W. A. Brown. 2013. "Long-Term Outcomes after Bariatric Surgery: Fifteen-Year Follow-Up of Adjustable Gastric Banding and a Systematic Review of the Bariatric Surgical Literature." *Annals of Surgery* 257 (1): 87–94.

Ogden, Jane. 1995. "Psychosocial Theory and the Creation of the Risky Self." *Social Science & Medicine* 40 (3): 409–415.

Ogden, Jane, Cecilia Clementi, and Simon Aylwin. 2006. "The Impact of Obesity Surgery and the Paradox of Control: A Qualitative Study." *Psychology & Health* 21 (2): 273–293.

Ong, Aihwa. 2006. *Neoliberalism as Exception: Mutations in Citizenship and Sovereignty*. Durham, NC: Duke University Press.

Orbach, Sue. 1978. *Fat Is a Feminist Issue: A Self-Help Guide for Compulsive Eaters.* New York: Paddington.

Parasecoli, Fabio. 2013. "Feeding Hard Bodies: Food and Masculinities in Men's Fitness Magazines." In *Food and Culture: A Reader,* 3rd edited by C. Counihan and P. Van Esterik, 284–298. New York: Routledge.

Patterson-Faye, Courtney J. 2014. "Plus Size Black and Latino Women: The Implications of Body Shape and Size for Apparel Design." In *Designing Apparel for Consumers: The Impact of Body Shape and Size,* edited by Marie-Eve Faust and Serge Carrier, 256–272. Philadelphia: Woodhead.

———. 2016. "'I Like the Way You Move': Theorizing Fat, Black and Sexy." *Sexualities* 19 (8): 926–944.

Pescosolido, Bernice A. 2013. "The Public Stigma of Mental Illness: What Do We Think; What Do We Know; What Can We Prove?" *Journal of Health and Social Behavior* 45 (1): 1–21.

Petersen, Alan, and Robin Bunton, eds. 1997. *Foucault, Health, and Medicine.* New York: Routledge.

Pietiläinen, K. H., S. E. Saarni, J. Kaprio, and A. Rissanen. 2012. "Does Dieting Make You Fat? A Twin Study." *International Journal of Obesity* 36 (3): 456–464.

Pollack, Andrew. 2013. "AMA Recognizes Obesity as a Disease." *New York Times,* June 18, 2013. www.nytimes.com.

Pollan, Michael. 2008. *In Defense of Food: An Eater's Manifesto.* New York: Penguin.

Popenoe, Rebecca. 2004. *Feeding Desire: Fatness, Beauty and Sexuality among a Saharan People.* New York: Routledge.

Puhl, Rebecca M., and Chelsea A. Heuer. 2009. "The Stigma of Obesity: A Review and Update." *Obesity* 17 (5): 941–964.

———. 2010. "Obesity Stigma: Important Considerations for Public Health." *American Journal of Public Health* 100 (6): 1019–1028.

Rapp, Rayna. 1999. *Testing Women, Testing the Fetus: The Social Impact of Amniocentesis in America.* New York: Routledge.

Raves, D. M., A. Brewis, S. Trainer, S. Y. Han, and A. Wutich. 2016. "Bariatric Surgery Patients' Perceptions of Weight-Related Stigma in Healthcare Settings Impair Postsurgery Dietary Adherence." *Frontiers in Psychology* 7:1497. www.frontiersin.org.

Reischer, Erica, and Kathryn S. Koo. 2004. "The Body Beautiful: Symbolism and Agency in the Social World." *Annual Review of Anthropology* 33:297–317.

Ristovski-Slijepcevic, Svetlana, Kirsten Bell, Gwen E. Chapman, and Brenda L. Beagan. 2010. "Being 'Thick' Indicates You Are Eating, You Are Healthy and You Have an Attractive Body Shape: Perspectives on Fatness and Food Choice amongst Black and White Men and Women in Canada." *Health Sociology Review* 19 (3): 317–329.

Robinson, S. A., J. B. Webb, and P. T. Butler-Ajibade. 2012. "Body Image and Modifiable Weight Control Behaviors among Black Females: A Review of the Literature." *Obesity* 20 (2): 241–252.

Rogge, Mary Madeline. 2004. "Obesity, Stigma, and Civilized Oppression." *Advances in Nursing Science* 27 (4): 301–315.

Rose, Nikolas, and Carlos Novas. 2007. "Biological Citizenship." In *Global Assemblages: Technology, Politics, and Ethics as Anthropological Problems*, edited by Aihwa Ong and Stephen J. Collier, 439–463. New York: Routledge.

Rothblum, Esther D. 2018. "Slim Chance for Permanent Weight Loss." *Archives of Scientific Psychology* 6 (1): 63–69.

Rothblum, Esther D., and Sondra Solovay, eds. 2009. *The Fat Studies Reader*. New York: NYU Press.

Rubino, Francesco, Ricardo V. Cohen, Geltrude Mingrone, Carel W. le Roux, Jeffrey I. Mechanick, David E. Arterburn, Josep Vidal, George Alberti, Stephanie A. Amiel, Rachel L. Batterham, Stefan Bornstein, Ghassan Chamseddine, Stefano Del Prato, John B. Dixon, Robert H. Eckel, David Hopkins, Barbara M. McGowan, An Pan, Ameet Patel, Francois Pattou, Philip R. Schauer, Paul Z. Zimmet, and David E. Cummings. 2020. "Bariatric and Metabolic Surgery during and after the COVID-19 Pandemic: DSS Recommendations for Management of Surgical Candidates and Postoperative Patients and Prioritisation of Access to Surgery." *Lancet* 8 (7): P640–648.

Sabin, Janice A., Maddalena Marini, and Brian A. Nosek. 2012. "Implicit and Explicit Anti-fat Bias among a Large Sample of Medical Doctors by BMI, Race/Ethnicity and Gender." *PLoS ONE* 7 (11): e48448. http://journals.plos.org.

Saguy, Abigail C. 2014. *What's Wrong with Fat?* Oxford: Oxford University Press.

Scheper-Hughes, Nancy, and Margaret Lock. 1987. "The Mindful Body: A Prolegomenon to Future Work in Medical Anthropology." *Medical Anthropology Quarterly* 1 (1): 6–14.

Segal, Naomi. 2018. "'A Petty Form of Suffering': A Brief Cultural Study of Itching." *Body & Society* 24 (1–2): 88–102.

Shange, Ntozake. 1975. *For Colored Girls Who Have Considered Suicide / When the Rainbow Is Enuf: A Choreopoem*. New York: Simon and Schuster.

Shildrick, Margrit, and Janet Price. 1998. *Vital Signs: Feminist Reconfigurations of the Bio/logical Body*. Edinburgh: Edinburgh University Press.

Sjöström, Lars, Anna-Karin Lindroos, Markku Peltonen, Jarl Torgerson, Claude Bouchard, Björn Carlsson, and Sven Dahlgren. 2004. "Lifestyle, Diabetes, and Cardiovascular Risk Factors 10 Years after Bariatric Surgery." *New England Journal of Medicine* 351 (26): 2683–2693.

Sjöström, Lars, Markku Peltonen, Peter Jacobson, Sofie Ahlin, Johanna Andersson-Assarsson, Åsa Anveden, and Claude Bouchard. 2014. "Association of Bariatric Surgery with Long-Term Remission of Type 2 Diabetes and with Microvascular and Macrovascular Complications." *JAMA* 311 (22): 2297–2304.

Skelly, Julia. 2018. "Skin and Scars: Probing the Visual Culture of Addiction." *Body & Society* 24 (1–2): 193–209.

Smith, Fran, and Jacqui R. Farrants. 2013. "Shame and Self-Acceptance in Continued Flux: Qualitative Study of the Embodied Experience of Significant Weight Loss and Removal of Resultant Excess Skin by Plastic Surgery." *Journal of Health Psychology* 18 (9): 1129–1140.

Smith-Morris, Carolyn. 2005. "Diagnostic Controversy: Gestational Diabetes and the Meaning of Risk for Pima Indian Women." *Medical Anthropology* 24 (2): 145–177.

———. 2006. *Diabetes among the Pima: Stories of Survival.* Tucson: University of Arizona Press.

Sobal, Jeffery, and Donna Maurer, eds. 1999. *Interpreting Weight: The Social Management of Fatness and Thinness.* New York: Walter de Gruyter.

Solomon, Harris. 2016. *Metabolic Living: Food, Fat, and the Absorption of Illness in India.* Durham, NC: Duke University Press.

Soto, Sandra H., Elva M. Arredondo, Holly B. Shakva, Scott Roesch, Bess Marcus, Humberto Parada Jr., and Guadalupe X. Avala. 2019. "Family Environment, Children's Acculturation and Mothers' Dietary Intake and Behaviors among Latinas: An Autoregressive Cross-Lagged Study." *Social Science & Medicine* 228:93–102.

Spencer, Karen Lutfey. 2018. "Transforming Patient Compliance Research in an Era of Biomedicalization." *Journal of Health and Social Behavior* 59 (2): 170–184.

Spitzack, Carole. 1990. *Confessing Excess: Women and the Politics of Body Reduction.* Albany: SUNY Press.

Springfield, Sparkle, Joanna Buscemi, Marian L. Fitzgibbon, Melinda R. Stolley, Shannon N. Zenk, Linda Schiffer, Jameika Sampson, Quiana Jones, Tanine Murdock, Iona Davis, Loys Holland, April Watkins, and Angela Odoms-Young. 2015. "A Randomized Pilot Study of a Community-Based Weight Loss Intervention for African-American Women: Rationale and Study Design of Doing Me! Sisters Standing Together for a Healthy Mind and Body." *Contemporary Clinical Trials* 43:200–208.

Staalesen, Trude, Monika Fagevik Olsén, and Anna Elander. 2015. "The Effect of Abdominoplasty and Outcome of Rectus Fascia Plication on Health-Related Quality of Life in Post–Bariatric Surgery Patients." *Plastic and Reconstructive Surgery* 136 (6): 750e–761e.

Stanford, Fatima Cody, Daniel B. Jones, Benjamin E. Schneider, George L. Blackburn, Caroline M. Apovian, Donald T. Hess, Sarah Chiodi, Shirley Robert, Ashley C. Bourland, and Christina C. Wee. 2015. "Patient Race and the Likelihood of Undergoing Bariatric Surgery among Patients Seeking Surgery." *Surgical Endoscopy* 29 (9): 2794–2799.

Stanford Health Care. 2019. "Hyperlipidemia." Accessed July 2019. https://stanford-healthcare.org.

Stoll, Laurie Cooper. 2019. "Fat Is a Social Justice Issue, Too." *Humanity & Society* 43:421–441.

Stover, Cassandra. 2014. "'Divulging the Eat Deets': Postfeminist Self-Surveillance on Women's Fitness Blogs." Thinking Gender Papers with the UCLA Center for the Study of Women, Los Angeles.

SturtzSreetharan, Cindi, Sarah Trainer, Amber Wutich, and Alexandra Brewis. 2018. "Moral Biocitizenship: Discursively Managing Food and the Body after Bariatric Surgery." *Journal of Linguistic Anthropology* 28 (2): 221–240.

SWNS. 2019. "Your Office Job Might Be Making You Fat." *New York Post.* June 11, 2019. https://nypost.com.

Tait, Melanie, and Alexis Sugden. 2018. "I Had 85% of My Stomach Cut Out. Am I a Traitor?" *Nib*, March 9, 2018. https://thenib.com.

Talukdar, Jaita. 2012. "Thin but Not Skinny: Women Negotiating the 'Never Too Thin' Body Ideal in Urban India." *Women's Studies International Forum* 35 (2): 109–118.

Taylor, Nicole. 2015. *Schooled on Fat: What Teens Tell Us about Gender, Body Image, and Obesity*. New York: Routledge.

Thereau, Jeremie, Thomas Lesuffleur, Sebastian Czernichow, Arnaud Basdevant, Simon Miska, David Nocca, Bertrand Millat, and Anne Fagot-Campagna. 2019. "Long-Term Adverse Events after Sleeve Gastrectomy or Gastric Bypass: A 7-Year Nation-wide, Observational, Population-Based, Cohort Study." *Lancet* 7 (10): 786–795.

Throsby, Karen. 2008. "Happy Re-birthday: Weight-Loss Surgery and the 'New Me.'" *Body & Society* 14 (1): 117–133.

———. 2012. "Obesity Surgery and the Management of Excess: Exploring the Body Multiple." *Sociology of Health and Illness* 34 (1): 1–15.

Tiggemann, Marika, and Julia K. Kuring. 2004. "The Role of Body Objectification in Disordered Eating and Depressed Mood." *British Journal of Clinical Psychology* 43 (3): 299–311.

Toma, Tania, Leanne Harling, Thanos Athanasiou, Ara Darzi, and Hutan Ashra-fian. 2018. "Does Body Contouring after Bariatric Weight Loss Enhance Quality of Life? A Systematic Review of QOL Studies." *Obesity Surgery* 28 (10): 3333–3341.

Townsend, Nicholas W. 2002. *The Package Deal: Marriage, Work, and Fatherhood in Men's Lives*. Philadelphia: Temple University Press.

Trainer, Sarah. 2012. "Negotiating Weight and Body Image in the UAE: Strategies among Young Emirati Women." Special issue. *American Journal of Human Biology* 24:314–324.

Trainer, Sarah, and Tonya Benjamin. 2017. "Elective Surgery to Save My Life: Rethink-ing the 'Choice' in Bariatric Surgery." *Journal of Advanced Nursing* 73 (4): 894–904.

Trainer, Sarah, Alexandra Brewis, Daniel Hruschka, and Deborah Williams. 2015. "Translating Obesity: Navigating the Front Lines of the 'War on Fat.'" *American Journal of Human Biology* 27 (1): 61–68.

Trainer, Sarah, Alexandra Brewis, Deborah Williams, and Jose Rosales Chavez. 2015. "Obese, Fat, or 'Just Big'? Young Adult Deployment of and Reactions to Weight Terms." *Human Organization* 74 (3): 266–275.

Trainer, Sarah, Alexandra Brewis, and Amber Wutich. 2017. "Not 'Taking the Easy Way Out': Reframing Bariatric Surgery from Low-Effort Weight Loss to Hard Work." *Anthropology & Medicine* 24 (1): 96–110.

Trainer, Sarah, Amber Wutich, and Alexandra Brewis. 2017. "Eating in the Panopti-con: Surveillance of Food and Weight before and after Bariatric Surgery." *Medical Anthropology* 36 (5): 500–514.

Trostle, James A. 1997. "The History and Meaning of Patient Compliance as an Ideol-ogy." In *Handbook of Health Behavior Research II*, edited by David S. Gochman, 109–124. New York: Springer.

Tucci, Sonia A., Emma J. Boyland, Jason C. G. Halford, and Joanne A. Harrold. 2013. "Stigmatisation of a Formerly Obese Young Female." *Obesity Facts* 6 (5): 433–442.

Turner, Bryan S. 1982. "The Discourse of Diet." *Theory, Culture & Society* 1 (1): 23–32.

———. 1984. *The Body and Society: Explorations in Social Theory*. Thousand Oaks, CA: Sage.

Umemura, A., W. J. Lee, A. Sasaki, and G. Wakabayashi. 2015. "History and Current Status of Bariatric and Metabolic Surgeries in East Asia." *Asian Journal of Endoscopic Surgery* 8 (3): 268–274.

Uranga, Romina María, and Jeffrey Neil Keller. 2019. "The Complex Interactions between Obesity, Metabolism and the Brain." *Frontiers in Neuroscience* 13:513.

Vartanian, Lenny R., and Jasmine Fardouly. 2013. "The Stigma of Obesity Surgery: Negative Evaluations Based on Weight Loss History." *Obesity Surgery* 23 (10): 1545–1550.

Vaz, Paulo, and Fernanda Bruno. 2003. "Types of Self-Surveillance: From Abnormality to Individuals 'At Risk.'" *Surveillance & Society* 1 (3): 272–291.

Vogel, Else. 2018. "Operating (on) the Self: Transforming Agency through Obesity Surgery and Treatment." *Sociology of Health & Illness* 40 (3): 508–522.

Wagenblast, Anne Lene, Line Laessoe, and Andreas Printzlau. 2014. "Self-Reported Problems and Wishes for Plastic Surgery after Bariatric Surgery." *Journal of Plastic Surgery and Hand Surgery* 48 (2): 115–121.

Waitzkin, Howard. 1989. "A Critical Theory of Medical Discourse: Ideology, Social Control, and the Processing of Social Context in Medical Encounters." *Journal of Health and Social Behavior* 30:220–239.

Warin, Megan. 2003. "Miasmatic Calories and Saturating Fats: Fear of Contamination in Anorexia." *Culture, Medicine and Psychiatry* 27 (1): 77–93.

Warner, Michael. 1999. *The Trouble with Normal: Sex, Politics, and the Ethics of Queer Life*. New York: Free Press.

Watson, Jonathan. 2000. *Male Bodies: Health, Culture, and Identity*. Milton Keynes, UK: Open University Press.

Weaver, Lesley Jo, and Emily Mendenhall. 2014. "Applying Syndemics and Chronicity: Interpretations from Studies of Poverty, Depression, and Diabetes." *Medical Anthropology* 33 (2): 92–108.

Weber, Max. 2002. *The Protestant Ethic and the "Spirit" of Capitalism and other Writings*. Translated by P. Baehr and G. C. Wells. New York: Penguin Books.

Wee, C. C., R. B. Davis, K. W. Huskey, D. B. Jones, and M. S. Hamel. 2013. "Quality of Life among Obese Patients Seeking Weight Loss Surgery: The Importance of Obesity-Related Social Stigma and Functional Status." *Journal of General Internal Medicine* 28 (2): 231–238.

White, Francis Ray. 2016. "Fucking Failures: The Future of Fat Sex." *Sexualities* 19 (8): 926–944.

Whitesel, Jason, and Amy Shuman. 2016. "Discursive Entanglements, Diffractive Readings: Weight-Loss Surgery Narratives of Girth & Mirthers." *Fat Studies* 5 (1): 32–56.

WHO (World Health Organization). 2019. "Obesity." Accessed July 2019. www.who.int.

WHO Expert Consultation. 2004. "Appropriate Body-Mass Index for Asian Populations and Its Implications for Policy and Intervention Strategies." *Lancet* 363 (9403): 157–163.

Willis, Martin, Keir Waddington, and Richard Marsden. 2013. "Imaginary Investments: Illness Narratives beyond the Gaze." *Journal of Literature and Science* 6 (1): 55–73.

Wind, Gitte. 2008. "Negotiated Interactive Observation: Doing Fieldwork in Hospital Settings." *Anthropology & Medicine* 15 (2): 79–89.

Wolf, Naomi. 1990. *The Beauty Myth: How Images of Beauty Are Used against Women*. New York: HarperCollins.

Wolf-Meyer, Matthew J. 2017. "Normal, Regular, and Standard: Scaling the Body through Fecal Microbial Transplants." *Medical Anthropology Quarterly* 31 (3): 297–314.

Wood, Michael H., Arthur M. Carlin, Amir A. Ghaferi, Oliver A. Varban, Abdelkader Hawasli, Aaron J. Bonham, Nancy J. Birkmeyer, and Jonathan F. Finks. 2019. "Association of Race with Bariatric Surgery Outcomes." *JAMA Surgery* 154 (5): e190029. http://jamanetwork.com.

Wutich, Amber, and Clarence C. Gravlee. 2010. "Water Decision-Makers in a Desert City: Text Analysis and Environmental Social Science." In *Environmental Social Sciences: Methods and Research Design*, edited by Ismael Vaccaro, Eric Alden Smith, and Shankar Aswani, 188–211. Cambridge: Cambridge University Press.

Yates-Doerr, Emily. 2014. "The Mismeasure of Obesity." In *Reconstructing Obesity Research: The Measures of Meaning, the Meaning of Measures*, edited by Megan McCullough and Jessica Hardin, 49–70. New York: Berghahn Books.

———. 2015. *The Weight of Obesity: Hunger and Global Health in Postwar Guatemala*. Berkeley: University of California Press.

Yi, Stella S., Siçmona C. Kwon, Laura Wyatt, Nadia Islam, and Chau Trinh-Shevrin. 2015. "Weighing In on the Hidden Asian American Obesity Epidemic." *Preventive Medicine* 73:6–9.

Zigon, Jarrett. 2008. *Morality: An Anthropological Perspective*. New York: Berg.

# INDEX

Page numbers in *italics* indicate Tables.

endocrinologist, 29

energy, 46, 75, 91, 115

ethnic minorities, 7, 151

ethnography, 2, 4, 12, 14–16, 131; background, 147–49; coding and analysis of, 151–53; interviews, 149–51; research, 147–53

exercise, 18, 22, 41, 61, 66, 81; daily, 70; excess skin and, 122; post-surgery, 87; pre-surgery, 31; requirements, 86

expectations: of culture, 65; management of, 135; of weight loss, 3

failure, 1–2, 51, 62, 104; dietary guidelines, 82–84; fear of, 116; feelings of, 112, 114; organ, 38

fat: acceptance, 12–13; activists, 22, 41; as derogatory term, 19; positivity, 12, 36, 52–53, 57

fat bodies, 1, 53

fatigue, 76, 86, 107–8

fatness, 12, 18

fats, dietary, 6, 21, 30, 79, 81, 112

fat stigma, 7–9, 12–13, 15, 20–21, 52, 138; among Asian Americans, 37; in Black community, 53, 57, 60; gendered response to, 54; psychosocial stress from, 28; in the US, 65. *See also* stigma

Fat Studies scholarship, 26

fatty liver disease, 39–40

feedback: negative, 84, 98; positive, 55, 98–99, 101; after WLS, 55, 84, 97

feelings: of failure, 112, 114; of intimidation, 99; negative, 56; after weight loss, 77–78

fiber, 30

fitness apps, 92

fitting, 4, 68, 93–96, 101–2, 104, 134

food, 105, *163–64*; absorption of, 4–6, 87, 107; diary, 29–30, 37; excretion of, 4; intake of, 80, 111, 112, 114; intolerances, 107–8; labels, 30, 113; preparation, 79; pureed, 81; restriction, 131; as reward,

119; sensitivities, 107; soft, 81; spices in, 81; thoughts of, 15, 102; tracking of, 113; water and, 31, 82, 85, 108

full-bodied, 56

future plans: fear of, 134; quality of, 72; without WLS, 47–48

GabiFresh, 67

gastrectomy, sleeve, 5, 31, 87

gastric band surgery, adjustable, 5, 87, 118

gastric bypass surgery, 91; laparoscopic Roux-en-Y, 5, 31, 45, 57–59, 72, 87, 107

gastrointestinal disorders, 132

Gatorade, 81

gender, 7–9, 32–38, 54, 60, 63, 124

genetics, 40, 105, 134

Gide, André, 130

glucose, insulin and, 40, 88, 91. *See also* diabetes

Goffman, Erving, 62

Graham, Ashley, 67

greediness, 81

habits, 114, 134–35

hair loss, 108

hard work, 61, 65–66

health: affirmation, 59; as balancing act, 106–10; after bariatric surgery, 106; history, *157*; improvements in, 89; public, 18, 21, 71, 138; risk, 70, 71; stigma, 62; after WLS, 88, 92, 106

"Health at Every Size," 12–13

health-care expenses, 22

health-care systems, 10, 70

health insurance coverage, 8, 48, 121, 127

healthy lifestyles, 18

heart attack, risk of, 40

heart disease, 3, 38–42, 88, 134

hernia, 110

HIV/AIDS, 9, 137

honeymoon period, 76, 101, 104, 131

humor, 61, 126

# ABOUT THE AUTHORS

SARAH TRAINER is a medical anthropologist. Her previous work has included ethnographic research in the United Arab Emirates and the US Southwest. She is currently the Research & Program Coordinator for a National Science Foundation–funded ADVANCE Program at Seattle University.

ALEXANDRA BREWIS is President's Professor of Anthropology at Arizona State University. She is the author of *Lazy, Crazy, and Disgusting: Stigma and the Undoing of Global Health* and *Obesity: Cultural and Biocultural Perspectives.*

AMBER WUTICH is President's Professor of Anthropology and Director of the Center for Global Health at Arizona State University. She is the author of *Lazy, Crazy, and Disgusting: Stigma and the Undoing of Global Health* and *Analyzing Qualitative Data: Systematic Approaches.*